PRIVATE PLACEMENT PROGRAMS

THE HOLY GRAIL

A COMPLETE AND COMPREHENSIVE GUIDE

SIR PATRICK BIJOU

This is not an offer to sell or solicit securities. This book is for general information purposes only and is not to be construed as a solicitation. The information contained within is based on relationships with providers in the international banking world where these endeavors operate.

This is not an offer to sell or buy instruments or other securities. It contains only generalized information for the education of the reader.

This book is geared towards providing exact and reliable information concerning the topic and issues covered. The publication is sold with the idea that the publisher is not required to render accounting, officially permitted, or otherwise, qualified services. If advice is necessary, legal, or professional, a practised individual in the profession should be ordered. From a Declaration of Principles which was accepted and approved equally by a Committee of the American Bar Association and a Committee of Publishers and Associations. In no way is it legal to reproduce, duplicate, or transmit any part of this document in either electronic means or in printed format. Recording of this publication is strictly prohibited, and any storage of this document is not allowed unless with written permission from the publisher. All rights reserved. The information provided herein is stated to be truthful and consistent. Any liability, in terms of inattention or otherwise, by any usage or abuse of any policies, processes, or directions contained within is the solitary and utter responsibility of the recipient reader. Under no circumstances will any legal obligation or blame be held against the publisher or the author for any reparation, damages, or monetary loss due to the information herein, either directly or indirectly. The information herein is offered for information purposes solely and is universally so. The presentation of the data is without a contract or any guarantee assurance.

....

This is not an offer to sell or buy instruments or other securities. It contains only generalized information for the education of the reader.

Published by BIJOUBOOKS

DEDICATION

This book is dedicated to my daughter Isabella, who is the inspiration of my life, and without her never-failing sympathy and encouragement, I could not have written this book.

ACKNOWLEDGEMENTS

I cannot express enough thanks to the International Court of Justice, the United Nations, the World Peace Tract, and all my fellow Ambassadors, especially brother Yosef Yomtov for their continued support and encouragement.

This project could not have been accomplished without the support of my friend and a remarkable editor and book formatting expert, Mr Bilal Qureshi. Thank you for the painstaking efforts and hours you have put into this project and for tolerating me.

Special acknowledgement to my Daughter Isabella and the love, understanding and support she has shown me over the years. To my late parents Easter and Eric, who are no longer here but always in my heart and thoughts.

My thanks go out to all the people who have supported me and helped complete this book directly or indirectly. I am overwhelmed in humbleness and gratefulness to acknowledge the depth of all those who have helped me put my ideas above the level of simplicity and into something tangible.

I want to express my special thanks to my godmother and life mentor, the remarkable Margret Brooks, who is probably the most knowledgeable and greatest banker I have ever had the privileged of knowing.

A special thank you to my grandchildren Tigger and Eden Lloyd and their beautiful parents Dominic and Luara for believing in me and for their unfailing love and support throughout the years.

Finally, to my caring, loving partner, Janice: my deepest gratitude. Your encouragement when the times got rough is much appreciated and duly noted. You have my heartfelt thanks. And, of course, my best friend and loyal companion, always by my side and inseparable, my loving Cockapoo puppy, Myla.

"No mountain is too high to climb if you have the right tools. Every obstacle has a solution, and the most challenging can be realized with imagination, creativity, and resilience."

Sir Patrick Bijou

TABLE OF CONTENTS

ABOUT THE AUTHOR

Sir Patrick Bijou is a Senior Judge for the ICJ-ICC, Ambassador for the United Nations, a British investment banker, philanthropist, and a published author. Sir Patrick specializes in the debt capital markets, private placements, equities, derivatives and futures trading. He has worked with multiple leading banks such as Wells Fargo, Deutsche Bank, Credit Agricole CIB, Merrill Lynch and others, apart from trading on Wall Street.

He has over four decade's experience in the financial field and has worked with numerous prolific clients, including governments, banking institutions, and corporations. He is also a renowned author and has published over 21 books across several genres.

Sir Patrick was born in Georgetown, Guyana, South America. At the age of five, he came to Britain when his father obtained a scholarship to study and has remained in the U.K. ever since. Having been brought up in London, he spent part of his education in England and completed his education in the USA, where he obtained his degrees in Business Studies and later an MBA in Economic and International banking.

As a notable investment banker, he has also worked on Wall Street, and is a skillful and highly experienced Tier 1 trader in the derivative and bond markets, and he also established MTN desks within various significant banks. He became responsible for the setup of the MTN & Private Placement Desk and dealer functions within Lloyds Bank PLC, and was the first trader for Lloyd's treasury for increasing the portion of self-led deals significantly from 4% to 32% in 2002.

Sir Patrick has tailored funding and investments for many different clients, including governments, banks and financial institutions, and has implemented over $16.B funding for socio-economic and humanitarian projects.

He has excelled as an investment banker and was awarded many accolades such as the Multiple Recipient, of the Wells Fargo "Valley of the Stars" award throughout his illustrious career. He was also distinguished by receiving the Wells Fargo "Circle of Stars" award, and was a Member of Wells Fargo's "Millionaire Club" and "Champion Circle". This further propelled him to then become the notable banker he is today. He was finally awarded his most distinguished accolade of all, a knighthood, for his services to banking and philanthropy.

His expertise is so profound that he was headhunted for a position within the International Court of Justice Redemption Department for his finance and international law proficiency to become a member of the Panel of Arbitrators of the International Centre for the Settlement of Investment Disputes. He currently sits as a Senior Judge of the ICJ-ICC. Sir Patrick manages to fit all these activities into his current role as Fund Manager for ProCapital, and is also distinguished as being a U.N. Ambassador.

He is also a Global Ambassador for the International Rights and Welfare Association (IRAWA), and Ambassador of the Royal Diplomatic Club. In May 2021, he was appointed Ambassador by The Academy of Universal Global Peace USA as a member of the governing board/trustees and awarded The Human Excellency Award and Presidency of the Commonwealth Entrepreneurs Club.

One of his most significant career achievements was creating a line of credit for international supply chains and SMEs for the public sector and government funding through PPP. He also helped create the Contract for Difference (CFD) economic phenomena and credit leverage ratio concepts, regarded as hugely pioneering, which all banks and trading institutions have adopted today.

His journey into content writing has allowed him to become an exceptionally motivated and enthusiastic author and professional communicator, experienced in proactive campaign-driven and responsive communications.

His platforms are at Credit Suisse Geneva and DBS Singapore, where he manages high yield investments with attractive returns for selective high net worth clients.

"Coming together is a beginning, keeping together is progress, and working together is a success."

Sir Patrick Bijou

INTRODUCTION

In a managed buy/sell trading program, the spread between the buying and selling of bank debentures creates profits by buying low and selling high to a predetermined exit buyer. Because traders cannot use their own money to operate a program, they look for financially qualified investors to provide collateral support for the initial purchase of a new issue asset.

In trading, as we are discussing it here, a trader has locked in the first issuance of some instrument – such as a standby letter of credit, a bank guarantee, or a medium-term note – while, at the same time, the next, or secondary buyer has been lined up and ready to take the asset at a higher price. However, the trader cannot execute the start trade without having shown new money, such as a line of credit; there is nothing to buy or sell. That is where the investor comes into play.

Typically, a credit line makes the trades work, and in order to get the credit line, the trader must show that an investor is proffering his cash or instrument assets to be monetized. In many cases, the investor becomes a joint venture partner in the process of this monetization. The investor money is never really touched – it simply acts as supporting collateral for the trade credit line. As the credit line is generally non-repayable, non-recourse or non-depletion, this means little to no risk to the investor of losing his money. This limits the risk of the underlying collateral being tapped in the event of a default. For additional safety, the bank blocks cash funds in an administrative hold, which prevents credit line depletion during the trade contract, or utilizes an acceptable instrument as the support. In the case of a bank instrument, the trader can rightfully use the instrument to support the credit line.

Because the trader already has the 'exit' buyer – the second buyer taking the asset at the predetermined higher price – the profit spread has also been predetermined.

When profits are generated, they are generally split so that the investor shares in the bounty, sometimes up to the full amount of the trade credit line, resulting in an 80 to 100 percent profit to the investor, sometimes more. Each program has different types of profit sharing with the trader, which are negotiated when the program is established with the client.

For illustration purposes, a new issue bank debenture may be purchased at about 40 percent of the face value. So, a €500m face value instrument may cost the trader €200m to buy. The trader uses the trade credit line to make that new issue purchase. Then an exit buyer who was pre-established at the beginning of the program may purchase it at 70 percent (or €350m). The difference is the profit made in the trade, of €150m. That is then used to pay profit to the investor (a shared percentage of the total profit), as well as the trader. When bank debentures trade multiple times during a month, this profit adds up handsomely. This is why an investor can see a profit on his money ranging from 80 to 100 percent of the amount of the trade credit line, and sometimes more (depending on the program).

The challenge for many investors is understanding the minimal risk for loss of principal, particularly if the money owned by the investor stays in his own bank account or is used to issue a cash-backed standby letter of credit. Small cap programs typically require movement of funds to a trader account in order to obtain the trade credit line. Few small cap programs, although there are some, can take under €100m and some offer an insurance policy against loss of principal. Several that we have seen do not offer this. One that we know of does.

Having understood the principles behind a managed buy/sell, the next question most potential investors ask is, 'what are the steps needed to engage with such a program?'.

Most investors need a minimum of $100m or €100m – either in cash in a commercial corporate bank account or the face value of a bankable instrument. That number is a little bit deceiving, because you have to factor in the trade credit line being anywhere from 70 to 80 percent of the value of the account. That 70 to 80 percent net must equal at least $100m. So, the real need is for the investor to have about $150m, to account for the deduction with the loan-to-value factored into the process.

A financially qualified investor, in order to avoid potential solicitation rules, is the one who moves first to establish the relationship. This is done with the submission of a Know Your Customer (KYC) and proof of funds set of documents which indicate the investor's desire and capacity to enter a program. While the preparation of these documents takes just a little time to complete, it fulfills the solicitation rules allowing the trading organisation to open the conversation and subsequently prepare the trade contract shortly after receipt by the appropriate authorized intake person.

In general, it takes a couple of weeks to arrange the trade commitments and the banks, along with approval from the authorities governing these programs, at which time the trading may proceed at the next opportunity to start.

With the noise of internet brokers misinforming people about these programs, building trust must first be mutual between parties. Without trust, there can be no transaction. Trust is the first thing any investor needs to feel is in place before too much discussion of a program is presented.

The fact is that managed buy/sell programs using bank debentures do exist, however actual providers are few and far between. The supply of these programs is small, and demand far exceeds it. Getting in the way of being connected to something real are usually the internet brokers, who smell money but do not have the relationships or knowledge of how these work, so, the likelihood of success is almost nil. When you have a trusted party to work with, who has authentic relationships and compatibility, it is possible to be included in a program. For most investors, this is the mechanism used to fund projects without debt or repayment.

The PPP market is changing and no longer limited to governments and MTNs, and industrial companies and banks can issue their own debt instruments. Debt notes such as Medium Terms Notes (MTN), Bank Guarantees (BG), and Stand-By Letters of Credit (SBLC) are issued at discounted prices by major world banks in the amount of $-billions every day.

These private placements can be structured to meet the specific requirements of investors in terms of maturity and coupon. They can be targeted to retail as well as institutional investors, bear fixed or foreign exchange/interest rate-linked coupon, and can include caps, calls, and other features as required by investors.

A constant theme running through the global non-bank finance market as it has evolved since the 2008 crash, has been private placement and buy/sell programs. Sadly, the whole sector has become tainted as unscrupulous individuals, with no real knowledge of how it operates, have persuaded the unaware to part with significant sums of money on the expectation that they were going to reap outstanding returns. So prevalent did these scams become that the FBI and other agencies actually put out warnings that these programs are, in themselves, a scam. Blame the internet, it's the cause of much grief in the market generally! It's probably true to say that less than 1% of what's on offer on the internet is real. But, nevertheless it is a genuine, private 'Tier-1' market place where financial instruments of many types (mostly MTN's) are transacted by independent traders and trading groups, operating across the world's top tier banks.

Clients considering entering this market to make the right decisions look to us for guidance, to find explanations on some of the obscure or unclear aspects of its secure investment opportunities.

All trading programs in the Private Placement arena involve trade with discounted debt notes in some fashion. Further, in order to bypass the legal restrictions, this trading can only be done on a private level. This is the main difference between PPP trading and 'conventional' trading, which is highly regulated. This is a Private Placement level business transaction that is free from the usual restrictions present in the securities market. It is based on trusted, long established private relationships and protocols. Conventional trading activity is performed under the 'open market' (also known as the 'spot market') where discounted instruments are bought and sold with auction-type bids. To participate in such trading, the trader must be in full control of the funds, otherwise he has no means of buying the instruments before reselling them.

However, in addition to the widely recognized open market there is a closed, private market comprising a restricted number of 'master commitment holders'. These are trusts, foundations and other entities with huge amounts of money that enter contractual agreements with banks to buy a limited number of fresh-cut instruments at a specific price during an allotted period of time. Their job is to resell these instruments, so they contract sub-commitment holders, who in turn contract exit-buyers. This form of pre-planned and contracted buy/sell is known as arbitrage, and can ONLY take place in a private market (the PPP market) with pre-defined prices. Consequently, the traders never need to be in control of the client's funds. However, no program can start unless there is a sufficient quantity of money backing each transaction. It is at this point that, the client, is needed because the involved banks and commitment holders are not allowed to trade with their own money unless they have reserved enough funds, comprising money that belongs to clients, which is never at risk.

The 'host' trading bank is then able to loan money to the trader against your deposit. Typically, this money is loaned at a ratio of 10:1, but during certain conditions it can be as high as 20:1. In other words, if the trader can 'reserve' $100 million of client funds, then the bank can loan $1 Billion against it, with which the trader can trade. In all actuality, the bank is giving the trader a line of credit based on how much client funds he controls, since the banks can't loan leverage money without collateral. Because bankers and financial experts are well aware of the 'normal' open market and of so -called 'MTN programs', but are closed out of this private market, they find it hard to believe that it exists. Bankers in top-tier, global banks (where this trading takes place) are ignorant that this trading exists within their own institutions because it happens at a level far removed from their own mainstream banking operations.

Private Placement trading safety is based on the fact that the transactions are performed as arbitrage. This means that the instruments will be bought and resold immediately with pre-defined prices. A number of buyers and sellers are contracted, including exit-buyers comprised mostly of large financial institutions, insurance companies, or extremely wealthy individuals. The arbitrage contracts, provision of leverage funds from the banks and all settlements follow long established and rapid processes. The issued instruments are never sold directly to the exit-buyer, but to a chain of market participants. The involved banks are not allowed to directly participate in these transactions, but are still profiting from them indirectly by loaning money with interest to the trader as a line of credit. This is their leverage. Furthermore, the banks profit from the commissions involved in each transaction. The client's principal does not have to be used for the transactions, as it is only reserved as a compensating balance ('mirrored') against the credit line provided by the bank to the trader.

CHAPTER 1

HISTORY OF PRIVATE PLACEMENT INVESTMENT PROGRAMS

In the 1990s, the trading in bank instruments was and is presently a multi-trillion dollar industry worldwide. The World's largest fifteen to twenty-five Holding Companies of North American and European Banks are authorized to issue blocks of debt instruments such as medium term notes, debenture instruments, and standby letters of credit at the behest of the United States Treasury for the United States Treasury Trust and Foundations and the United States Federal Reserve. The Instruments issued are backed by a Treasury undertaking.

The genesis of this marketplace was the 1945 Bretton Woods Conference of world's leaders. The principles originally championed as answers to post World War II economic stability are still the impetus for the operation of these transactions today. These transactions started some fifty years ago, have grown and been continuously modified, and as described in this article are Private Placement U.S. Treasury and Federal Reserve investment transactions administered by select Western Banks.

A short historical summary will help to understand the origin of these transactions and the reasons why the Treasury backed, private bank instrument marketplace has remained strong and viable notwithstanding the great social, political and economic changes the world has experienced during the last half century.

With World War II having come to a close, the leading political and economic authorities of the world met in Bretton

Woods, New Hampshire. Their purpose was to formulate a common plan to rebuild the war's massive devastation and to impose global restraints upon forces which had twice led to world chaos during the first half of the Twentieth Century and left economic collapse in its wake.

To accomplish this goal, these leaders sought to empower universally recognized international institutions capable of effectuating and preserving political order and capable of encouraging and facilitating world economic trade and cooperation. The World's leading economists advocated the establishment of an international banking system which administered a universally accepted "currency". It was believed that a centralized world authority, and a standard world currency, with fixed exchange rates among the various currencies of the world was the formula for the stimulation of universal economic growth and the maintenance of economic balance and stability though the economies of the world.

John Maynard Keyes urged the adoption of a standard currency. The political realities of the Nation State's autonomy, however, inevitably precluded the adoption of a uniform currency. As an alternative, the international Leaders resolved to adopt the United States Dollar as the standard world currency for international trade. It was gold backed and the most stable currency. This adoption of the United States Dollar as the world's standard currency for international trade was the milestone which triggered the development of the bank instrument marketplace. The Bretton Woods Conference gave birth to the United Nations, the World Bank, the International Monetary Fund (IMF) and the Bank of International Settlements (BIS).

The World Bank was structured to function in a manner consistent with traditional commercial banks. It was created to act as lender to the poorer and less developed countries. Funding for the World Bank came from the assessment of the more industrialized countries. Today, it takes deposits from more than

140 member Governments and lends to the lesser developed countries in need of international capital.

The International Monetary Fund was created to work in conjunction with the World Bank. While the defined role of the IMF has been adjusted through the years, its basic purpose has remained the same: administer global economic stability and political harmony through targeted lending to member countries to facilitate growth, to maintain relative stability among the various world currencies and to avoid collapse in times of crisis.

Most of the world's economies experienced great post World War II expansion. With this expansion came increased international trade and the need for more and more United States Dollars to accommodate this growth. In permitting the U.S. Dollar to be adopted as the world's standard currency, the role of the United States Treasury and the United States Federal Reserve expanded.

To protect the dollar's value while increasing the dollar's availability, the Treasury commenced to work with the World Bank, the IME, the BIS and through the Federal Reserve, and the largest Western European Banks. They developed a system of issuing uniform financial bank instruments in U. S. Dollar denominations in accordance with the new and universally accepted financial standards. In doing so these U.S. Agencies and International Institutions merely incorporated the existing basic operating procedures of the major Western European Banks.

The United States banks manage their asset liability by offsetting short term deposits against long term loans while Western European banks fund their customers' long term borrowing needs through the issuance of various bank financial instruments including Medium Term Notes and Letters of Credit. A plan was enacted to permit the Western European Banks to issue financial instruments in United States Dollar denominations pursuant to the expressed authority of the U. S. Treasury through the U.S. Federal Reserve. In enacting this system, the Treasury/Federal Reserve authorized the Western European Banks to capture the expatriated U.S. Dollars from the world marketplace and with the new credit created, issue these 'new" Dollars into circulation in specific geographical locations where investment was needed, over the controlled life of the instrument. The implementation of this system following the Bretton Woods Conference provided a means for the U.S. Treasury and Federal Reserve to control the rate and volume and placement location of the U.S. Dollars being introduced into the global marketplace.

In its attempt to further solidify the universal acceptance of the U.S. Dollar as the standard world currency, the Bretton Woods Conference had fixed the price of Gold backing the U.S. Dollar at $35.00 an ounce. During the 1950s and the 1960s the price of gold in the open market had increased to a price nearly ten times that amount. The need to back the U.S. Dollar with gold valued at $35.00 an ounce while simultaneously providing sufficient U.S. Dollars to accommodate the increased needs of the international marketplace created significant stress on the United States Monetary system. The United States did not have enough gold to continue issuing the dollars necessary to continue to support international economic expansion.

On August 15, 1971, facing a threatened speculative run on the U. S. gold reserves, President Richard Nixon renounced America's promise to convert paper dollars into gold upon demand. With this executive proclamation the United States abandoned the gold standard. In the absence of the gold backed standard currency, the idea of fixed exchange rates among all currencies of the world became passe, and by 1973 the IMF, The World Bank, and the Bank of International Settlements had abandoned the idea of fixed exchange rates.

Within the territorial limits of the United States the U.S. Federal Reserve exerts influence upon the domestic economic trends by the regulation of domestic bank reserve requirements and the adjustment of the Federal Discount Rate. While these may be internally effective tools, they are inadequate to provide the international control demand in the global marketplace. The United States Treasury expanded the roll of the Federal Reserve System to monitor the International markets separate and apart from domestic duties. In implementing the International System of world order, the United States Treasury through the Federal Reserve has the largest World Banks issue bank financial instruments in significant U. S. Dollar denominations. As these instruments are issued and sold the U. S. Dollars are extracted from circulation and the new credits are created in exchange for the new bank instruments, and the control over the Global U. S. Dollar money supply is affected. These transactions are meaningful because the bank instruments are of such significant dollar amounts that the effect of these sales will have a direct impact upon the volume of the U. S. Dollar in circulation within a particular local economic system. Once the Federal Reserve has collected in the Dollars they can be reinserted into targeted segments of the global economy in accordance with the United States Treasury and the G-8 Nations determined policies.

The same system is the foundation wherein the IMF discretely attempts to maintain world order. As economic, political and social factors alter the relationships of the Nations of the World, the IMF is equipped to respond through the power of responsible administration of financial aid. Loans may be granted to member countries to fund various individual projects which are beneficial to its citizens and mankind in general. Should a Central Bank of an individual country run into a deficit in its balance of payments, the IMF is able to supply short term financing to a member country. Functioning in this manner, the IMP can interject an immediate fix to the short term instability of an individual county while at the same time avoiding calamitous consequences to the other nations with whom the unstable country may have contracts.

A review of past events reveals the extent of the IMF's role as: The force behind the bailout of Mexico, the 10 Billion-dollar loan commitment to Russia, the attempts to bring stability to Africa and to undermine the oppressive authority of African Overlords, the industrial development of Eastern Europe, the reconstruction of Bosnia, and the development of free markets in South America.

However, these targeted loans come with definite strings attached. The funding of such loans maybe conditioned upon the the particular country demonstrating to the World Bank or the IMF officials that it has reduced its inflation rate, reduced its import tariffs, opened its markets to external forces, ceased destroying its rain forest, terminated policies inconsistent with basic human rights, taken steps to eliminate corruption, cut internal spending in certain areas, adjusted objectionable internal policies and is acting in accordance with universally recognized concepts of human dignity.

By the sale of Bank Instruments, the IMF is able to promptly respond to issues in a targeted fashion. This system avoids the need to submit requests to the various member counties for the use of politically budgeted funds and avoids the parochial, partisan, political processes of the parliaments of various Nation States.

The Bank of International Settlements (BIS) is a little known private institution based in Basel, Switzerland. It also performs a critical function in the preservation of order in the global monetary system Control of this institution is actually vested in private individuals, and not in governmental officials. The principal functionaries are the Private Central Bankers from the world's industrialized countries. Like the IMF, the Bank of International Settlements functions in the nature of a world economic security net and clearing house. It is capable of moving billions of dollars from one country to another to expeditiously correct potentially disruptive financial imbalances between countries, and to effectuate the prompt administration of financial first aid to individual Nations and financial institutions in major crisis situations. The BIS also helps maintain the relative stability of the world currencies as well as the global system as a whole.

The Medium Term Notes are issued by the largest World Banks at the instructions and authority of the U.S. Treasury directly or through the Federal Reserve and distributed through the largest banks using a well-established private marketing system. These marketing systems of Private Treasury Trading Trusts, Foundations and Federal Reserve Accounts exclusively market these instruments and these accounts are administered by the participating banks. The proceeds generated by the sale of these instruments are retained by the U.S. Treasury or the Federal Reserve and reintroduced into the market place when deemed appropriate. These funds may be used to fund loans made by the INIF to its member countries. By funding specific projects, the INIF can monitor the proceeds and certify that the funds are being used as agreed.

These Private Trading Entities regularly purchase these instruments on the initial issue or Primary market and the pricing is at a negotiated discount. The instruments are immediately sold to a well-defined private and discrete market at the market rate or at secondary market prices. This new profit is new credit created that can be used for financing of U. S. Treasury registered and Approved Projects. As indicated in the Federal Reserve Bulletin, Anatomy of the Medium Term Note market," August, 1993 page 765, these transactions involve "riskless principal" as all of the instruments bought are sold prior to purchase.

In the Private Placement Program transactions, trading is conducted on the strength of the U.S. Treasury Department Approval of the holder of the funds after they have been shown to be good, clear, clean and non-criminal in origin. It is the value of the funds as evidenced to the Treasury Trust or Foundations, or the Federal Reserve, and not the funds themselves that finance the purchase of the instruments by the participating Private Placement Transaction.

In the event that the instruments have been issued for a World Bank or IMF project, the funds are generated by the sale of the instruments by the Private Transaction Accounts and are available for use in funding the loan commitments made by IMF or other such international agency. The instruments are commonly five hundred million dollar notes with a ten year maturity bearing interest of seven and one half percent, backed by a Treasury Instrument of like terms, and purchased at a discount and resold to major institutions at the market rates.

Through the implementation of this system, the U. S. Treasury and the Federal Reserve cause dollars to be moved from one country to another in a fashion consistent with the economic and political policies of the G-8 + Nations, the United States Government, The World bank, The IMF and the United Nations. In so doing the participants are able to effect foreign aid and the IMF is able to significantly fund their commitments without resorting to individual assistance from the treasuries of its member states.

The Private Transaction Accounts operate with a profit motivation and they may have Private Placement Participation from private individuals and other private entities which must be screened and cleared by the administering agencies. The Investment Manager Limited provides private individuals and other private entities access to this market in the form of accepting deposits of Private Placement Funds. Entry requires The Investment Manager Limited to obtain a clearance and Approval of the Depositor, from the United States Treasury Department/Federal Reserve for each Private Placement Deposit. This process may be initiated by submitting necessary documentation including proof of good, clear, clean funds of non-criminal origin, together with the appropriate bank documentation. (The format of necessary documentation is available upon request).

The United States Treasury rules are applicable to all banks who have administration and distribution arrangements with the Treasury to do this business in U.S. Dollar denominations. Recent enactments by the U.S. Treasury have extended the application of these rules to all participating foreign banks issuing instruments in U. S Dollars as well as all domestic banks. Some of the limitations include: type of capital banks may use for such activities, the manner in which participating capital may be procured, the manner in which the profits can be divided and accounted for, and to whom and under what circumstances of this activity can be made.

The form of security offered to participants in the Private Placement Transaction will be assignable Deposit Receipts from the Custody Safekeeping Accounts of the Investment Manager Limited that hold the Private Placement Deposit. The Custody Safe Keeping Account will hold the cash deposit or securities equal to or of greater value than the original Deposit.

The Treasury rules have a broad impact upon the nature and scope of all banks activities. Banks are precluded from using funds held on deposit within the institution for use in these transactions. The rules require that the participant be the legal owner of the funds and banks are prevented from soliciting clients and funds for participation in a trading transaction.

As a consequence of these restrictions and in response to the continual need for capital to initiate and complete Approved Projects, these transactions are established in a discreet, Private Placement Program Transaction which functions as the Private Placement Transaction. To participate with a Private Placement Transaction, the clearance of the participant and the depositor's funds by an authorized representative of the United States Treasury is essential. After the funds have been screened as good, clear, clean, and of non-criminal origin, and U. S. Treasury approval has been procured, the participant is in a position to place the funds in a Custody Safe Keeping Account or Corporate Account, at a nominated World Bank acceptable to the Depositor and The Investment Manager Limited.

The Treasury Approval is significant as it represents that the funds are clear and the approval is extended to the established Bank Account and authorized by the Treasury rules, it also represents that disclosure about the details of the transaction my take place, and it represents that the earnings on the deposited funds are legally exempt from the limits imposed upon banks pay out restrictions set by the U. S. Federal Reserve discount rate limitations. It aslo means that the bank may deliver to the Established Bank Account an Assignable Depository Receipt as security for the deposited funds.

A commonly offered security is that of a Deposit Receipt or an Assignment for the deposit, which is issued by the Established Bank Account of The Investment Manager Limited through the Administering Bank. The Safekeeping Receipt or Assignment is accompanied by limiting instructions in which the Administering Bank agrees to maintain a level of funds equal to the funds deposited by an "A+" rated Bank or U. S. Treasury instruments equal or greater to the total of the deposited funds.

The Investment Manager Limited commits the value of the funds in the Custody Safe Keeping Account to a Treasury Trust or Treasury Foundation Transaction Account, who administers all of the trading that creates new credit for the financing of Approved Projects. New credit is created and generated by the repeated use of the value of the funds deposited to finance successive buy and sell transactions in the Treasury Transaction Accounts.

In February 1997, The Treasury Department issued new rules for the distribution of the new created credit and these rules are regularly being updated and amended.

The U.S. Treasury Department enforces all of theft rules to ensure compliance with their directives. This process is closely regulated through U.S. Treasury Compliance Officers who are assigned to audit the business activities of the various participants.

Private Placement Program Transactions

All of the above speaks to the movement of US Dollars from one location to another for their application and uses in areas of need. The US Treasury also makes the Bank Instruments of 7.5 percent interest, with a term of ten years available to Project Managers to see that Projects are completed in those areas of need. The US Treasury and the Federal Reserve from time to time, make arrangements for Approved Projects and for Approved Depositors who have funds that the owner will make available to enter into an atmosphere of a Bank Secure Transaction, wherein approved Bank Trading Accounts are established, and the Bank Instruments will be purchased directly from the Treasury nominated and appointed Syndicate of Major Western Banks through the Treasury approved Trading Account. In the account we established for the trading purpose, the Treasury makes the Bank Instruments available to this account at a discount to the Open Market.

When these Instruments are purchased and then sold at market rates the profit is new credit that is then used to finance the Approved Projects. In this transaction, the dollars are accumulated in a Geographical Area where there is an excess of US Dollars and moved to a location of approved projects to he invested therein.

In this business one of the main considerations is, at the end of the term of the ten years when the 7.5% interest, ten year term instruments become due, they are paid at the full face value of 100 percent, thus repaying the discount "new credit" and the interest paid for ten years thereon. These instruments are the responsibility of the US Treasury and hence the American People. Therefore, you will subject to Treasury Compliance Officers monitoring in these transactions at various times and places.

WHAT ARE PRIVATE PLACEMENT PROGRAMS AND TRADE PLATFORMS

Trading Platforms are pools of capital that invest in a wide variety of financial instruments including stocks, bonds, commodities, ETF's and foreign exchange. These pools of capital may be a number of legal entities; however, the most common is known as a PPP, an acronym for Private Placement Programs. Private Placement Trading Programs are not offered to the general public. They are exactly what their name implies, offerings of membership interest to a select group of chosen investors who meet certain financial requirements.

The minimum investment in these Private Placement Programs can often be quite high and require a lockup period, where the capital is committed to the Trade Program for a certain amount of time. The minimum investment levels and principal commitment periods vary depending on the type of investments and the objective of the investment. One year lock ups are not uncommon and in some investments the lock up period may be even longer. Lock ups serve a very important function. They provide the Trade Platform Managers and Platform Traders with time in which to obtain results for the investors. Platform Traders want to know that the capital allocations they have been given to trade are for a long enough period of time to allow a particular trading strategy time to mature.

If you were to look at the returns of outstanding Platform Traders you would see profitable results over time; however, in the short term they may have a period of negative returns. If your interest is in traders with no down periods, please read no further, as they do not exist, contrary to popular belief. There is no such thing as free money. Trading involves risk. Every investor dreams of opening the door today and finding tomorrows Wall Street Journal, but this only exists in fantasy. Platform Trading requires hard work, tremendous discipline, patience and superb talent. The fact is very few people have the gifts to be a successful trader. The Platform Traders at the very top of their peers are rewarded with staggering wealth. Platform Traders utilize many strategies to help determine profitable trades, such as macro analysis, price theory, fundamental analysis, value analysis and many more investment strategies. What superior and outstanding Platform Traders can do is make enough winning trades over time, irrespective of what strategy they may use to accumulate trading profits. However, a number of their trades will not be winners. A large part of successful Private Placement Program trading is risk management; controlling losses and preserving investment capital.

One of the very basic risk management techniques utilized by Private Placement Program Traders is only risking a very small percentage of the investment capital on every trade. It is usually between one half and two percent on a particular trade. If a trade loss hits a defined percentage allocation, the trade is closed out. The average investor has an extremely difficult time taking a loss. In fact, it is a human tendency to hold on to losing trades and cut winning trades short, which is the very opposite of what great Platform Traders do. Risk management systems can get very complex and Platform Traders often write complex algorithms to manage risk when there are many positions and trade strategies running all at once.

The advent of the computer has radically revolutionized trading, just as it has every facet of our lives. Modern Trading Platforms are heavily dependent on mathematics and the hard sciences. Most Platform Traders today have advanced formal education and training in mathematics, probabilities, physics, computer science, economics, and engineering. Trade rooms are more similar to busy computer driven laboratories than the old image of guys in a boiler-room shouting into two telephones at one time. Almost all orders are input electronically and trades are matched up by sophisticated software. Private Placement Programmers and software engineers are indispensable to successful Private Placement Programs and Trade Platforms.

As mentioned earlier, Platform Traders have many products to trade and a huge number of global exchanges to execute the trades. The most well-known exchange in the world is the New York Stock Exchange (NYSE). When Platform Traders make a trade, that trade is executed on an exchange. The NYSE, CME, NYMEX, ICE, CBOE and NASDAQ are the largest U.S. exchanges. In Europe the LSE, Euronext and Frankfort Exchange are largest. In commodities much of the execution is done on the Globex, an electronic exchange. Platform Traders use the exchanges to buy and sell trillions of dollars of stocks, bonds, currencies, gold, oil, euro-dollars, CMO's, ETF's and hundreds of other securities, currencies, and derivatives in efforts to make profits for themselves and investors.

Private Placement Program Traders can make profits by buying a particular instrument or by shorting, (selling it) betting the price will go down. Some Platform Traders buy and sell similar instruments simultaneously, betting on the change in price between the two instruments; this is called arbitrage and spread trading. Other Platform Traders employ option strategies, such as writing options, writing straddles, strangles, butterflies and condors. Option strategies can quickly become extremely complex and are a highly specialized area of trading which requires extraordinary expertise.

Private Placement Trading Platforms utilize margin to buy and sell all of the various instruments they trade. Margin is simply a partial payment for the instrument. Most people are familiar with margin on stocks. Margins are met with cash, period. Contrary to what some people may believe, the only instrument that is good for backing a trade position is cash. When a profit is made, it is credited to the Trade Platforms books that day; when a loss is taken it is debited from the Trade Platforms books that day. Private Placement Platform Trading is a cash business; gains and losses are marked to market each day. Trade Platform Managers should know by between midnight and two a.m. each trading day where they stand. The Private Placement Trade Platforms maintain what is called a customer segregated account with an FCM. This account is where the Trade Platform Investors' funds are held. An independent capital account is established for each Trade Platform Investor in order to provide accurate accounting on a monthly or quarterly basis. The Private Placement Platforms' funds are deposited into a master segregated funds account to be used for margin in trading.

Goldman Sachs, Merrill Lynch, ABN AMRO, MF Global, JP Morgan Chase, Credit Suisse, Deutsche Bank and Bank of America are all FCMs. These companies, as well as handling trades for independent Trade Platforms for many years, have had their own internal proprietary trading desk or Trade Platforms. Some of these trade desks are famous such as Goldman's Alpha Fund, Morgan Stanley's PDT (Process Driven Trading) Platform and Deutsche Bank's legendary SABA Trading Program, led by Boaz Weinstein. The new regulatory environment is forcing many of the banks to divest themselves of proprietary Trading Platforms. This is making for a large talent pool comprising the best and brightest traders available for Private Placement Programs, Private Hedge Funds and Trading Platforms.

Private Placement Programs and Trading Platforms often use what is known as notionalization or notional funding to increase the leverage that the Trade Platform may use. The Trading Platforms may leverage its trading capital as much as ten times, meaning that One Hundred Million Dollars ($100,000,000) may be traded as it was a Billion Dollars ($1,000,000,000). Leverage, while giving the ability to greatly increase the returns on cash can also lead to significant loss. The old adage that "leverage is a double-edge sword" is very true. Notionalization absolutely must be constantly monitored and adjusted, depending on margin requirements and market conditions. The Private Placement Platform Managers have investment committees that are responsible for determining notional trading levels. Notionalization is a very powerful tool for the Private Placement Trading Platforms.

In conclusion, when it comes to Private Placement Programs, the minimum investment can be high and the risk can be high as well, depending on the various methods being used. However, the reward is typically great, great enough to easily justify the investment and risk for one who has the means with which to get involved in such an investment. Constant methods are always in place in order to mitigate risks.

Understanding Notionalization

The Private Placement Platform Managers have investment committees that are responsible for determining notional trading levels. Notionalization is a very powerful tool for the Private Placement Trading Platforms.

One of the main benefits of investing in managed futures is the ability to do so through Notional Funding in a separately managed account – whereby you don't have to put up a cash deposit equal to the program's minimum investment amount in order to invest in that program. For example, it is possible to trade the $1,000,000 Three Rock Global Macro program (QEP Investors only) with a cash deposit of just 200k.

If you are saying, so what.... you can put up just a portion of the investment amount in all sorts of investments: stocks via a margin account, real estate via a mortgage, art via a credit card; you are missing the one big difference. That difference is that there is a cost to buying stocks on margin or purchasing real estate with a mortgage. That cost is the cost of money or the interest rate you pay to borrow the funds to purchase the investment in which you are interested.

With notional funding, there is no borrowing of money and therefore no interest rate and no cost of money. How can there be no borrowing? Because we're not talking about someone loaning you $1 million to meet the minimum (or about trading a smaller version of the program with $200K), we're talking about having $200,000 traded as $1,000,000 via the use of notional funding.

But as an old history professor we knew would say – 'that begs the question' – 'What is Notional Funding?' And when we answered notional funding is funding an account through the use of notional funds, he would again say that begs the question: 'What are Notional Funds?' We should have known not to use the word in the definition.

What Is Notionalization

Notional funding, for those that don't know, is the ability to fund your account below its nominal value (fully funded value), but to still trade that account as if it was at its nominal value. This is becoming increasingly common in the institutional investment world, with an increasing number of CTAs offering this too. In the last few years, with the backing of the NFA and the CFTA, managers are now even allowed to quote their performance on this basis (as a percentage return on a fully funded basis, even if it is partially funded).

If, for instance, you wanted to invest with a money manager that had a minimum investment of $100K, you could either fully fund your account with the $100K, or, if notional funding was offered, you could partially fund your account - say, with only 50K - but still have that account traded as if it was $100K. If the manager made 20% in that year, you would have made 20K (a 20% gain on a nominal basis), but a 40% gain on a notionally funded basis. Obviously, the same is true on the downside, in terms of the proportionally increased volatility. In this case, your account would be considered 50% funded.

Institutional investors have increasingly been favorable to this, since it allows them to have a limited amount of capital at any one manager, limiting business risk with the manager in addition to FCM/custodial risk, since the remaining portion of your capital would be held elsewhere. If manager A accepted notional funding of 20% on a 500K minimum, the investor would only actually invest 100K with manager A, and would be free to use the remaining $400K to diversify with other presumably uncorrelated managers or simply allocate it to principal protected investments. They would still have the upside of a $500K account with that manager, while the downside on that account would strictly be limited to 100K, which in this case is the equivalent of a 20% drawdown.

Obviously the viability of such a strategy presupposes having a clear understanding of the investment program's return/drawdown expectations. It would be insane to fund an account at 20% of the fully funded level (as with the above example) if there was a significant potential for a 20% drawdown, since that would result in a margin call. Therefore, the percentage of the fully funded level allowed by managers is a function of their drawdown expectations, in addition to margin requirements. Many will offer different levels of funding (20%, 30%, 50%, etc.); as a rule, though, the lower the level of funding, the higher potential gains on a cash-on-cash basis, but with a higher risk of margin call.

This is surely not a new concept; and, really, it is somewhat of a strange concept that I think doesn't always intuitively sit well with people. Chris, I hear you thinking, isn't all of this partial funding the same as increased position risk on a cash basis. Yes, it is. That is exactly right, at least in terms of execution, although conceptually it is very different. I believe that Tdion was one of the few to address this in one of his threads - having the money in your account actually being risk capital, rather than not truly being risk capital for you on an emotional/financial level.

For example, if an investor was to invest in a fund that had a maximum drawdown expectation of 20%, he should be prepared to lose 20% (and realistically some more) since that is within expectation. However, if the fund was to drawdown to 40% on the same investment, would he really be prepared to lose that much? Most people, I would venture, probably wouldn't be, especially if they have specific investment expectations ahead of time. They would likely pull their account at some point below 20%, since any risk significantly below that wouldn't be palatable; that is to say, they really aren't treating the vast majority of their account as risk capital at all. If asked, they would likely justify this large cash portion as being there for margin purposes - but, of course, you don't need nearly that much for margin purposes in forex (or commodities), which is what makes all of this possible for such instruments.

Now for the negatives. If you were to invest on a notional basis with a manager, your account would experience significant volatility on a cash basis, significantly magnifying both your cash losses and gains. Would you be able to deal with this? Well, that is probably going to be a question of whether you are actually treating the investment from a fully funded perspective. For instance, if someone invests 20% of the nominal level (say 100K again, for a 500K minimum), you must actually have 500K, and must actually be following one of the aforementioned strategies with that money. If you have done such things - and that money is truly diversified in uncorrelated/principal protected investments - it would be much easier to perceive the process in the desired way, and potentially be quite profitable with limited risk. On the other hand, if you only actually had 100K to invest, put it all with the same manager on a 20% funded basis, the volatility might well get to you, and ultimately cause you to prematurely pull the investment, or feel that you lost everything (rather than simply 20%) if that account was to go bust on a cash basis.

Further, even if one was treating the process sensibly, and diversified among various managers, you are still banking on correlation between the managers remaining constant (or, if you are doing this as a private investor, the different trading strategies with which you diversify). If, for example, you were with 5 different managers, with 20% funding with all of them - if all of them simultaneously went into drawdown (and even if the nominal drawdowns were perfectly acceptable), there could be considerable total portfolio volatility.

Notionally Funding a Trading Systems or Managed Futures Account

When an investor looks at the performance of a trading system or Commodity Trading Advisor, one of the most significant statistics is what is the required minimum account size. It makes no sense considering trading systems or managed futures that have $100,000 minimums if the investor only has $50,000 to invest.

However, it is valuable to know that frequently the investor can start with less than the minimum through notional funding. For example, an investor could notionally fund a managed futures or trading systems account at the $50,000 level but tell the manager to trade at a nominal $100,000 level. In other words, the account will trade as though there were $100,000 in it even though there is not. The investor is simply making use of added leverage.

In the previous example this means that the account will be trading at 2-to-1 leverage. Meaning the investors will have gains and losses at twice the level. Had the investor only put up a third of the nominal amount minimum then he would see gains and losses at 3 times the level and so on.

Why those using Trading Systems or Managed Futures Might Want to Consider Notional Funding

Notional funding can be an efficient use of capital, because frequently a trading system or managed futures account will not come anywhere close to using all the money in the account. For example, in Hoffman Asset Management's case we have a margin-to-equity ratio of generally less than 10%. What this means is that for every $100,000 invested, generally speaking, we will be using less than $10,000 at any given time for margin. The remaining $90,000 sits on the sidelines stagnant. Although it is true that interest on those unused funds can be earned, most investor's feel they could do better investing those funds elsewhere. Often time's high net worth individuals or institutions will even put NOTHING in their accounts and trade 100% notionally. The question for investors should be "how can I calculate a reasonable notional level in which to invest".

We feel the answer to that question is one that can be computed based on several statistics. Specifically, what is the maximum drawdown expected and what is the maximum margin that might be needed. For example, Hoffman Asset Management (as of this writing) has had a maximum drawdown of about 17% on a $125,000 nominal account size. This means a $21,250 drawdown in cash terms. The maximum margin usage is about 15% on $125,000 or, about $18,750 in cash terms.

To compute a notional investment amount, we suggest that an investor add the maximum expected drawdown and the maximum expected margin usage. This figure would give the investor the absolute minimum they could invest in the account without having a margin call.

In the previous example, if an investor had started on the worst possible day, and had a $21,250 drawdown, and simultaneously had the maximum margin usage of $18,750, he would have needed a $40,000 of cash in the account to fund that

$125,000 nominal account size. Once again, some institutions and individuals who are not worried about margin calls may even decide to fund the account with less than that (or zero).

Benefits to the Trading Systems Or Managed Futures Investor

This allows for the smaller, but more aggressive investor to participate in the program without needing to tie up the entire amount in cash. This will amplify their gains and losses at the added leverage level they are using. If, for example, the manager made a 30% return with a 17% drawdown, then the investor at a 2-to-1 leverage ratio would have experienced 60% gains with a 34% drawdown.

Notional Funds

Notional funds represent the difference between a managed futures investment's minimum investment amount and the amount of cash an investor is willing to put towards a managed futures program at that time. An investor may not have the full amount of the minimum, or wish to only put up a portion of the minimum and use the rest for another investment. In a way; notional funds can be thought of as added money which is used to bridge the gap between the cash outlay an investor is willing to put towards a managed futures program at that time, and the stated minimum amount of that program.

A quick example is probably the easiest way to describe it. Take the aforementioned Three Rock program (QEP Investors only) with its minimum investment amount of $1,000,000. An investor does not actually have to have all of that money in their account in order to trade the program. Levels of notional funding vary between managers, but for this example, Three Rock will allow clients to use notional funds to cover up to 80% of the investment minimum.

The actual cash balance plus the notional funds balance equals the required minimum investment amount of $1 million. Another way to think of how this works is to imagine having that $200,000 account, but telling the manager to trade is as if it was $1,000,000.

If you're asking "how the heck can you trade more than what you have in your account?" – let us explain further.

To understand how an investor can use these notional funds, we must first back up a step and understand how a managed futures advisor arrives at their minimum investment amount. ***Minimum investments could, or perhaps should, be further split up into three distinct levels, specified as:***

The Margin Minimum: the technical minimum amount needed to actually place the trades on the exchanges.

The Drawdown Minimum: the amount for an investor to withstand any eventual drawdown of the investment.

The Window Dressing Minimum: the amount to make the percentage drawdowns and returns attractive to the greatest number of investors.

Margin Amount: The first part of the minimum investment amount is the amount technically needed to place trades. This is what the exchanges and clearing firms refer to as the margin requirement. Any account which wishes to trade a futures contract on a regulated futures exchange like the Chicago Mercantile Exchange must first have enough money in the account to cover the performance bond requirement of the exchange (the margin). This insures that the exchange can make the trader who takes the other side of the trade good should the trade go against the account.

Margins can sort of be thought of as the amount of money which could be lost on that position in a single day – and the exchanges and clearing firms make sure each account has that much money – or else the whole system doesn't work. If this wasn't in place, where would a winner get their winnings from – the loser could disappear.

Drawdown Amount: The second part of the minimum investment amount is the amount an investor needs to withstand any eventual drawdown. Again, this is another technical level of sorts, in that an account must have at least that amount in order to stay above zero. If the investment has the possibility of losing $150,000 for example, in the normal course of operation, then an investor better have at least that amount in order to proceed. If they didn't, they would have to get out of the investment during the normal ups and downs of the investment.

Think of it like a tank of gas; if you are driving 100 miles and need 5 gallons of gas to get there, you better have at least 5 gallons of gas in the car – or else you'll never get there.

Window Dressing Amount: The third part of the minimum investment amount is the amount needed to make the percentages appealing to potential investors, or "window dressing" amount. Unlike the margin amount, it is simply a subjective amount the advisor computes in order for the average returns and risk of his or her program to come out "nicely," for lack of a better term.

Imagine an advisor with average annual returns of $100,000 and drawdowns of $50,000. If that advisor sets his minimum at $100,000 – the average annual return in percentage terms is 100% with a 50% drawdown; while if the advisor sets his minimum at $1,000,000 – the average annual return in percentage terms is 10% with a 5% drawdown. While the returns in dollars are exactly the same, the advisor would likely find much more success raising money with the $1 Million minimum amount, because investors will ignore programs with large drawdowns such as the 50% drawdown number. The difference between the desired minimum and the minimums needed for margin and drawdown is the window dressing amount, and it is often this amount which can be "notionalized."

If we look at a fictitious CTA program with a $1 million minimum investment, and 15% average margin usage, and 25% max drawdown as an example, those levels would be:

Window Dressing Amount

Understanding that up to 80% of a managed futures program's stated minimum investment amount can be nothing more than window dressing gets us a step closer to understanding how you can use notional funds, when investing in a managed futures program.

It should be clear that while an investor actually needs both the 'technical amount' for margins and 'drawdown amount' to stay alive, the investor doesn't necessarily need the window dressing amount. If it is only there to make the returns and drawdowns more palpable for most investors; an investor who can stomach much larger percentage gains/losses (you will have the same dollar gains/losses) doesn't need window dressing.

How can you use notional funding?

For those investors who don't want the window dressing, (those who can handle 3 to 5 times the percentage gains and losses), notional funding is perhaps the most efficient form of investing available to investors. Once investors understand that the window dressing amount is only to make them feel better about how much (in percentage terms) they have made or lost – they are free to take that window dressing amount and use it for other purposes.

Notional funding also allows for the trading of multiple managed futures programs with a single cash allocation. Assume an investor wants to put $900K into managed futures. An investor could use all of those funds on one manager, or could trade a balanced managed futures portfolio of Three Rock (QEP) (1 million), Degraves Global Diversified (QEP) (1 million), Red

Rock Global (1 million), totaling $3 Million in initial investment amounts, with just the $900K in cash.

This would represent leverage of roughly 3.3 to 1 in the account ($900K traded as $3 Million), and the investor would see percentage gains and losses on his $900K that are 3.1 times what an investor putting up the full $3 Million would see.

Now comes the fun part touched on in the beginning of our discussion. The cost of doing this is zero. There is no interest rate charged on the notional amount like you have in the stock market when buying shares on margin or when buying a house with a mortgage. This is because there isn't any real money behind the notional funds, thus you aren't borrowing any money and thus there is no charge for the notional funds you employ. The notional funds are, in a way; nothing more than the amount of leverage you are taking on. The more notional funds you use; the more leverage you are applying to your investment.

What are the risks of notional funding?

While there is no physical cost to notional funds, one "cost" is that the fees charged by the manager are on the nominal amount of the investment (meaning the full minimum amount), not the cash balance in the account. So if the program you're participating in has a 2% management fee, that will balloon to an 10% annual fee on your cash amount if you used 20% cash with 80% notional funds to meet the minimum. Likewise, commissions will have a much bigger impact on the account in percentage terms.

It is important to note, however, that the fees and commissions will not be any different, in dollar terms, than they would be if fully funding the account. Consider a $1,000,000 minimum investment program, which an investor invests in using $250,000 cash and $750,000 notional funds (25% cash/75% notional). The 2% management fee on this account would be charged on the $1,000,000 minimum nominal level of the account, meaning the charge would be $20,000. That $20K charge would be the same for an investor doing 100% cash/0% notional, 50% cash, 50% notional, and our 25% cash/75% notional example; but it would represent a 4% charge ($20K/$500K) for the 50%/50% account, and an 8% charge ($20K/$250K) for the 25%/75% account.

So while leverage through notional funding increases the percentage amount of fees and commissions, it has no effect on the dollar gains and losses. The key to understanding notional funds is to understand that while the percentages change – the dollars do not. The $20,000 in fees does not become larger – they stay at $20,000 no matter how much notional funds you use. They only become larger as a percent of the cash in your account, and only when the cash in your account gets smaller. So 2% of $1 MM = 4% of $500K = 8% of $250K. They all equal $20,000.

There is also a greater risk that you may lose more than you deposited in the account when using notional funds. If a $1 Million minimum program loses $500K, and you are notionally funding that account with just $250K (having $250K traded as $1 Million), your account will have lost $250K more than you deposited in it, and you will owe that money to the clearing firm. Of course, even if you had fully funded the account, you would still lose the same $500K (again, the dollar amount of gains and losses does not change, only the percentage amount), and whether you notionally fund or fully fund – there is always the possibility with a futures investment of losing more than you deposit in your account.

The last negatives to consider are the mental anguish you may go through seeing percentage drawdowns 4 times those that are reported (but again, you're still losing the same amount of dollars) and the nervousness you may encounter when/if a drawdown takes the account down to within a few hundred dollars of a margin call. And finally, if the account goes on a margin call in which you have to deposit more money into the account in order to keep trading with the program, the risk that you choose to cease trading the program instead of adding more money, and then miss out on the upside when and if the program rebounds.

CHAPTER 2

PRIVATE PLACEMENT PROGRAMS, HOW HIGH ARE YIELDS

Seemingly every day there are hundreds of more people learning about the private placement business, usually either through online research or word of mouth. Once an exclusive opportunity which was limited to just a few privileged individuals, the private placement business is now full of thousands of "professional brokers". As you would expect, some of them are very successful, but the other 99% are not!

You may ask yourself, why are "private placement programs" growing so fast when it is such a tough business in which to succeed? Well it's unfortunately because of the nature of most humans to chase the dollar, and claims of fast money. Let's face it, if you're rich, it is rather intriguing to consider something that can double your money every month, or "better"!!

With all of the recent hype about private placement programs, the most common question I have received over the last few years is:

I've heard of all kinds of programs out there, and I want to know, what returns are actually possible in REAL private placement programs?

Since this is such a frequent question and a critical topic to understand, we felt that an article explaining private placement yields was essential.

Below, we have listed different investment levels, and will explain what your opportunities, risks, and prospective yields could be if you found a REAL private placement trader.

Please note, this is not a solicitation or description of any programs associated with InsideTrade LLC. It is rather an explanation of information we have attained from reliable sources that have been successful in the private placement business. All returns shall be considered hypothetical, and for informational purposes only.

Various Investment Levels

1 Million: This is the level that most investors lose money, or have less than expected success. Whether it is because they fell for the "piggy back" program, "Bank of America" program, "PING" program, "Bullet" program, or the bank instrument/ proof of funds program, most are never successful. Though there are real programs at 1M, they do NOT trade bank instruments, and offer far lower returns.

MAX POSSIBLE RETURNS: 20% per month

10 Million: At this level, you may be able to find legitimate private placement programs, but your success depends on if the trader will accept such a small file. Sometimes there may be other larger files applying concurrently that you can be pooled with, but your yields won't be as high as the larger file. In this case, at such a small level, it is still very tough to even be placed in a REAL bank instrument trading program. As you may know, bank instruments are cut in 100M+ increments, and even with a steep discount, you still need over 65M to purchase just one note.

MAX POSSIBLE RETURNS: 10% per week

50 Million: Usually at this level, you can find a trader that will combine your file with another concurrent applicant to meet the minimum needed to purchase a discounted bank instrument. Though this is possible, it is not guaranteed that you can enter into a program unless you find a REAL trader, who is happy to make an exception for you.

MAX POSSIBLE RETURNS: 20% per week

100 Million: At this level, the trader can purchase instruments with the line of credit that is drawn against the client's collateral. Typically, traders can make spreads of about 7-15 points on each trade (ex. buy 65% of face value, sell at 72%). In addition, there is no need to combine the account with another client, since the client's funds are sufficient to purchase the note alone. Needless to say, this dramatically increases your potential returns, and opens up opportunities for project funding and humanitarian developments.

MAX POSSIBLE RETURNS: 40% per week

As you may already know, there are many programs out there that may talk the talk, but when it comes to actually paying out, most of them disappear, or change the expected yields at the last minute. Though yields can be even higher for some opportunities, it is very unlikely that you will find a safe and stable program earning more profit than the numbers listed above.

Unfortunately, everyone knows that brokers run the business, and the traders "hide in the shadows" until the client's information has been attained. For most desperate brokers, the goal is to attain as many files as possible. In having this goal, many brokers twist words and sugar coat information to get more applicants. As you can see, it is not uncommon to have inflated and unrealistic yields communicated to clients. In fact, it has become less common to speak with experienced brokers with reasonable yield expectations, than it is to speak with uneducated brokers with big promises.

Though it may be needless to repeat, be careful and use common sense when entering private placement transactions.

Just like everything else, if it sounds too good to be true, it usually is.

HOW TO COMPLETE "DUE DILIGENCE" IF INVESTING IN PRIVATE PLACEMENT PROGRAMS

When considering a private placement program, you always need to be skeptical of the people offering the opportunity. Since there are only a few traders in the world, the chances of you finding even one real trader are pretty small. Unfortunately, most people looking for a program have the odds stacked against them from the beginning. With this in mind, we felt it was critical to explain common methods of "vetting" a private placement trader.

Private Placement Due Diligence Tips

1. Trust your Instinct

Always trust your gut feeling on the trader, and never let "high returns" distract you from the transaction at hand. Also, be careful when trusting your "gut feeling", and make sure you are following common sense, rather than greed and hope.

2. Trader Experience

When you first speak with the trader, ask him about his background, and what lead him to become a trader of bank instruments. If you are well versed in finance or private placement, it should be rather easy to tell who has legitimate experience, and who doesn't. Also, ask them how they developed such unique relationships with top banks, and exactly how the profits are generated in these transactions. If you hit them with a number of questions, there is usually an obvious stumbling point that you may need to examine further.

3. Estimated Profits

If you ever hear a trader "guaranteeing" profits, then hang up the phone. No one by law can guarantee specific profits in a private placement transaction, they can only state historical returns. Though it may sound like the opportunity of a lifetime, it isn't. Think about it, if they really were a legitimate trader that managed millions of dollars, they wouldn't be breaking the law for just one more client. Also, if you ever hear someone speak of returns higher than 50% per week, no matter what the size of the deal (ex. 10 B), it is likely to fail. As you know there is an economic slump, especially in the international banking system, which has led to smaller margins on trades, leading to smaller net profits to clients.

4. Business Standing

When you speak to the trader, collect their business information and the state in which they are incorporated. Once you receive this information you can check the Secretary of State website, and make sure they are a legitimate business. At that time, it is also important to see how long they have been in business, and who the officers are under that corporation. Once you retrieve the information of everyone with legal interest in the company, you can then make sure there are no pending legal suits against them, and proceed to background checks.

5. Background Check

Once you have the information of the trader and company, it would be in your best interest to use whatever sources you can to complete a thorough background check. This check should be on not only the trader, but the others who are registered with the trader's company. Also, it would be a good idea to check out the closest people to the trader who introduced you to the transaction.

6. Trader's Country of Origin

If the trader is located within the USA, then you have a much better chance to recover any damages if something were to happen. On the other hand, if the trader is located in Europe or overseas, it may be much tougher to organize and win a court battle, especially if you are not a European citizen. In essence, your money could possibly be lost if something was to happen with a private overseas investment.

7. Trading Banks Involved

To complete the transaction, you will need to most likely SWIFT, or block funds in favor of the trader's account. If there is a big name bank involved that's a plus, but most of the time the trading bank is not huge (ex. not UBS/ HSBC). If there are smaller less known banks involved, don't be worried, it's normal. The most important aspect to focus on is the country of the bank, if it is backed by other banks, its history, and the banks size in relation to other banks in that country. This will give you an idea if something disingenuous may be ready to occur, or if you are clear to carefully move forward.

8. Change in Program Procedures

Make sure that the original process the trader described is the process you are completing. In many fake private placement programs, the "trader" or brokers may use the "bait and switch" technique. For those who don't understand this strategy, it involves explaining program details in a biased manner which makes the client feel extremely comfortable, and then switching around the final steps at the last second. Needless to say, this is dangerous, and is usually associated with fake private placement programs.

9. Private Placement Contract

Typically, a private placement contract is a Joint Venture agreement where the trader gets a certain % of the profits (30-50%). The thing is, the contract has no references to specific returns, and usually is rather vague as to the responsibilities of the trader, and what they are trading. Once again, this is a sticking point for some clients, but if you understand the laws associated with private placement programs, you would understand why the contract is structured this way.

10. The First Few Payments

You will never know if you have a real private placement program until it has paid out far more than the principal that has been blocked, or conditionally assigned. With this in mind, don't celebrate until you reached this point, and always be diligent with your attention to detail. The basic rule of thumb is if the transaction isn't smooth from the beginning, it is likely to fail in the end.

In summary, the private nature of these programs may make some feel uncomfortable, but the opportunity is out there to be seized. If you are interested in searching for the right trader, just refer to the tips above, and you will be armed with information that will make your search for more efficient.

"Ping" Programs, Are they Real or Not?

Every day we speak to investors who expect to leave money in their account, and collect huge profits from private placement investments. From where did this false expectation arise? As usual, it was created by misinformed private placement brokers who wanted to increase the number of new applications. Unfortunately, it did just that, while also creating a false expectation for new clients with interest in private placement.

The idea behind a "PING" private placement program is that the client leaves the money in their own account, and the trading bank checks on it to make sure the full balance is still available. This verification of the funds by the trading bank is referred to as "PINGING" the account, and supposedly is done on a daily or weekly basis to ensure the balance remains stable. This is also the same premise behind an "administrative hold", which many inexperienced brokers will refer to as well.

For many of the beginners in the business this may make sense in theory, but the problem is simple, THERE IS NO COLLATERAL IN PLACE. For the trader to be able to access discounted bank instruments, they must have liquid collateral to purchase the notes. This liquid collateral MUST be derived from the client's assets, which are usually blocked or conditionally assigned to the trader for the period of the trade. Once the assets are blocked or assigned to the trader, they can access a line of credit against the client's collateral, and start trading on behalf of the client to generate profit. Since "PINGING" the account leaves the client's funds unencumbered and no assets in favor of the trader, the bank will NOT give the trader a line of credit, and therefore, the "program" will more than likely produce excuses, rather than returns.

The fact is, private placement traders always need a form of collateral to access a line of credit, and a "PING" structure does not provide this. Without this line of credit, the bank instrument is never "cut" and trading will never begin. Despite what you are told, EVERY investment has a degree of risk to it, and typically the investments which offer higher potential returns, have higher levels of risk as well.

If you are a reader, and have closed a "PING" transaction in the past, please post your experiences, but after 7+ years of consistent effort, we feel this structure is nothing more than a sign of future disappointment.

IMPORTANT TIPS FOR PRIVATE PLACEMENT PROGRAMS

In 2009, there are now more people than ever who are looking for private placement programs. Even with such a small and "private" niche, approximately 3000 prospective brokers/investors type "private placement program" into Google every month. With this recent growing interest, a flood of undereducated individuals have tried to enter the business, and in response, it is now more polluted with fraud and misrepresentation than ever. Since I have met a number of people who were victims of their own ignorance, I felt it was critical to outline a few key points about Private Placement Programs.

Top 10 Tips for Private Placement

1. NEVER establish a relationship through email or Skype, phone is the ONLY way to feel people out.

Do you think that someone who has closed a private placement transaction would want to develop relationships through email or Skype? I don't think so. Anyone who is successful, and not trying to hide something, values their time.

The only way to establish relationships in the private placement business is to speak over the phone, or meet face to face. People assess your tone and confidence, among other things, and email/Skype are much less effective since you are only communicating through written format. The fact is, you need to be able to feel someone out when you are working with "private investments".

2. If you are looking to find a private placement program with less than 10M, the trader will NOT be trading bank instruments.

When you ask brokers what they are trading to generate these high returns, most say they are "buying and selling MTN's and BG's". The fact is, bank instruments are issued in 100M notes, and you need serious money to purchase one. The only way you could even get a 10M client into a private placement, is if it was pooled with other clients to meet the minimum cost of the discounted note. (Ex. 100M Note, 35% Discount, Trader Buys for 65M, Need More than 6 Clients with 10M)

If you ever find a 1M program, they must be trading in some other market, or it just doesn't make sense unless they are pooling money. In short, when dealing with such private transactions, pooling money is very dangerous. One bad apple can ruin the entire bunch, and you can waste tons of time and money chasing dreams. If there is an investigation due to complaint from anyone, the entire pool of money would be frozen for months, and sometimes it can even be years.

The point is, don't waste your time unless you have the capital. There are other investments at 1M that have GREAT yields and a whole lot more transparency.

3. NEVER tolerate long broker chains in a private placement program.

Private placement deals never get done when there are more than 4 brokers involved (including the program manager and client rep). This is something that is critical when trying to get a deal done in the private placement business. As many of you know, there can be over 10 brokers in a deal at time. Think about it, even if you closed the deal, the paycheck wouldn't even be worth the mediation you would need to constantly perform.

The key point to remember is, if you can't work your way quickly through the chain, you will be completely wasting your time.

4. Only work with brokers/traders who have closed a transaction before.

Though there may be THOUSANDS of people out there who claim to have a private placement connection, most of them never closed a deal. This can be something they have worked at for years upon years, with no success at all. Think about it, what are the chances that anything will change? To ensure you are not wasting your time, put the pressure on from the beginning. If you are aggressive on the phone and ask them immediately if they have been paid, you can tell by their response and tone if they are legit. Use that technique, as well as their level of intellect and experience, as your guide.

5. Use your gut instinct. NEVER BLIND YOURSELF by thinking about the money you are promised. Focus on the transaction now, and celebrate later.

The most critical and frequent mistake is focusing on the money, and not the private placement transaction at hand. Sit back and let this one soak in, there is some serious danger associated with following the zero's and not common sense.

When clients hear about the "huge returns", many make excuses for the inconsistencies that evolve over the course of most fake transactions. Look straight ahead at what you have or DON'T have, and keep the money and celebration for after the transaction. Private Placement Program deals are never closed by those who are greedy, or those who put the cart before the horse.

6. ONLY work with brokers/traders who can answer questions COMPLETELY to your satisfaction.

The thing that irritates me the most is that many brokers try to sell private placement programs like they are used cars. With this "pitch" comes promises of RIDICULOUSLY OVERESTIMATED returns, and miscommunication about the application process.

The fact is, you are not supposed to "sell" or even "offer" private placement programs, they are an invitation only opportunity. In short, if you aren't blown away by their professionalism, both written and verbal, then don't waste your time. There is a new breed of idiots trying to get rich quick in the private placement business, and you never want to find yourself to have been their "Guinea Pig".

7. Ratios are your friend, speak to as many people as possible and create rules to qualify new possible leads. Never settle for something that feels less then genuine.

Today, there are literally thousands of people in the private placement program business. In fact, when we did our last count, there were over 40,000 "brokers" who have been in the business at some point over the last 5 years. Think about this for a second, there are maybe 100 of those people who are connected to a real opportunity, and as expected, those people are the hardest to find. It is a lot easier to get in touch with someone with no past success, than someone who is rich from past deals, and really doesn't need the transaction.

If you want to be successful, you have to relentless. First, pick up a phone and contact everyone you see out there online, Second, rip emails from every related keyword you can think of to build contact lists. Third, keep notes and rate everyone to make sure you have records of the people with whom you were impressed. Once you send out some email blasts, and speak to thousands of people, you will then know the realism of your goals. Remember, ratios are your friend in the private placement program business. If you settle early, you may regret it later.

8. If there is a famous or public name attached to a private placement program, demand to speak with them to ensure you are in fact connected.

Though there are a few well known people in the private placement program business, you always want to make sure the name isn't just "bait" from the brokers. If you come across someone who drops a name, be suspicious, but demand to speak with this "well known" person. If you can verify that they are attached to the deal, then you might be on the right path. Remember, there are only a few hundred people connected to a real private placement program in the entire world, so don't be too convinced by just a "name".

9. ALWAYS follow non-solicitation laws, and NEVER state or guarantee the expected returns. All Private Placement Programs are based upon a "best efforts basis", and NEVER state guaranteed returns.

If you speak with someone, and they tell you that they can "guarantee" a very high return, then hang up the phone. If this happens, I can guarantee you one thing, they have never closed a deal in the private placement business, and they do not understand the non-solicitation laws. If you state approximate or forecasted returns to someone before they go through compliance, without using the term "historical", you are breaking the law and can be thrown in jail by the authorities. Private Placement Programs are no joke, you either do it right without luring people in, or you can pay some severe consequences.

10. PING programs DO NOT EXIST in the REAL private placement program business. Please stop promoting them, they NEVER work!

We will make it simple for you to understand, PING programs NEVER WORK. No bank will extend a line of credit to a trader that has no client collateral client in place. If your money is sitting in your account, and they are supposedly "PINGING IT" on regular basis, the lending bank has no authority to seize the collateral in the case of a default by the trader since it isn't in their hands. The fact is, banks do not lend 100M to some random person unless they have collateral which can be liquidated to replace what was loaned. Even if the trader says they have their own line of credit ready, it doesn't matter because they legally can't trade their own money. They must use the collateral of another to stimulate the line of credit to start trading for profit.

On the other hand, if the cash backed collateral is blocked, conditionally assigned, or the trader is made a temporary beneficiary of the asset, the transaction can take place.

KEY POINT: If a client expects to keep their money in their own account, and just miraculously make high returns with no risk, they are BLINDING THEMSELVES with hope, rather than looking at the transaction with common sense. Remember the idea of the self-fulfilling prophecy? Well, you can't blind yourself to the realities in this business, or you will be breaking fast.

Remember, for every successful investor who completes a private placement transaction, there are another 1000 who waste time following their hopes and dreams, rather than common sense. For those who are interested in learning more about private placement, and alternative investment opportunities, please contact us via phone. We have worked successfully in the private placement business for several years, and are very experienced in various high yield investments.

Top 10 "Red Flags" for Private Placement Programs

With the recent increase in private placement, project funding, and bank instrument related fraud, it is now more crucial than ever to identify suspicious actions. Though this may seem like common sense, the problem is, until our blog was created there was no reliable information source which defined truth and dispelled myth. As we have done with all of our articles on private placement programs, this list of common "red flags" will provide unique insight and invaluable tools to help you on your path to success.

By staying attentive to common warning signs, such as the ones we will discuss below, you can approach each private placement transaction with diligence and realism. Though many of these tips may seem simple at first, applying them correctly can be the difference between a life of wealth, and a trip to the "school of hard knocks". Take a look below, these tips can save you millions!

Top 10 Red Flags for Private Placement Programs

1. Private Placement Programs with VERY High Returns: If you hear about a private placement investment yielding over 50% per week, it is UNLIKELY to fulfill its promises. Unless you have over 100M, and are extremely lucky, you are barking up the wrong tree. Please review our article on private placement program yields for more information.

2. Programs which "Piggy back" or Pool Investors to Meet a Minimum: Pooling investors for private placement programs is risky, and unfortunately, it is quite frequent in today's private placement world. The problem is, if you have a large number of investors in a private placement, there is a good chance that one will "cry wolf" because they feel uncomfortable due to the lack of transparency. Once that happens, which it usually does, the SEC, FBI, etc. will begin an investigation that could last years, freezing everyone's assets.

3. "Ping" Programs, or "Administrative Holds": Private placement "ping programs", or programs that require administrative holds, are everywhere but rarely ever work. The problem is simple: there is no collateral on hand to stimulate the line of credit for the private placement trader. Many inexperienced private placement brokers push these deals, NEVER succeeding despite years of efforts.

4. Claims of "No Risk" for the Investor: In any alternative investment, there is always risk. This is especially true for private investments, due to their unregulated nature and high risk strategies. Despite what many brokers may say, private placement programs DO carry risk. To be successful in any private placement, you must always collateralize your funds, and assign them to the trader. If the trader defaults on the line of credit, the funds of the investor can be seized.

5. No One Typically Vouches for their Success with the Trader: If you are investing in a private placement program, ALWAYS be sure to speak with someone who has been

successful with the trader. Investors who choose to move forward with a private placement program which hasn't been vouched for are taking a huge risk. To state the obvious, acting as a "guinea pig" is not the best decision when seeking private placement.

6. The "Program Manager" Slips Up: If you ask the same questions twice, and the program manager changes their answers even slightly, you should dig deeper to look for more inconsistencies. Think of your conversation with the representative and trader of the private placement program as a psychological analysis. Every response, tone, and answer should be assessed to ensure you are comfortable before moving forward.

7. Traders that Accept Leased Bank Instruments: If a private placement trader accepts a leased bank instrument, move on before you waste your time. No REAL private placement program will accept funds which you do not have full control over. Though leased bank instruments have become extremely popular, in all reality, you have a one in a million shot of being successful. For more information, visit our article on the FACTS of bank instrument leasing.

8. Private Placement Programs that Accept Hard Assets: If you have hard assets, and are looking to get into a private placement program, then please be safe. Unfortunately, there is a liquidity crisis worldwide, and it is very tough to get banks to loan against illiquid assets. In all honesty, your best bet is to sell the asset, and invest a portion of the earnings into a private placement program.

9. "Bullet Programs", or Short-term "Leveraged" Programs: Short term or "bullet programs" typically promise extremely high yields, and very rarely work. Most real private placements last 40 weeks, due to the contractual agreements between the trader and their exit buyers who purchase the medium-term notes (MTN)/bank guarantees (BG). Usually, short term programs

claim to "leverage" the funds, and by doing so, "create immensely higher returns".

10. The Old-Fashioned Bait and Switch Technique: If a private placement program seems too good to be true, look out for the infamous "bait and switch" technique. In many cases, private placement brokers will paint a rosy picture of the process, and then switch the terms once the investors are so excited that they are ready to do whatever they need to get the "high returns". This is very common, so investors must ALWAYS be aware of this unfortunate scenario when verifying the details of any program with the trader.

Though there are plenty of actions which can be considered "red flags" in private placement, we have listed the most common scenarios above. If you remember nothing else from this article, a good rule of thumb is: if it sounds too complicated, or too good to be true, it usually is.

As with any other material we publish, reading can teach you a lot, but applying the knowledge and tips we provide is far more important. We didn't write this article for fun, look for any sign of inconsistency, and act if needed before it's too late. Remember, common sense is your friend, and when you choose to follow hope over rational thought, the oasis will always disappear when you arrive.

TOP 10 SECRETS FOR PRIVATE PLACEMENT PROGRAM (PPP) TRANSACTIONS

This year many financiers and high net-worth individuals are looking to use private placement programs, also known as managed buy/sell programs, for funding commercial real estate deals or humanitarian projects. The current economy has created a sea of "brokers" attempting to enter the trade will little or no knowledge about private placement traders or transactions.

Moreover, the misrepresentation and new fraud in the private placement industry has pushed more traders to work with repeat clients and the trend is moving toward using only liquid capital for entering trade. To prevent high net-worth individuals and businessmen from the headaches of dealing with these brokers, we have outlined a few secrets/tips to help guide people to success.

1. Work with professionals. Within a few phone calls or meetings, you should be able to see the knowledge someone has about private placement platforms and programs. The character of individuals you meet will show itself and you should work only with those that act with respect and can answer questions in an intelligent manner.

2. Transact business via the phone or in person. NEVER attempt to waste your time going back and forth over email or Skype. Although this may be an initial form of communication, it should not be the only one.

3. Consider programs that are 100M and above. Banking instruments such as Medium-Term Notes (MTNs), Bank Guarantees (BGs), and Treasury Bills (T-bills) are purchased in 100M notes. There are a few instances, such as when a new trader is starting out, where a pool of investors will put together 10M sums of money together to purchase one note, but it is rare.

4. Beware of large broker chains. These are also known as daisy chains. They are usually full of misrepresentation and conflicting information. Plus, so many of them are worried about getting circumvented in the private placement program that they will hesitate to put you in touch with someone that can actually perform a transaction! Your time will be wasted filling out NCNDs.

5. Focus on a successful transaction. Most people become so blinded by the money involved that they become paranoid, refuse to work with certain people, become greedy, try to circumvent their partners/brokers, and in the end everyone loses.

6. Network. Create as many resources in the private placement world as possible, qualify new leads, and refuse to work with anyone that is not genuine. Not only will the sheer numbers help you execute a private placement program transaction, but it will also help you learn about the industry and even gain contacts that may help you in other aspects of your business.

7. Avoid PING programs. Ping programs simply do not exist. A line of credit that the trader uses must be drawn upon an asset or account that does not move or else the bank issuing the LOC takes an unnecessary risk in case the LOC is not paid back.

8. Follow the rules. ALWAYS follow non-solicitation laws that regulate what you can and cannot say regarding private placement programs, medium term notes, bank guarantees, and T-bills. A "best efforts basis" is a term often used when describing returns. Never guarantee any type of returns. You may, however, mention "historical" returns but, as any high net-worth individual or investor knows, past performance is no guarantee of future performance.

9. Keep track of progress. Keep a record of who has what connections or what team has performed in the past. Work with those that are professional and knowledgeable in the field and keep an organized folder of any documents that may have come across your desk.

10. Do not only focus on Private Placement Programs. Remember, this form of funding is not the only one available for commercial real estate or humanitarian projects. Many foundations may have money set aside for projects and there are also private lenders, venture capitalists, and angel investors that can help you obtain the funding you need for your businesses.

CHAPTER 3

EXPLANATORY NOTES OF PRIVATE PLACEMENT PROGRAMS

1. PREFERRED TRANSACTIONS. What we are looking for, principally, is this: (i) Clients who are informed, sophisticated, motivated, decisive, respectful and cooperative, and who have full ownership and control over their capital; (ii) largescale cash funds or bank instruments only, Preferably Minimum 1-10 Million Euros or thereabouts and (iii) straightforward, uncomplicated fact situations. No historical instruments, No LTNs, No CMOs, No IBOEs, No gray/blue screen or "restricted access" interbank screen transactions. No hard assets. No commercial securities. No developing countries "sovereign" instruments (Except Venezuelan Bonds). No government funds. Private investors only.

2. ACCEPTED COUNTRIES/BANKS. We are able to operate the World Programs in most countries in the world – with the exception of Mainland China and those nations subject to trade embargo or deemed state sponsors of terrorism. Our preference, certainly, is that the client's assets be held in a branch of a major, international bank (U.S./Western European banks and the like). We can, though, in many instances, work with established national/regional banks. Good banks with SWIFT capability in Russia, Eastern Europe, the Middle East and Asia, for example.

3. BLOCKING/RESERVING ASSETS. The trade platforms have a variety of means at their disposal for blocking/reserving the client's cash fund/bank instruments for trading purposes, depending on the nature of the transaction. From use of a SWIFT Guarantee, to "internal blocking" of the client's assets without SWIFT's. The trade platforms will try to accommodate the client's preferences as best they can. That said, clients would be well-advised not to tie the platform traders' hands unduly by limiting what procedures are acceptable.

4. CASH FUNDS. The client must be the legal owner of cash funds held on deposit. Earned funds from legitimate business activities or funds acquired via legal inheritance. No leased, borrowed, encumbered, or "pre-blocked" funds, or funds that have been assigned or pledged to the client. Funds restricted for use, nontransferable or otherwise non-transactable cannot be used.

5. BANK INSTRUMENTS. We can utilize bank instruments in trading – Certificates of Deposit, Bank Guarantees, Letters of Credit, etc. - depending on the circumstances surrounding their issuance. And we can, in certain instances, work with instruments acquired by the client from a third-party; say, for example, to facilitate project funding. The client, though, must be willing to fully disclose the circumstances surrounding the issuance of the bank instrument, including the presence of any terms or conditions affecting the instrument's use. And the third-party (who will need to clear "compliance") must be willing to assist the transaction as necessary. Madrid lawyers.and.economists@gmail.com

6. ASSISTING CONSULTANTS WITH BANKING, ETC. We can, in certain instances, directly assist Consultants with their banking, helping them to open accounts in one of the Western European banks, with whom we work very closely. Alternatively, we can provide Consultants with access to an independent lawyer/Paymaster who can set up bank accounts, arrange off-shore companies and trusts and offer tax planning as required or other various PROGRAM FEATURES.

7. MULTIPLE TRADE PLATFORMS. Clients enjoy privileged access to four (4) of the seven (7) largest Traders/trade platforms in the world. These are the preeminent Traders/trade platforms in the business; highly skilled and supremely qualified, with all the necessary approvals and registrations – and the muscle and "firepower" – to get the job done correctly.

8. "ONE-TO-ONE" PLATFORM TRADING. Clients are offered an unparalleled opportunity to work directly with a major Trader/trade platform without a meddlesome "trade group" interposed between the parties, therefore blocking access.

9. A WIDE RANGE OF PROGRAM OPPORTUNITIES. Multiple Traders/trade platforms means multiple program opportunities and a greater selection with more flexibility. We offer standard program opportunities - but also tailor-made offerings, custom-designed by the platform traders to satisfy the client's specific requirements.

10. HIGH-YIELD PROGRAM EARNINGS. The Program offers clients attractive, high yield returns; these are earnings realized from platform trading of investment-grade bank debenture instruments. Discussions regarding yield amounts are best left to direct talks between the client and the trade platform that accepts the transaction.

11. CLIENTS NEEDN'T TRANSFER THEIR ASSETS. The trade platforms utilize a variety of procedural means at their disposal to "block/reserve" the client's principal for trading purposes, from use of a SWIFT Guarantee, to "internal blocking" of the client's assets without SWIFT's.

12. NO PROJECT OBLIGATIONS. There are no formal project requirements.

Clients, though, are encouraged to utilize their Program earnings to finance viable and sustainable business expansion and commercial and humanitarian projects that promote economic growth and improve quality of life.

STEPS FOR APPLYING TO A PRIVATE PLACEMENT PROGRAM

- The client provides a proof of funds and passport copy along with their compliance package. Most of the assets that people try to apply with CAN'T be used for any REAL private placement program. These include ITR's (Irrevocable Trust Receipt), SKR's (Safe Keeping Receipt), T Strips (Treasury Strips), junk bonds, asset-backed bonds, hard assets, real estate, and more. As you can expect, most of the applications at this stage are unacceptable, and fraudulent.
- The Trade group submits the application to the compliance department for review. Within hours, most real traders will know if the asset and owner are legitimate. Also, at this time, the criminal background and origin of the funds are explored to ensure they are dealing with a clean applicant. In addition, if the client has over 100M, real trade groups typically either know of the applicant, or have seen the person try to apply before. There is a very small circle of real traders, so when someone applies with large assets, the word gets around rather fast.
- The Client passes due diligence, speaks with the trader, and receives the contract. Most clients have NEVER been involved with a legitimate private placement before. With that being said, many will show the contract to their attorneys, who have never been through this as well, and they may advise against proceeding due to a lack of familiarity. Needless to say, this can kill the deal, or may make the PPP investor feel uncomfortable. The problem you will run into over and over at this stage is transparency, and gaining trust from the client. Due to the private nature of the private placement business, there is

only so much information the trader can reveal, and this is a common obstacle.

- The Client signs the contract, and then the trader countersigns it to make it official. Once the client signs the contract, there are still a number of potential obstacles before you can "close the deal". If a client signs the contract and does not complete the transaction, they may be reported to the authorities, and by doing so, they will be permanently prevented from participating in any private placement program in the future. As we said before, there is a small circle of real traders, and if they label a potential client as a non-performer, it is rare that any other REAL trader will spend their time to work with them.
- The Client contacts their bank to complete the private placement transaction. Banks are in the business of making money, and customer requests are secondary to the profit of the bank. When a client asks to block, conditionally assign, or transfer their funds, they are cutting into the pockets of the bank, which we know they don't stand for very well. If the bank loses that asset off their books, they actually lose over 25x that amount in potential loans from their country's central bank (FED/ECB). With this in mind, most banks stall with excuses, since that will frustrate most customers enough to kill the transaction. Even though this may be an obstacle, this should never be a deal killer since it is the client's money, not the banks. To complete a deal, you either need a bull's personality or a great relationship with the bank, otherwise you may encounter problems with the final steps.
- The Client's funds are blocked, conditionally assigned, or transferred to the trade group in accordance with the contract. Very few trade groups request that the client

transfers ownership of their assets. If they do request this, be very cautious, and expect something is not as it seems. Most private placement traders ONLY need a conditional assignment of assets, temporary beneficiary access, or the blocking of the assets in their favor for the period of the trade. This allows them to access a line of credit which they trade for the client, specific to their contract agreement. Also, so you know, PING programs are 99.9% fake, since they do not allow the trader to access the line of credit, they need to start trading. No bank will loan without collateral, and since "PINGING" the account is not sufficient assurance to the bank that is has collateral in place, it typically never works. It is just another ignorant broker creation and is most often part of a bait and switch strategy.

- The Trader accesses the line of credit from the trading bank. The trader is the only one who can access a line of credit against blocked assets. No one who is trying to complete a scam will ever be able to draw a huge line of credit on blocked assets. The bank completes thorough due diligence on anyone to which it loans, and when that loan involves millions of dollars, it is far more diligent. In short, no bank will offer a line of credit for millions to someone who they do not thoroughly trust, so there is not a lot of worry about when blocking assets in someone's favors.
- The Trader uses their line of credit to have discounted bank instruments issued from the bank. First, the issuing bank sells the instrument directly to the trader for a significant discount (ex. 60% of face value). After the trader buys the instrument, they then sell it to the commitment holder/exit buyer (ex. 66% of face), who then sells it to their commitment holder for a higher price (72% of face). This continues until someone purchases it

with the intent to hold the note to collect the coupon/interest, and the difference between the discounted note and its value at maturity. This is the basic idea of how profit is generated in Private Placement Programs that use bank instruments.

- The Client receives payment of profits weekly or according to the contract. Once everything it set up with the banking, it is a very smooth process to get continual profits into your account. Typically, the first payment is made within 10-15 banking days after trading has started so they can ramp up the account to purchase larger notes. After the first payment, the client will receive disbursements on a weekly basis, or whatever their contract specifies. Most clients and brokers would be best served in setting up international bank accounts, or better yet, they can have an account at the bank where the trading is occurring. This will prevent the need to send external wires through different countries and banking systems. All profits would be internally transferred "ledger to ledger", and would not attract as much attention.
- The Client uses profits to fund projects and retains the rest for personal use. Most real private placement programs are intended to fund humanitarian projects in underdeveloped nations. Typically, 60-70% of the program's profits must go to projects, while the remaining 30-40% is for "administrative use". In essence, the 30-40% can be used at the client's discretion, but you must make sure you are funding projects as well. The platform does not regulate this, but the FED oversees all of the companies who have applied and received money in these types of programs.
- Once the client completes this 40-week trading process, they can re-enter, but they must have projects into which they can funnel the profits. Most private placement

contracts are for 2 years, and are renewed upon expiration if both parties choose.

Private Placement Programs, Blocked Funds, Administrative Holds & the Tooth Fairy

The Tooth Fairy is a wonderful myth of childhood. Children would place their tooth under their pillow and wake up excitedly the following morning to find a shiny coin under their pillow; this is a childhood joy many of us experienced. Alas, the sad reality is there is no Tooth Fairy; the money came from mom and pop's pockets. There is no free money in life.

Blocked funds and administrative hold procedures reside in the same mythical village as the Tooth Fairy, Santa, and the Easter Bunny. Let's imagine you wish to buy a rare automobile. You are lucky enough find a 1967 Ferrari P4, you are indeed very fortunate, and the seller tells you there are two other wealthy potential buyers. He wants a deposit of 10 percent to hold the car for you. You tell him that's not a problem; I have been searching worldwide for years for such a car here is my check. The dealer deposits your check in his account only to be told by his bank it is not good funds. What! It was written on funds in a blocked account. But not a problem for the dealer, he simply sells the car to one of the other buyers with real money. Your blocked funds could not facilitate a transaction and your P4 belongs to a buyer operating in the real world.

The trading of real financial instruments in Private Placement Memorandums, such as CMO's, Treasury Bonds, Securities, MTN's, CD's, Commodities and Currencies, is no different than the example of the rare car purchase. Sellers of securities want to be paid in cash. Platform trading relies on the ebb and flow of billions of dollars every day.

Trading platforms also rely on heavy utilization of leverage to generate high returns. Leverage in turn is dependent on margin utilization. To see how margin works let's take an example most people are familiar with, buying real estate.

If you buy a house for $100,000 and you pay a down payment, let's say 10 %, you pay $10,000 cash and a bank lends you the balance. You are controlling a $100,000 investment with $10,000. This is leverage. You have significantly leveraged your $10,000. In fact, your leverage is 10 to 1 or 10x. If the house was to double in price, you have made a $100,000 on your investment. Of course, you have to deduct expenses, although still a nice return. The $10,000 you put down on the house was a cash payment. Think about it. When have you made a down payment, paid a utility bill, paid taxes, or paid for anything with blocked funds? When a trade platform places a trade, they use a deposit called margin. Let's say a trader wants to buy 1,000,000 shares of stock and that stock, XYZ stock, is trading at $50 a share. He is going to utilize leverage by buying on margin. Margin in the U.S. is set by the Federal Reserve at 50% under Regulation T.

The trader draws $25,000,000 from the customer's segregated funds account at the broker dealer through which he is executing and the broker/dealer pays the seller through an exchange such as the New York Stock Exchange, the Chicago Mercantile Exchange, the London Stock Exchange, or an Over the Counter Exchange. The broker/dealer lends him the other $25,000,000 and charges him an interest rate called the broker loan rate. Now let's say the investors in this particular trade platform have all invested with blocked funds or funds on administrative hold. The institution that sold your trader $50,000,000 of XYZ stock wants to be paid. If they don't get paid in cash your trader gets no stock and it is a D/K or a busted transaction. Your trader needs $25,000,000 cash to pay the seller. Remember the broker/dealer is going to lend the platform 50%, so $25,000,000 has been paid. Where does the trader get his $25,000,000? Well, he would get it from the investors in the trading platform; however, their funds are blocked. He can perhaps look at a bank statement where he may see the blocked funds, although he cannot use them to trade. So he uses his own funds to buy the stock. Now, think about this. He is going to risk his own money in order to pay you the profits. Why? The answer is he is not. All trading of any financial instrument requires a buyer and a seller. It does not matter what financial instrument, whether it be CMO's, MTN's, Bonds, Stocks, Commodities, Metals or Currencies. Stop and ask yourself; would you accept blocked funds for selling any asset of yours?

Every financial transaction on earth matches a buyer and a seller. The buyers and sellers may be banks, governments, insurance companies, institutions, shadow governments, or ultra wealthy individuals. There is one unassailable fact; the seller wants to be paid. You cannot pay with blocked funds. You cannot pay with funds on administrative hold. You can pay with cash, period. An investor can borrow against real financial assets, such as real estate, stocks, bonds, gold, etc. However, the trading platform is not a bank and it is not in the business of lending investors money. Investors can make their own loan arrangements and then invest into the trade platform the only thing that will facilitate the platform's margin requirements, cash.

In addition to every financial transaction having a buyer and a seller, every transaction has some level of risk. Let's come back to our trader's purchase of $50,000,000 of XYZ stock. The trade platform is required to maintain a margin to equity ratio by regulation. If the price of XYZ drops $10 per share, the platform needs to deposit additional $5,000,000 cash with the broker/dealer. Where does that come from, from the investors in the platform? The broker/dealer is not going to accept some inane concept of we have the $5,000,000 but it is blocked. They need cash in 3 business days. By now, if you are deeply into the fantasy of free money, you are saying to yourself, this poor writer does not understand that there is no risk and a secret government trading platform in Switzerland wil accept blocked funds. I would say to you; you are most likely beyond help because avarice has blocked any sense of logic you may have.

No one is going to give you hundreds of millions of dollars unless you are fortunate enough to win a national lottery or inherit the money. There is no free money. Trading is a capital-intensive business and it is a highly liquid business. Capital freely flows between buyers and sellers. It moves around the globe on a 24-hour basis. Blocked funds would be an anathema to trading. If such a thing really existed it would only serve to impede the very life blood of trading, which is the rapid flow of capital between buyers and sellers.

Important Aspects of Any Private Placement Program Deal

The goal is to prevent clients/brokers from wasting their time and risking their money. To achieve this, we will explain the two most important aspects of any private placement Program deal: "Collateralizing Funds" and "Profit Distribution". For more information on these critical subjects, please refer below. As you will see, we discuss problems, solutions, and a lot more!

"Collateralizing Funds"

The problem with most private placement programs is the risk factor. If you're blocking funds via a ("MT760") in favor of a "trader's trust", you are collateralizing your assets in favor of that trust. This means your funds are at risk if the trader was to default on the line of credit they drew against your asset. In addition, the cost for blocking funds is typically 1-2% of the face value, which is paid upfront to the bank. That is not the scenario in which you want to be involved. You have upfront fees, the trader is controlling your money, and there is no clear idea of what you're investing into at this juncture.

The solution to this problem is a customized Trust structure. If you set up your own trust, and transfer your money into it, you retain control. All the trader can do is manage your account within the conditions of the contract. Not only can you see all of the activity in the account, but all profits are sent directly back to you. At that point, you pay the trader their share, not the other way around.

Please note, if the money cannot be moved from the client's bank, they can send an MT 760 to their own trust account. By collateralizing funds in favor of yourself, through your trust, you have removed the risk. Now all you have to do is find a trader who can facilitate a line of credit against that MT 760. If the trader is real, they can get an LTV of 75-85% against the MT 760. Once you have attained the line of credit, it is time to trade! As you can see, the trust is the key component. Without it, you would be sending that MT 760 to the "trader's trust account", not your own trust account.

"Profit Distribution"

The problem with most "trades" is banking delays are inevitable. If you are receiving Millions from an international account, over and over again, it is bound to raise red flags. The fact is, money doesn't move as easily as it used to. Since 9-11, anti-money laundering laws have made it harder and harder each year. In a typical private placement offer, your profits would be repatriated weekly. Due to recent law changes, this is no longer a reasonable strategy.

The solution to this problem is the Trust. By establishing a trust prior to the trade, you create a safe place to accumulate profits. This will allow you to build your profits in a tax friendly jurisdiction, and if you decide to repatriate the funds, you can do so. The key is, you must disclose your incoming transfers appropriately, while sending larger amounts less frequently.

In summary, most "programs" do not require the structuring of a trust. If a client tries to enter a trade program without a properly structured trust, they will always fail. The only other option is if a client bought into an existing trust which was already involved in private placement. This is not an opinion; it is a fact of the business. Every real platform will require the investor to structure a trust. If they don't, it is ALWAYS a waste of time.

UNDERSTANDING BANK INSTRUMENTS, FROM BANK TO END INVESTOR

With so many people trying to broker private placement programs and bank instrument sales, we felt that it was critical to outline the entire process from instrument creation to maturity.

To truly understand the purpose and functions of bank instruments, we must first define what a bank instrument in fact is.

By definition, bank instruments are asset backed notes issued by a bank to an investor which mature over 5-10 years, collecting an annual coupon ("interest") until it matures at its pre-defined value.

For those who don't understand why debt instruments, bonds, or notes are created, let's explain it all in 2 sentences: Companies, or in our case banks, create paper notes ("IOU's") which they sell to investors, guaranteeing a certain annual interest and maturity value. This allows the investor to collect their expected profit, while the bank accesses immediate cash to meet capital requirements for additional financing opportunities.

Unlike its boring cousins (bonds), the bank instrument is rather complex, and is typically referred to as a "hybrid note". Unique amongst most debit financing notes, bank instruments: collect high annual interest rates, are backed by top rated banks, and are issued ONLY in amounts of 50 Million EURO or greater. Though those are intriguing qualities, the key is: bank instruments can be purchased at a discount from face value, and traded to investors in the secondary market.

Since we understand this topic is rather complex, we created a 5-step summary to clarify the details of how bank instruments evolve. This will explain the relation of bank instruments to private placement programs, and the investment benefits to purchasing bank notes.

Bank Instrument Steps to Maturation

1. Once the investor or trader has been cleared through compliance, the issuing bank will "cut"/create an instrument (Medium Term Note or Bank Guarantee), naming the investor or trader as the sole beneficiary. This instrument will have a predefined interest rate (0-7.5%/yr.), and a value on the date of its maturity. At this point, the purchaser would more than likely pay a discounted rate to the issuing bank, ranging from 60-90% of face value, depending on their relationships and the instrument's size.
2. If the investor chooses to hold the note, they just collect interest and exercise the value upon maturity. If the initial purchaser was a "trader", they would have a pre-defined "exit buyer" to buy the note at a higher value (ex. Trader buys at 65, sells at 74). As you can see with spreads like that, if the trader can consistently access instruments, they can organize a very profitable private placement program.
3. Once the first purchaser has purchased the note, they will usually resell it to another buyer at a higher price. Though the buyer isn't purchasing the note directly from the bank, many private placement programs are run by middlemen who fit right here in the process. Usually, they will purchase the note, and make a profit similar to what was made off of them (ex. Buy at 74, sell at 81). People in this

position are usually high net worth individuals, large corporations, hedge funds, etc.

4. The final middle man repeats the process the others have done, but they look for a different type of buyer. In this case, the note has been traded several times, and is at a smaller discount than it originally was. For many that may not be appealing, but for some that seems intriguing and less "risky". Since everyone can verify the instrument has been owned by several companies ("seasoned"), institutional buyers such as pension funds, hedge funds, mutual funds, and other low risk ventures flock for security and higher yields. As expected, the final middle man usually sells the note to an institutional buyer for a profit similar to what was made off of them (ex. Buy at 81, sell at 90).
5. The final purchaser holds the note, collecting the difference between the discount they paid vs. face value, and the annual interest until the time of its maturity. Though the information above is accurate, the spreads per trade may vary depending upon a number of variables. To state the obvious, different traders, banks, relationships, and strategies can make prices/profits fluctuate.

THE MOST COMMON REASONS WHY INVESTORS ARE NEVER ABLE TO ENTER INTO A PRIVATE PLACEMENT PROGRAM:

The most common reasons why investors are never able to enter into trading are:

1. They contact with people who say they are "the platform" and of course that´s false or in most cases they have a contact with "An intermediary Platform", which is different to a Trading Platform or a Trader. The trading platform or the Trader Office never contact clients. That is not their business. The first person who contacts the

client is the Program Manager from the Trader Office after the operation and engagement with the client is submitted and approved.

2. They don't have enough money or they have bought/leased a POF/BG which is in Euroclear or DTC, but in fact they do not have the money and of course they cannot invest what they do not have.
3. They don't have the money in an "acceptable" bank. They have the money in an offshore bank that doesn't allow the verification "bank to bank" or in a bank that is not recognized for any bank authority.
4. They don't have full control of the money (or the asset), because they rented, leased the instrument and of course they do not have the right to block the money or the instrument. They can´t issue a Swift MT-760 because they aren´t the owner of the asset.
5. They don't have a good explanation from the origin of the money, so this kind of money is not valid to enter the program. The money must be good, clean, clear, and of noncriminal origin.
6. They don't have workable assets. In most of the cases the assets are not good for trading because they are not banked from a real bank, that is to say they are just in a security house, but they do not have an SKR from the bank. It´s not incorporated in the Financial Banking System.
7. They try to proceed according to their own rules and this is not the way to enter into Private Placement Programs. The rules and procedures are set by the trader and are the same for everybody, so if the investor can not comply/accomplish this rule, the investor cannot participate in this financial opportunity.
8. They do not follow the required procedure: (8.1- Presentation of Documentation. 8.2- Due Diligence. 8.3-

Presentation of the Program Manager and Blocking asset agreement. 8.4- Submission of the trading pre-contract. 8.5- Presentation of the trader and signing the Trading Contract.

9. They do not collaborate enough with the Trader or the Trading Group.
10. The client has an asset that doesn't allow the verification bank to bank.
11. They delay the delivery of documents or send non-confirmed documents.
12. They are on a "Black List" or under investigation. These are the main reasons why a potential client cannot pass compliance or Due Diligence and will not be able to enter into trading. These are the main reasons that everyone must understand and be able to comply with, in order to pass compliance and enter into trading.

Differences Between Private Placement Program and Public Offerings

The securities are sold to a group of investors in the private placement of shares, whereas in a public offering the securities are offered to the public.

Private placement of shares can be issued by both public and private Companies, whereas in the case of a public offering the Company is either listed or will be listed after the offer is made.

This placement deal may not be required to be registered with a regulator, whereas the deals in which securities are offered publicly have to be registered with a regulator.

How Do Private Placement Programs Affect the Share Price of a Company?

The private placement of shares, if done by a private company will not affect the share price because they are not listed. However, for a public listed Company, this placement will lead to a decline in share price at least in the near term.

This placement leads to dilution of the ownership of the existing shareholders to a proportion of the size of this placement. This is because new shares are issued and the holdings of the existing shareholders remain the same. Let us see an example:

Let the number of shares outstanding before the private placement of shares be 10 million and the Company has proposed to offer 1 million equity shares in the private placement. Thus, this would result in dilution of ownership of the existing shareholders by 10%.

This dilution of a share normally leads to the decline of the share price; the impact of this placement can be considered as similar to that of a stock split. However, such an impact can be seen only in the short-term, as a long-term effect on the price would take into account the utilization of funds by the Company raised during this placement. If the Company does a private placement of shares to raise capital for a project which could provide better returns, extra profits and revenue from such a project will impact the share price thus pushing it higher.

Private Placement Program Advantages

The following are the top 5 private placement advantages

Long Term Advantage – If it is a debt security, the Company issues private placement bonds which generally have a longer time to mature than a bank liability. Thus, the Company will have more time to pay back the investors. This is ideal for the situations where the Company is investing in new businesses that would require time to earn and grow. Further, if this placement is based on equity shares; they are generally sold to strategic investors with a "buy-and-hold" strategy. These investors invest for a longer duration and also provide strategic inputs on running the business. Thus, the Company benefits from having a long-time relationship with the investor.

Less Execution timeframe – As the market for this placement has matured this has increased standardization of documentation, better terms, and pricing and increased the size of raising funds. Further, the issuer does not have to register and market such a fundraising exercise with the regulator, hence it can be executed in lesser time and cost. If the issuer is issuing private placement bonds that will be privately held, he may not be required to get credit rating which will further reduce the cost to be paid to the credit agency.

Diversification of Fundraising – Fundraising by this placement helps the Company to diversify the Company's funding sources and its capital structure. It aids the Company in raising capital when market liquidity conditions are not good. It helps the Company to organize the capital structure in terms of debt-equity structure and help it to manage its debt obligations.

Lesser Regulatory Requirements – This placement requires limited public disclosures and is prone to less regulatory requirements than that would be needed in a public offering. Thus, the Company would negotiate the deal privately and offer the securities at a negotiated and fixed price.

Sell to Accredited Investors – This placement issuer can sell complex securities to the investors participating in the issue because such an issue will be limited to a select group of investors (accredited investors). Further, they would understand the potential risk and return on such securities transactions.

Private Placement Program Disadvantages

The following are the top 2 private placement disadvantages

Difficulty in Finding a suitable investor – First and foremost, the disadvantage of a private placement of shares would be to find a suitable investor. Further, the investor may have a limited amount of funds to invest and may set certain targets to be achieved whereby he would invest the funds.

Higher Returns Requirement – The investors may require more return because of the risk they are taking by investing privately. If the investment is for private placement bonds, they may ask for higher interest rates or annual coupons because of the risk they take for unrated bond securities and illiquid securities. If investment in a private Company is by an issue of equity shares, they may ask for higher equity ownership or board positions because of the liquidity risk of their investment. Further, even if the Company is publicly traded and it chooses to offer private placement shares, the investors would do a due diligence and some clauses on such an offer like annual dividends or shares to be issued at cheaper than market rates as they would have to lock-in their stake (not to be sold in open market) for a certain time period.

CHAPTER 4

THE BASIC REASONS FOR PRIVATE PLACEMENT PROGRAMS

MONEY CREATION

First and foremost, PPOPs exist to "create" money. Money is created by creating debt.

For example: You as an individual can agree to loan $100 to a friend, with the understanding that the interest for the loan will be 10%, resulting in a total to be repaid of $110. What you have done is to actually create $10, even though you don't see that money initially.

Don't consider the legal aspects of such an agreement, just the numbers. Banks are doing this sort of lending every day, but with much more money. Essentially, banks have the power to create money from nothing. Since PPOPs involve trading with discounted bank-issued debt instruments, money is created due to the fact that such instruments are deferred payment obligations, or debts. Money is created from that debt.

Theoretically, any person, company, or organization can issue debt notes (again, ignore the legalities of the process). Debt notes are deferred payment liabilities.

Example: A person (individual, company, or organization) is in need of $100. He generates a debt note for $120 that matures after 1 year, and sells this debt for $100. This process is known as "discounting". Theoretically, the issuer is able to issue as many such debt notes at whatever face value he desires – as long as borrowers believe that he's financially strong enough to honor them upon maturity.

Debts notes such as Medium Terms Notes (MTN), Bank Guarantees (BG), and Stand-By Letters of Credit (SBLC) are issued at discounted prices by major world banks in the amount of billions of USD every day.

Essentially, they "create" such debt notes out of thin air, merely by creating a document.

The core problem: To issue such a debt note is very simple, but the issuer would have problems finding buyers unless the buyer "believes" that the issuer is financially strong enough to honor that debt note upon maturity. Any bank can issue such a debt note, sell it at discount, and promise to pay back the full-face value at the time the debt note matures. But would that issuing bank be able to find any buyer for such a debt note without being financially strong?

If one of the largest banks in Western Europe sold debt notes with a face value of €1M EURO at a discounted price of €800,000, most individuals would consider purchasing one, given the financial means and opportunity to verify it beforehand. Conversely, if a stranger approached an individual on the street with an identical bank note, issued by an unknown bank, and offered it for the same sale price; most people would never consider that offer. It is a matter of trust and credibility. This also illustrates why there's so much fraud and so many bogus instruments in this business.

LARGE DEBTS' INSTRUMENTS' MARKET

As a consequence of the previous statements, there is an enormous daily market of discounted bank instruments (e.g., MTN, BG, SBLC, Bonds, PN) involving issuing banks and groups of exit-buyers (Pension Funds, large financial institutions, etc.) in an exclusive Private Placement arena.

All such activities by the bank are done as "Off-Balance Sheet Activities". As such, the bank benefits in many ways. Off-Balance Sheet Activities are contingent assets and liabilities, where the value depends upon the outcome of which the claim is based, similar to that of an option. Off-Balance Sheet Activities appear on the balance sheet ONLY as memoranda items. When they generate a cash flow they appear as a credit or debit in the balance sheet. The bank does not have to consider binding capital constraints, as there is no deposit liability.

NORMAL TRADING VS. PRIVATE PLACEMENT

All trading programs in the Private Placement arena involve trade with such discounted debt notes in some fashion. Further, in order to bypass the legal restrictions, this trading can only be done on a private level. This is the main difference between this type of trading and "normal" trading, which is highly regulated. This is a Private Placement level business transaction that is free from the usual restrictions present in the securities market.

Usually, trading is performed under the "open market" (also known as the "spot market") where discounted instruments are bought and sold with auction-type bids. To participate in such trading, the traders must be in full control of the funds, otherwise they lack the means to buy the instruments and resell them. Also, there are fewer arbitrage transactions in this market, since all participants have knowledge of the instruments and their prices.

However, in addition to the open market there is a closed, private market wherein lies a restricted number of "master commitment holders". These holders are Trusts with huge amounts of money that enter contractual agreements with banks to buy a limited number of fresh-cut instruments at a specific price during an allotted period of time. Their job is to resell these instruments, so they contract sub-commitment holders, who in turn contract exit-buyers.

These programs are all based on arbitrage transactions with pre-defined prices. As such, the traders never need to be in control of the client's funds. However, no program can start unless there is a sufficient quantity of money backing each transaction. It is at this point the clients are needed, because the involved banks and commitment holders are not allowed to trade with their own money unless they have reserved enough funds on the market, comprising unused money that belongs to clients, never at risk.

The trading banks can loan money to the traders. Typically, this money is loaned at a ratio of 10:1, but during certain conditions this ratio can be as high as 20:1. In other words, if the trader can "reserve" $100M, then the bank can loan $1B. In all actuality, the bank is giving the trader a line of credit based on how much money the trader/commitment holder has, since the banks won't loan that much money without collateral, no matter how much money the clients have.

Because bankers and financial experts are well aware of the open market, and equally aware of the so-called "MTN-programs", but are closed out of the private market, they find it hard to believe that the private market exists.

ARBITRAGE AND LEVERAGE

Private Placement trading safety is based on the fact that the transactions are performed as arbitrage transactions. This means that the instruments will be bought and resold immediately with pre-defined prices. A number of buyers and sellers are contracted, including exit-buyers comprised mostly of large financial institutions, insurance companies, or extremely wealthy individuals.

The issued instruments are never sold directly to the exit-buyer, but to a chain of clients. For obvious reasons the involved banks cannot directly participate in these transactions, but are still profiting from it indirectly by loaning money with interest to the trader or client as a line of credit. This is their leverage. Furthermore, the banks profit from the commissions involved in each transaction.

The client's principal does not have to be used for the transactions, as it is only reserved as a compensating balance ("mirrored") against this credit line. This credit line is then used to back up the arbitrage transactions. Since the trading is done as arbitrage, the money ("credit line") doesn't have to be used, but it must still be available to back up each and every transaction.

Such programs never fail because they don't begin before all actors have been contracted, and each actor knows exactly what role to play and how they will profit from the transactions. A trader who is able to secure this leverage is able to control a line of credit typically 10 to 20 times that of the principal.

Even though the trader is in control of that money, the money still cannot be spent. The trader need only show that the money is under his control, and is not being used elsewhere at the time of the transaction.

This concept can be illustrated in the following example. Assume you are offered the chance to buy a car for $30,000 and that you also find another buyer that is willing to buy it from you for $35,000. If the transactions are completed at the same time, then you will not be required to "spend" the $30,000 and then wait to receive the $35,000. Performing the transactions at the same time nets you an immediate profit of $5,000. However, you must still have that $30,000 and prove it is under your control.

Arbitrage transactions with discounted bank instruments are done in a similar way. The involved traders never actually spend the money, but they must be in control of it. The client's principal is reserved directly for this, or indirectly in order for the trader to leverage a line of credit.

Confusion is common because most folks seem to believe that the money must be spent in order to complete the transaction. Even though this is the traditional way of trading -

buy low and sell high – and also the common way to trade on the open market for securities and bank instruments, it is possible to set up arbitrage transactions if there is a chain of contracted buyers.

This is why client's funds in Private Placement Programs are always safe without any trading risk.

HIGH YIELD

Compared to the yield from traditional investments, these programs usually get a very high yield. A yield of 50%-100% per week is historically possible.

For example: Assume a leverage effect of 10:1, meaning the trader is able to back each buy-sell transaction with ten times the amount of money that the client has in his bank account. In other words, the client has $10M, and the trader is able to work with $100M. Assume also the trader is able to complete three buy-sell transactions per week for 40 banking weeks (one year), with a 5% profit from each buy-sell transaction:

(5% profit/transaction) (3 transactions/week) = 15% profit/week Assume 10x leverage effect = 150% profit... PER WEEK!

Even with a split of profit between the client and trading group, this still results in a double-digit weekly yield. This example can still be seen as conservative, since first tier trading groups can achieve a much higher single spread for each transaction, as well as a markedly higher number of weekly trades.

CLIENTS

The involved clients (program clients) are not the end-buyers in the chain. The actual real end-buyers are financially strong companies who are looking for a long term, safe investment, like pension funds, trusts, and insurance companies. Because they are needed as end-buyers, they are not permitted to participate "in-between" as clients. The client who participates in a PPOP is just an actor in the picture along with many other actors (issuing banks, exit-buyers, brokers, etc.) who benefit from this trading. Usually, the client does not interact with others involved in the process.

PROGRAM STRUCTURE

Normally, a trading program is nothing more than a pre-arranged buy/sell arbitrage transaction of discounted banking instruments. Theoretically, a client with a large amount of funds (on the level of $100-500M USD) could arrange his own program by implementing the buy/sell transaction for himself; however, in this case he needs to control the entire process, initiating contact with the banks and the exit buyers at the same time. This is not a simple task, considering the restrictions in place.

For a client it is much simpler (and usually more profitable) to enter a program where the trader and his trading group have everything in place (the issuing banks, the exit buyers, the contracts ready for the arbitrage transaction, the line of credit with the trading banks, all of the necessary guarantees/safety for the client, etc.). The client needs only to agree with the contract proposed by the trader, disregarding any other underlying issues.

It is further advantageous for the client to enter a program with a substantially lower amount of money and benefit from the line of credit offered by the trading group.

NON-SOLICITATION AND NON-DISCLOSURE

As a direct consequence of the PPOP's environment where this business has to take place, a non-solicitation agreement has to be strictly followed by all parties involved. This agreement strongly influences the way the participants can interact with each other. Sometimes non-solicitation agreements foster scam attempts, due to the fact that at an early stage it is often difficult for the clients to recognize reliable sources with whom to be in contact.

There is another reason why so few experienced people talk about these transactions: virtually every contract involving the use of these high-yield instruments contains very explicit non-circumvention and non-disclosure clauses forbidding the contracting parties from discussing any aspect of the transaction for a specified number of years. Hence, it is very difficult to locate experienced contacts who are both knowledgeable and willing to talk openly about this type of instrument and the profitability of the transactions in which they figure. This is a highly private business, not advertised anywhere nor covered in the press, and is closed to anyone but the best-connected, most wealthy entities that can come forward with substantial cash funds.

HOW BANKS AND BROKERS CAN PROFIT

Banks are not allowed to act as clients in such programs. However, they are able to profit indirectly in different ways. This fact permits some private brokers, trading groups, and clients to take part in this process that otherwise would only be a banking matter. The assets coming from private clients are necessary to start the process. These private, large funds are the mandatory requirement for the buy/sell transactions of banking debt instruments. Brokers are necessary to introduce the clients to the trading groups. Thus, each of the involved parties takes their part in the sharing of the benefits, commissions for banks and brokers and proceeds for trading groups and clients).

PROJECTS

The purpose of this type of trading is to finance projects, not generate tremendous profits for the client. These may be for-profit or non-profit and can be funded as a result of this trading.

Since this type of trading generates such large amounts of money on the market, measures must be taken to keep the inflation low. One way to do this is to adjust the interest rates, but this usually has little or no effect. A better way to minimize inflation is to let some of the profit be used for different projects that need funding, such as rebuilding infrastructure in regions of the world that have experienced catastrophes or war.

PROCESS SYNTHESIS

The complete process involving the issuing of debt-notes, the arbitrage transactions, the programs, and the projects is a result of combined market forces. Banks have a method of increasing their revenues and profits, clients are able to finance different ventures, and borrowers are able to access loan funds. There is a supply and demand for such instruments, and as long as the supply and demand exist then also this kind of trading will exist.

PROCESS SUMMARY

The following is a summary of the process involved for entering a PPOP:

A client with a minimum of €100M applies for a Private Placement Opportunity Program.

This business is entirely private. To get access to these investment programs, the client needs to send his preliminary documentation to a broker whom the client trusts to be in direct contact with the trading group. That means a Client Information Sheet, a copy of their passport, and a bank statement showing the balance of funds being committed for trade. It is generally required that the bank statement be signed by two authorized bank officers to make it full bank responsibility. There is no other way for the client to get in contact with the trading group.

After the client has sent his own paperwork (their Passport, Client Information Sheet, and recent bank statement showing cash on deposit), the trading group will investigate the applicant. If the response is positive, the program manager in the trading group will contact or meet with the client. If the investigation is not favourable, the program manager will contact the broker and tell him that the client did not qualify.

In the body of the contact with the client, the trader will explain the program terms/conditions to the client, and outline the guarantees and requirements to start the program. The client will get instructions to open a new sole signatory bank account at the trading bank for transferring the funds there.

The client will receive a contract which states the total gross yield, the percentage of the gross profit reserved for projects, the percentage for the trading group and the percentage for profit participation fees to be deducted for brokers/intermediaries. The net return to the client will be wired to another account that can be located in any bank worldwide. If the client accepts the contract, the contract is signed and the program is ready to start.

The trader is now able to leverage the client's reserved money 10 times, and is now able to back up the arbitrage transactions with that money, through a credit line that remains in the bank account that is screened before each arbitrage transaction. Trading now continues, and the profit is paid out per the contract terms to the client.

The programs work with cash only or gold bullion. This fact means that the client will only be accepted with liquid funds. Recent rulings by the G20 prohibit the use of an asset other than cash or gold bullion in a bank vault. A line of credit must be established and drawn down into an account at a bank, where it is lodged and blocked.

Analysis Of Risk Involved In Private Placement Program Contracts

Finalizing Private Placement Program contracts with clients can be a stressful process because of problems encountered along the way.

FROM THE CLIENT'S SIDE

The applicant client will not be able to meet directly with the trader in this business. The main reason why there's a broker-intermediary chain is because the people in the trading groups have no time or interest in meeting all the people who are just fishing for information, and/or who fail to qualify because they don't have enough money, or have useless bank instruments.

If you're a qualifying client, truly connected intermediaries/ brokers should be able to place you in contact with a performing trading group. Don't attempt to find a trader on your own: Most so-called traders in the financial world are not involved in this kind of trading and are not educated to their existence. Those few traders who are keep a low profile and would never talk with a client who hasn't been cleared. In fact, they cannot until the client passes the international KYC (Know Your Customer) compliance.

When it comes to cases of non-performance, the problem is usually on the client side. The client doesn't qualify for a variety of reasons; he doesn't have enough money, the bank is too small or is located in the wrong country, he cannot move his funds, etc.

Oftentimes deals are killed because the broker and/or intermediary don't understand the process, and inject themselves, more concerned about a fee than about allowing the two principals (Client and Trader) to interact without interference.

Some of the most common reasons why clients are never able to enter this kind of trading are:

- They don't have enough money or workable assets.
- They don't have the money in an acceptable bank.
- They don't have full control of the money (or of the bank instruments).
- They don't have a good explanation of the origin of the money.

- They do not follow the required procedure.
- They do not collaborate enough with the Trading Group.
- They delay the delivery of documents or send fake or non-confirmed documents.
- Their identity cannot be confirmed.
- They are blacklisted or under investigation.

Remember that the trading group does not have to give any explanation why the client doesn't pass through the clearance.

Clients should understand what is required to qualify:

A minimum of $100 Million EURO or USD in cash located in a major bank in Western Europe, USA, Canada, Hong Kong, Singapore, or Australia. Additionally, the money needs to be traceable with a non-criminal history.

The client, or company if one is represented, should be clearly identified.

Once cleared, clients are invited to the table, but their acceptance is never guaranteed, regardless of their assets or prominence.

The client himself must be the one and only person with whom the trading group engages. He is not allowed to let his lawyer or any other person perform or act on his behalf, brokers included. If the client does not speak English and needs assistance, then he must sign a Limited Power of Attorney for a translator. The LPOA will only be accepted for communication purposes, and the client must still sign all the documents.

Clients who have the least amount of money are always placed last in the queue. A client with €100M will get more attention than a client with €10M. Clients who have assets other than cash or AU bullion in a bank vault will also always be placed last in the queue, if they are accepted at all. Assets other than cash or gold bullion must be monetized to provide cash for the trading account.

It is difficult for any client to ensure that he meets the right people; those few intermediaries and brokers who know the process and who are working with a performing trading group. The best he can do is to educate himself and not be lured by those who claim that their program will give the highest yield. He must also be patient, and trust the legitimate intermediary or broker. There is no way that the client will directly meet with the trade group before he has been cleared.

If for any reason the client is dissatisfied with the broker and/or intermediary, then another one can be obtained.

These are some of the main risks the client can meet:

Nothing will come out of the trade; no contract and no profit, just frustration after weeks/months of waiting.

Clients or their intermediaries and/or brokers are "shopping around" with client documents, which sooner or later will result in blacklisting.

The client is told that he must move his funds out of his own control; to an escrow account, etc.

The client is told that he must buy or lease a bank instrument for his money. In the worst-case scenario, this instrument is a fake or impossible to use.

The client is told that he must pay upfront fees, because a leverage of his funds must be done, or some bank instrument must be discounted, or banking fees must be paid, etc. The upfront fees paid are lost, and nothing more will happen.

FROM THE BROKER'S AND INTERMEDIARY'S SIDE

There is a common misuse of such terms as brokers, intermediaries, and facilitators. The fact is, these are not official terms in banking or finance, but such terms are used within trading groups and in their communication between each other. Although a broker or an intermediary can claim that they are in direct contact with a person carrying that title, it is not a guarantee of anything. Any person can fraudulently call himself a trader, or a commitment holder, or whatever. And since such positions cannot be verified (at the first stage), such titles can be meaningless as seen from the clients' point of view.

There is almost always a chain of the trading group, a broker and intermediary, and the client. This is for two reasons. Firstly, trading groups, brokers, and intermediaries are not allowed to solicit; the Client must start by asking for information.

Secondly, this protects all parties involved with the trading group. Brokers may work through several intermediaries, and vice versa intermediaries. A chain of more than one or two intermediaries connected directly between the two Principals, in general, is not acceptable to some program providers.

A good broker should also screen the potential clients, filtering the most promising applicants and at the same time collecting from them the proper documentation. In this way, the trading group receives workable documentation from the broker.

The most common risks or problems that a broker, an intermediary or a facilitator can meet with in this business are:

- They may need to investigate dozens of clients before finding a qualified applicant.
- They may discover the assets of a client to be unworkable after weeks or months of processing.
- They may have difficulty qualifying themselves with new clients because they cannot show any past performance or past contracts. The relationship with the client is just a matter of trust at an early stage.

There could be several levels involved for the intermediaries. The closest one to the trading group (sometimes called also facilitator) is the most important person. This person should have a direct contact with the trading group. Any other broker beneath the facilitator has a lower value in the hierarchy. The broker and/or the intermediary can have problems showing the client his level in the hierarchy at an early stage.

PROCEDURES FOR PRIVATE PLACEMENT PROGRAMS

WITH VENEZUELAN GLOBAL BONDS

1.- Personalized Analysis and Assessment

Our team of economists and lawyers will at all times be responsible for advising the client in a detailed and personalized manner. Depending on the client's assets, each case will be studied independently and the best way to proceed will be proposed with the key intention of completing the operation successfully.

Advice at all stages of the process: From the explanation of this kind of financial opportunity and how yields rise to the required banking and corporate documentation that the client should provide to be later presented at the Trader's Office.

Possibility of carrying out any kind of face meeting in Madrid (Spain) or, if not possible, traveling to the city where the investor is located. This last option will be available depending on the characteristics of the client's assets.

2.- Submission of Documentation

The client must provide all required documentation for the submission of the operation at the Trader's office:

*** Set Compliance:** After the initial contact with the client and after studying the viability of the operation, the client will be provided with the compliance set (Set of documents) for its proper completion and signature. For greater efficiency and ease, our firm will complete 90% of the compliance set so the client will simply need to review it and proceed to sign it.

***Passport:** DIN-A4 size and in any of the following formats: PDF, JPG, BMP or PNG.

***Asset:** The Proof of Funds and all bank documents must be manually signed by two bank officials currently in charge of the client's account. Electronic signatures will not be accepted. In the case of documents requiring a verification by the Euroclear system/DTCC, it will be imperative to print the 12 pages.

IMPORTANT: We do not accept any kind of procedure that prohibits all telephone calls from bank to bank, since this is necessary to verify and ensure that we are dealing with a real signer of the account and that funds and/or assets are not the object of "leasing".

*RWA (799/760) FROM THE CENTRAL BANK OF VENEZUELA. In some cases, RWA 799/542.

3.- Due Diligence and Asset Verification:

Once the operation is submitted at the Trader's office, we will immediately proceed to the verification of the assets and the realization of the "Due Diligence" (under study for acceptance) of the client and the submitted assets. The client must not be connected with the mafia, drug traffic, weapons, or any other illegal activity. Also, the asset must be good, clear, clean, with a non-criminal origin and must be freely available for the customer.

4.- Available Options to block the Assets:

The investor will have to block the VENEZUELAN GLOBAL BONDS OR FUNDS VIA: *Swift MT-799 and MT-760: The client's bank issues a Swift MT-799 prior notice and a Swift MT-760 Block to the bank the Trader appoints on the contract. The recipient of the MT-760 will be "the Trader's Company ".

5.- Program Manager Contact

Once the previous inquiries are successfully completed, within a maximum of 48-72 hours, the Program Manager will contact the client directly by phone. The aim of this call, in addition to the Program Manager's formal presentation, is to inform the kind of program the client will have access to, the profitability, and also to agree on the different possible ways to block the assets.

6.- Signature Trading Contract

After the client and the Program Manager agree on the blocking way and clarify every possible matter that may arise on the conversation, the client will be offered several options to sign the Trading Agreement:

Option 1.- Signing the Trading Contract via email and later, when the signing for the opening of the customer's account takes place, and the ratification of the Trading Agreement will be performed before the Trader. (Fast option)

Option 2.- The client and the Trader agree on a day and time to sign the Trading Contract in person. (This option is not available for all cases since it will depend on the characteristics of the submitted assets).

PROCEDURES FOR PRIVATE PLACEMENT PROGRAMS

With LTNs from the Central Bank of Brazil

1.- Personalized Analysis and Assessment

Our team of economists and lawyers will at all times be responsible for advising the client in a detailed and personalized manner. Depending on the client's assets, each case will be studied independently and the best way to proceed will be proposed with the key intention of completing the operation successfully.

Advice at all stages of the process: From the explanation of this kind of financial opportunity and how yields rise to the required banking and corporate documentation that the client should provide to be later presented at the Trader's Office.

The possibility of carrying out any kind of face meeting in Madrid (Spain) or, if not possible, traveling to the city where the investor is located. This last option will be available depending on the characteristics of the client's assets.

2.- Submission of Documentation

The client must provide all required documentation for the submission of the operation at the Trader's office:

*** Set Compliance:** After the initial contact with the client and after studying the viability of the operation, the client will be provided with the compliance set (Set of documents) for its proper completion and signature. For greater efficiency and ease, our firm will complete 90% of the compliance set so the client will simply need to review it and proceed to sign it.

***Passport:** DIN-A4 size and in any of the following formats: PDF, JPG, BMP or PNG.

***Asset:** The Proof of Funds and all bank documents must be manually signed by two bank officials currently in charge of the client's account. Electronic signatures will not be accepted. In the case of documents requiring a verification by the Euroclear system/DTCC, it will be imperative to print the 12 pages.

IMPORTANT: We do not accept any kind of procedure that prohibits all telephone calls from bank to bank, since this is necessary to verify and ensure that we are dealing with a real signer of the account and that funds and/or assets are not object of "leasing".

*RWA (799/760) FROM THE CENTRAL BANK OF BRAZIL or any TOP BANK.

In some cases, RWA 799/542.

3.- Due Diligence and Asset Verification:

Once the operation is submitted at the Trader's office, we will immediately proceed to the verification of the assets and the realization of the "Due Diligence" (under study for acceptance) of the client and the submitted assets. The client must not be connected with the mafia, drug traffic, weapons, or any other illegal activity. Also, the asset must be good, clear, clean, with a non-criminal origin and must be freely available for the customer.

4.- Available Options to block the Assets:

The investor will have to block the LTNs VIA:

* Swift MT-799 and MT-760: The client's bank issues a Swift MT-799 prior notice and a Swift MT-760 Block to the bank the Trader appoints on the contract. The recipient of the MT-760 will be "the Trader's Company". In some cases, via swift MT-799 and MT-542.

5.- Program Manager Contact

Once the previous inquiries are successfully completed, within a maximum of 48-72 hours, the Program Manager will contact the client directly by phone. The aim of this call, in addition to the Program Manager's formal presentation, is to inform the kind of program to which the client will have accesss, the profitabilities, and also to agree on the different possible ways to block the assets.

6.- Signature Trading Contract

After the client and the Program Manager agree on the blocking way and clarify every possible matter that may arise on the conversation, the client will be offered several options to sign the Trading Agreement:

Option 1.- Signing the Trading Contract via email and later, when the signing for the opening of the customer's account takes place, and the ratification of the Trading Agreement will be performed before the Trader. (Fast option)

Option 2.- The client and the Trader agree to a day and time to sign the Trading Contract in person. (This option is not available for all cases since it will depend on the characteristics of the submitted assets).

HERITAGE FUNDS PROGRAM

This Program is offered by a Government Agency and it is only for accounts holders at HSBC Hong Kong.

Minimum 500M USD/Euros

Maximum 10T USD/Euros with 2B Tranche Per Day

1. Terms and Requirements:

Proof of funds / Bank Statement / Account requirement / Account must be on HSBC Internal Screen.

2. Transaction Procedures:

1. Investor Agrees to this Procedure and returns and signs Consulting Fee Agreement and provides Company documents, Corporate Resolution (if a Corporation), A-size Color copy of signatory passport and Bank Statement.
2. Asset Manager completes due diligence with the FED.
3. In the morning, Investor takes Asset manager to the counter of HSBC to obtain a printed Bank Statement.

4. The same morning Asset Manager and Investor sign a Co-operation Agreement and other documents inside HSBC, Hong Kong. The same day afternoon, the Asset Manager assists Investor with opening a Receiving Account.
5. Transaction period is One Year and pays Monthly. Profit is 100% per Month, shared as follows: China Bank Group 50%, Investor 40%, Program Manager 10%.
6. Both parties sign the Co-operation Agreement, to confirm the smaller amounts from 500M upwards will be put together on traders' side untill it reach 5B USD/EUROS, so your investors must be prepared for a certain waiting period, for profit sharing, and to protect the interest of all parties, so that the transaction can be completed. The terms and conditions of the Co-operation Agreement must be adhered to by both parties.

3. Profit Sharing:

1. The Co-operation Agreement profit sharing will prevail.
2. Sharing Formula is as follows, and profits will be wired directly to the accounts of all beneficiaries.
3. Sharing:
   I. China Bank Group profit per Month: 50 %
   II. Investor profit per Month: 40%
   III. Program Manager per Month 10%
   IV. Asset Manager to assist beneficiaries with making payment on local taxes.
4. Investor agrees to pay 5% consultant fees to all parties concerned, as soon as the profits arriving at the account are allowed to move.
5. Under this transaction, Investor's funds in the deposit account will not be moved, blocked, pledged, or depleted. Instead of blocking one of the trading officers must be added with a second signature on the client's account, with no right whatsoever to move the funds. At the end of the

trading this signature will be withdrawn. There is no risk, or damage to the account.

Investor agrees not to move the funds in the account during the transaction period on good faith, and is free to handle the account as he desires at the end of the transaction.

PROCEDURES FOR CHINESE CITIZENS

Due to the problems currently existing with people of Chinese origin for access to a PPP (Private Placement Program) and due to the refusal of the Fed (Federal Reserve), we offer two viable procedures to provide access to this financial opportunity to a Chinese citizen.

The two available procedures are:

1.- Assignment of a person (not a Chinese citizen) in the bank account where resources are deposited

The client assigns his bank account to a person of his confidence. This person is assigned with limited powers. He may not transfer the funds from the account. The program will be processed and signed by this new person assigned as "Account Signatory."

There are two available options to block the asset:

(a) SWIFT MT-799 and MT-760: The client's bank issues a Swift MT-799 pre-advice and a Swift MT-760 block to the bank the Trader appoints on the contract. The recipient of the MT-760 will be "the Trader's Company ". This option implies a higher cost for the client, but it is the classic one because it is more comfortable for the Trader.

(b) Authorization to manage the account: The client authorizes the Trader as a signatory to indistinctly manage the account where the resources are deposited, with the EXCEPTION of transferring funds from the account. The Trader's intervention at the client's bank will be solely and exclusively to request a letter to block the amount of invested funds. The client is the only signatory allowed to move funds. This option is more economical for the client, since it avoids the cost of Swift issuance and the time loss that bureaucratic procedures imply. (Option only for account in Europe)

3.- Issuance of BG (Bank Guarantee)

The owner of the funds instructs his bank to issue a new BG using like collateral through his resources. The amount of BG will be decided between client and bank. The client will appear as "Applicant" (owner) and "Beneficiary" will be the Trader´s company once the trading contract is signed.

Once the BG is issued, the client has 2 available options:

(a) SWIFT - The client´s bank issues a SWIFT MT-799 at Trader´s bank. Once recaptioned the Swift, client and Trader sign the trading contract. (Conditioned to reception of Swift MT-760). After signing the contract, the client issues a Swift MT- 760 at the Trader´s bank designed in the contract.

#COURIER – Client sends a copy of BG (scanned) to Trader and he will open a bank account to the client in a TOP 5 Bank where the BG will be deposited via banking courier. The BG will be blocked internally.

Important: The investor will receive a monthly report by one of the best auditing companies in the world, "PriceWaterhouse Coopers", which will detail every transaction made by the trader and the profit driven in each transaction.

[INSERT APPLICANT LETTERHEAD IN HEADER SPACE]

RULES TRADING

Date: XXX X XXXXX

To: Economists & Lawyers

None of the customary standards and practices that apply to normal, conventional business, investing and finance, apply to "trading/transaction-programs". Personal business and financial success have virtually nothing to do with who you are and what you know, but almost everything to do with what you are and whom you know.

It is a "privilege" to be invited to participate in one of our Private Placement Transaction Programs. It is not a "right." These programs deliver unparalleled yields in combination with absolutely no program-related risk. The trading administrators and managers have a virtually endless supply of financially qualified applicants.

All things considered, the trading administrators and their banks will favor the applicant who provides the best paperwork.

An applicant should never underestimate what the trading entities can obtain regarding knowledge about him. Failure to provide full disclosure will disqualify the disingenuous.

Generally, these programs exist to finance humanitarian projects, not to generate more money for the wealthy. Clients who have such projects usually receive preferred treatment and the highest yields.

Clients must first prove that they are qualified, not the other way around. Until the client is accepted by Compliance, the Traders, and Trading Banks, no placement can occur. The U.S. Patriot Act has introduced obligatory stringent compliance procedures, which lengthens the time required to receive clearance.

Face-to-face interviews with compliance officers and program management are occasionally required, but generally not necessary.

Any arrogant or demanding personality will be guaranteed to be rejected.

Only the principal owner of funds (or bank confirmed Mandate) is required as signatory. Corporations must empower an Officer or Director as sole, exclusive signatory by using a Corporate Resolution.

Not only do the funds have to be on deposit in a top bank; they must also be in an acceptable Western (preferably) jurisdiction. If not, the funds must be moved to an acceptable jurisdiction, or else responsibly endorsed by an acceptable bank in an acceptable venue.

It is felony fraud to submit documents or financial instruments that are forged, altered or counterfeit. Such papers are promptly referred to the appropriate law enforcement agencies for immediate criminal prosecution.

[INSERT APPLICANT LETTERHEAD IN HEADER SPACE]

The practices, procedures and rules are determined by the U.S. Federal Regulatory Authorities, Western European Central Banks program management, licensed traders, and trading banks. It is their decision who to accept and who to reject. Contract terms, yield, schedules, etc., are made to fit their needs and schedules -- and not the caprices or demands of the investors.

This marketplace is highly regulated and strictly confidential, and absolute confidentiality by the investor is a key element of virtually every contract. A client who breaks confidentiality will precipitate instant cancellation of this contract, often with severe financial consequence.

Submission of the application documents to more than one management group at a time is termed "shopping." If an investor "shops" he can expect that this fact shall be quickly disseminated and known among the program management groups who maintain close communication -- and he will then be accepted by none – and rejected ("blacklisted") by all!

Signature:

SEAL OF COMPANY

Name/Title: Company: Passport Number: Date of Issue:

Date of Expiry:

Country of Issuance:

THE MOST COMMON REASONS WHY INVESTORS ARE NEVER ABLE TO ENTER INTO A PRIVATE PLACEMENT PROGRAM

The most common reasons why investors are never able to enter into trading are:

1. They contact with people who says they are "the platform" and of course that´s false. The trading platform or the Trader Office never contacts the clients. That is not their business. The first person who contacts the client is the Program Manager from the Trader Office after the operation is submitted and aproved.
2. They don't have enough money or they have bought/leased a POF/BG which is in Euroclear or DTC but in fact they do not have the money and of course they cannot invest what they do not have.
3. They don't have the money in an "acceptable" bank. They have the money in an offshore bank that don´t allow the verification "bank to bank" or in a bank that is not recognized for any bank authority.
4. They don't have full control of the money (or the asset), because they rented, leased the instrument and of course they do not have the right to block the money or the instrument. They can´t issue a Swift MT-760 because they aren´t the owner of the asset.
5. They don't have a good explanation from the origin of the money, so this kind of money is not valid to enter the program. The money must be clean, clear, and non-criminal origin.
6. They do not have workable assets. Most of the cases the assets are not good for trading because they are not banked from a real bank, that is to say they are just in a security house but they do not have an SKR from the bank. It´s not incorporated in the Financial Banking System.

7. They try to proceed according to their own rules and this is not the way to enter in Private Placement Program. The rules and procedures are set for the trader and are the same for everybody, so if the investor can not comply/accomplish this rule, the investor cannot participate in this financial opportunity.
8. They do not follow the required procedure:
   8.1-Presentation of documentation.
   8.2-Due Diligence.
   8.3-Presentation of the Program Manager and Blocking asset agreement.
   8.4-Submission of the trading pre-contract.
   8.5-Presentation of the trader and signing the Trading Contract.
9. They do not collaborate enough with the Trader or the Trading Group.
10. The client has an asset that don´t allow the verification bank to bank.
11. They delay the delivery of documents or send non-confirmed documents.
12. They are on a "Black List" or under investigation. These are the main reasons why a potential client cannot pass compliance or Due Diligence and will not be able to enter into trading. These are the main reasons that everyone must understand and be able to comply with in order to pass compliance and enter into trading.

(FORMAT MT799 - PRE-ADVICE- SAMPLE)

PRIORITY: NORMAL MESSAGE OUTPUT REFERENCE:
CORRESPONDENT INPUT REFERENCE:
MESSAGE HEADER SWIFT OUTPUT: MT799
SENDER:
RECEIVER:
BANK NAME:
ADDRESS:

ACCOUNT No.:
ACCOUNT NAME:
SWIFT:
BANK OFFICER:
TELEPHONE No.:
TRANSACTION REF.:
MESSAGE TEXT
AS ADVISED AND INSTRUCTED BY OUR CLIENT ****CLIENT NAME*****, WE STAND READY TO ISSUE A SWIFT MT760 TO ****BANK NAME*** ****************, FOR THE BENEFIT OF ***********RECIPIENT BENEFICIARY NAME******, ACCOUNT NUMBER: 00000000000, IN THE AMOUNT OF ******AMOUNT IN WORD******** (€/USD 000,000,000.00) ONLY. THE VERBIAGE FOR THE MT760 TO BE ISSUED SHALL BE AS FOLLOWS:
QUOTE
WE, *****BANK NAME*****, ****************BANK ADDRESS***************; HEREBY CONFIRM WITH FULL BANK RESPONSIBILITY THAT OUR CLIENT, ******CLIENT NAME***************, AS OF THIS DATE, HAS AN CASH BACKED ****BANK INSTRUMENT TYPE**** ISSUED BY ***ISSSUER BANK NAME*****, FACE VALUE ***AMOUNT IN WORDS***** (€/USD 000,000,000 ONLY), NUMBER 000000000, CUSIP No. 000000000, IN THE ABOVE REFERENCED ACCOUNT WITH US.
WE FURTHER CONFIRM THAT THIS ****BANK INSTRUMENT TYPE**** IS HEREBY RESERVED/BLOCKED IN YOUR FAVOUR FOR THE BENEFIT OF ***********RECIPIENT BENEFICIARY NAME******, DULY REPRESENTED BY *******REPRESENT NAME*****, AND THAT THIS BANK INSTRUMENT SHALL REMAIN BLOCKED FOR A PERIOD OF THIRTEEN (13) CALENDAR MONTHS, FROM THE DATE OF THIS SWIFT, FOR THEIR FULL USE AND BENEFIT.
WE FURTHER CERTIFY THIS SWIFT CONFIRMATION REPRESENTED HEREIN SHALL BE FREELY ASSIGNABLE, DIVISIBLE, CALLABLE AND TRANSFERABLE AS PER THE BENEFICIARY INSTRUCTIONS AT NO CHARGE TO HIM. WE CONFIRM THAT THIS SWIFT HAS BEEN ISSUED UNDER FULL BANK RESPONSIBILITY AND THAT THE VALUE IS AVAILABLE TO THE NAMED BENEFICIARY "***********RECIPIENT BENEFICIARY NAME******".
WE CONFIRM THAT THIS BANK GUARANTEE IS UNRESTRICTED, DIVISIBLE, TRANSFERABLE, ASSIGNABLE AND CALLABLE, FREE OF

ANY LIENS OR ENCUMBRANCES, CLEAN AND LEGALLY OBTAINED AND ARE FREELY AVAILABLE FOR INVESTMENTS.
WE ALSO CONFIRM THAT THIS CALLABLE BANK CONFIRMATION SWIFT IS A FULLY CONFIRMED BANK INSTRUMENT WHICH MAY SERVE AS COLLATERAL TO SECURE ANY LOAN, CREDIT LINE OR CREDIT FACILITIES.
THIS SWIFT IS VERIFIABLE ON A BANK TO BANK BASIS BY A NOMINATED BANK MANAGER/OFFICER CONTACTING THE UNDERSIGNED. WE FURTHER CONFIRM THAT A CERTIFIED COPY OF THIS SWIFT SHALL BE COURIER TO YOUR BANKING CO-ORDINATES WITHIN 5 (FIVE) BANKING DAYS.
THIS BANK INSTRUMENT IS SUBJECT TO THE UNIFORM CUSTOM AND PRACTICE (1993 REVISION) UNDER INTERNATIONAL CHAMBER OF COMMERCE PUBLICATION NUMBER 500.
UNQUOTE
PLEASE ADVISE YOUR CLIENT, (TD..........) AND ACKNOWLEDGE AND CONFIRM YOUR ACCEPTANCE. END OF SWIFT TEXT MESSAGE
YOURS TRULY,

....

....

BANK OFFICER NAME BANK OFFICER NAME TITLE
TITLE

PRIORITY: NORMAL

(FORMAT MT760- SAMPLE)

MESSAGE OUTPUT REFERENCE:
CORRESPONDENT INPUT REFERENCE:
MESSAGE HEADER
SWIFT OUTPUT: MT 760 MESSAGES IN (AUTHENTICATED FORMAT GUARANTEE)
SENDER:
RECEIVER:
BANK NAME:
ADDRESS:
BRANCH:
ACCOUNT NAME: Emirates Financial FZE. ACCOUNT NUMBER:
SWIFT TRANSFER CODE:
BANK OFFICER:
TITLE:

PHONE:
FAX:
TELEX:
COUNTRY CODE:
TRANSACTION REF.:
MESSAGE TEXT
WE, *****BANK NAME*****, ****************BANK ADDRESS***************; HEREBY CONFIRM WITH FULL BANK RESPONSIBILITY THAT OUR CLIENT, ******CLIENT NAME***************, AS OF THIS DATE, HAS AN CASH BACKED ****BANK INSTRUMENT TYPE**** ISSUED BY ***ISSSUER BANK NAME*****, FACE VALUE ***AMOUNT IN WORDS***** (€/USD 000,000,000 ONLY), NUMBER 000000000, CUSIP No. 000000000, IN THE ABOVE REFERENCED ACCOUNT WITH US.
WE FURTHER CONFIRM THAT THIS ****BANK INSTRUMENT TYPE**** IS HEREBY RESERVED/BLOCKED IN YOUR FAVOR FOR THE BENEFIT OF ***********RECIPIENT BENEFICIARY NAME******, DULY REPRESENTED BY *******REPRESENT NAME*****, AND THAT THIS BANK INSTRUMENT SHALL REMAIN BLOCKED FOR A PERIOD OF THIRTEEN (13) CALENDAR MONTHS, FROM THE DATE OF THIS SWIFT, FOR THEIR FULL USE AND BENEFIT.
WE FURTHER CERTIFY THIS SWIFT CONFIRMATION REPRESENTED HEREIN SHALL BE FREELY ASSIGNABLE, DIVISIBLE, CALLABLE AND TRANSFERABLE AS PER THE BENEFICIARY INSTRUCTIONS AT NO CHARGE TO HIM. WE CONFIRM THAT THIS SWIFT HAS BEEN ISSUED UNDER FULL BANK RESPONSIBILITY AND THAT THE VALUE IS AVAILABLE TO THE NAMED BENEFICIARY "***********RECIPIENT BENEFICIARY NAME******".
WE CONFIRM THAT THIS BANK GUARANTEE IS UNRESTRICTED, DIVISIBLE, TRANSFERABLE, ASSIGNABLE AND CALLABLE, FREE OF ANY LIENS OR ENCUMBRANCES, CLEAN AND LEGALLY OBTAINED AND ARE FREELY AVAILABLE FOR INVESTMENTS.
WE ALSO CONFIRM THAT THIS CALLABLE BANK CONFIRMATION SWIFT IS A FULLY CONFIRMED BANK INSTRUMENT WHICH MAY SERVE AS COLLATERAL TO SECURE ANY LOAN, CREDIT LINE OR CREDIT FACILITIES.
THIS SWIFT IS VERIFIABLE ON A BANK TO BANK BASIS BY A NOMINATED BANK MANAGER/OFFICER CONTACTING THE UNDERSIGNED. WE FURTHER CONFIRM THAT A CERTIFIED COPY

OF THIS SWIFT SHALL BE COURIER TO YOUR BANKING CO-ORDINATES WITHIN 5 (FIVE) BANKING DAYS.
THIS BANK INSTRUMENT IS SUBJECT TO THE UNIFORM CUSTOM AND PRACTICE (1993 REVISION) UNDER INTERNATIONAL CHAMBER OF COMMERCE PUBLICATION NUMBER 500.
UNQUOTE
PLEASE ADVISE YOUR CLIENT, (TD..........) AND ACKNOWLEDGE AND CONFIRM YOUR ACCEPTANCE. END OF SWIFT TEXT MESSAGE
YOURS TRULY,

....	....
BANK OFFICER NAME	BANK OFFICER NAME
TITLE	TITLE

HOW TO UNDERSTAND PRIVATE PLACEMENT PROGRAMS AND THE HIGH PROFITS

In general, these programs (Private investment programs-PPP and Buy - Sell Trading Programs) get a very high profit compared to the common benefit available to traditional investments Most people do not believe that a yield of 50% to 100% a week is possible. It is more a problem of knowledge of the work programs and lack of experience in trading with financial instruments and especially understanding of how the financial system works and how money is created.

Suppose a leverage of 10:1 is used, which means that the trader is able to make a copy of each sale transaction with 10 times the amount of money the investor has in his bank account. Let's say the investor has 20 Million Euros, so the Trader is able to work with 200M Euros. Now let's assume that the Trader is able to make a purchase and sale transactions per day for 4 days a week for 40 banking weeks, and that the benefit is 10% for each sale transaction. That makes 10% x 4 = 40%, and the multiplier effect of the gain will be 10 times higher, that is to say 400% per week.

Then, this return will be divided between the investor and the Trader or Trading Group, but the final net return to investors will remain a double-digit weekly performance! Also note that the above example can still be considered conservative because, the leverage can be higher, the trader can get a much larger margin for each transaction, and also a higher number of transactions will improve the final performance.

We understand that these returns may seem high, but that is because we are comparing them with a traditional investment.

RULE 144A

Rule 144A — Private Resales of Securities to Institutions

Preliminary Notes

1. This section relates solely to the application of section 5 of the Act and not to antifraud or other provisions of the federal securities laws.
2. Attempted compliance with this section does not act as an exclusive election; any seller hereunder may also claim the availability of any other applicable exemption from the registration requirements of the Act.
3. In view of the objective of this section and the policies underlying the Act, this section is not available with respect to any transaction or series of transactions that, although in technical compliance with this section, is part of a plan or scheme to evade the registration provisions of the Act. In such cases, registration under the Act is required.
4. Nothing in this section obviates the need for any issuer or any other person to comply with the securities registration or broker-dealer registration requirements of the

Securities Exchange Act of 1934 (the Exchange Act), whenever such requirements are applicable.

5. Nothing in this section obviates the need for any person to comply with any applicable state law relating to the offer or sale of securities.
6. Securities acquired in a transaction made pursuant to the provisions of this section are deemed to be restricted securities within the meaning of Rule 144(a)(3).
7. The fact that purchasers of securities from the issuer thereof may purchase such securities with a view to reselling such securities pursuant to this section will not affect the availability to such issuer of an exemption under section 4(2) of the Act, or Regulation D under the Act, from the registration requirements of the Act.

Definitions

For purposes of this section, qualified institutional buyer shall mean:

Any of the following entities, acting for its own account or the accounts of other qualified institutional buyers, that in the aggregate owns and invests on a discretionary basis at least $100 million in securities of issuers that are not affiliated with the entity:

Any insurance company as defined in section 2(a)(13) of the Act; Note: A purchase by an insurance company for one or more of its separate accounts, as defined by section 2(a)(37) of the Investment Company Act of 1940 (the "Investment Company Act"), which are neither registered under section 8 of the Investment Company Act nor required to be so registered, shall be deemed to be a purchase for the account of such insurance company.

Any investment company registered under the Investment Company Act or any business development company as defined in section 2(a)(48) of that Act;

Any Small Business Investment Company licensed by the U.S. Small Business Administration under section 301(c) or (d) of the Small Business Investment Act of 1958;

Any plan established and maintained by a state, its political subdivisions, or any agency or instrumentality of a state or its political subdivisions, for the benefit of its employees;

Any employee benefit plan within the meaning of title I of the Employee Retirement Income Security Act of 1974;

Any trust fund whose trustee is a bank or trust company and whose participants are exclusively plans of the types identified in paragraph (a)(1)(i)(D) or (E) of this section, except trust funds that include as participants individual retirement accounts or H.R. 10 plans.

Any business development company as defined in section 202(a)(22) of the Investment Advisers Act of 1940;

Any organization described in section 501(c) (3) of the Internal Revenue Code, corporation (other than a bank as defined in section 3(a)(2) of the Act or a savings and loan association or other institution referenced in section 3(a)(5)(A) of the Act or a foreign bank or savings and loan association or equivalent institution), partnership, or a Massachusetts or similar business trust; and Any investment adviser registered under the Investment Advisers Act.

Any dealer registered pursuant to section 15 of the Exchange Act, acting for its own account or the accounts of other qualified institutional buyers, that in the aggregate owns and invests on a discretionary basis at least $10 million of securities of issuers that are not affiliated with the dealer, Provided, That securities constituting the whole or a part of an unsold allotment to or subscription by a dealer as a participant in a public offering shall not be deemed to be owned by such dealer;

Any dealer registered pursuant to section 15 of the Exchange Act acting in a riskless principal transaction on behalf of a qualified institutional buyer; Note: A registered dealer may act as agent, on a non-discretionary basis, in a transaction with a qualified institutional buyer without itself having to be a qualified institutional buyer.

Any investment company registered under the Investment Company Act, acting for its own account or for the accounts of other qualified institutional buyers, that is part of a family of investment companies which own in the aggregate at least $100 million in securities of issuers, other than issuers that are affiliated with the investment company or are part of such family of investment companies. Family of investment companies means any two or more investment companies registered under the Investment Company Act, except for a unit investment trusts whose assets consist solely of shares of one or more registered investment companies, that have the same investment adviser (or, in the case of unit investment trusts, the same depositor), Provided That, for purposes of this section:

Each series of a series company (as defined in Rule 18f-2 under the Investment Company Act) shall be deemed to be a separate investment company; and Investment companies shall be deemed to have the same adviser (or depositor) if their advisers (or depositors) are majority-owned subsidiaries of the same parent, or if one investment company's adviser (or depositor) is a majority-owned subsidiary of the other investment company's adviser (or depositor);

Any entity, all of the equity owners of which are qualified institutional buyers, acting for its own account or the accounts of other qualified institutional buyers; and Any bank as defined in section 3(a)(2) of the Act, any savings and loan association or other institution as referenced in section 3(a)(5)(A) of the Act, or any foreign bank or savings and loan association or equivalent institution, acting for its own account or the accounts of other qualified institutional buyers, that in the aggregate owns and invests on a discretionary basis at least $100 million in securities of issuers that are not affiliated with it and that has an audited net worth of at least $25 million as demonstrated in its latest annual financial statements, as of a date not more than 16 months preceding the date of sale under the Rule in the case of a U.S. bank or savings and loan association, and not more than 18 months preceding such date of sale for a foreign bank or savings and loan association or equivalent institution.

In determining the aggregate amount of securities owned and invested on a discretionary basis by an entity, the following instruments and interests shall be excluded: bank deposit notes and certificates of deposit; loan participations; repurchase agreements; securities owned but subject to a repurchase agreement; and currency, interest rate and commodity swaps.

The aggregate value of securities owned and invested on a discretionary basis by an entity shall be the cost of such securities, except where the entity reports its securities holdings in its financial statements on the basis of their market value, and no current information with respect to the cost of those securities has been published. In the latter event, the securities may be valued at market for purposes of this section.

In determining the aggregate amount of securities owned by an entity and invested on a discretionary basis, securities owned by subsidiaries of the entity that are consolidated with the entity in its financial statements prepared in accordance with generally accepted accounting principles may be included if the investments of such subsidiaries are managed under the direction of the entity, except that, unless the entity is a reporting company under section 13 or 15(d) of the Exchange Act, securities owned by such subsidiaries may not be included if the entity itself is a majority-owned subsidiary that would be included in the consolidated financial statements of another enterprise.

For purposes of this section, riskless principal transaction means a transaction in which a dealer buys a security from any person and makes a simultaneous offsetting sale of such security to a qualified institutional buyer, including another dealer acting as riskless principal for a qualified institutional buyer.

For purposes of this section, effective conversion premium means the amount, expressed as a percentage of the security's conversion value, by which the price at issuance of a convertible security exceeds its conversion value.

For purposes of this section, effective exercise premium means the amount, expressed as a percentage of the warrant's exercise value, by which the sum of the price at issuance and the exercise price of a warrant exceeds its exercise value.

Sales by persons other than issuers or dealers. Any person, other than the issuer or a dealer, who offers or sells securities in compliance with the conditions set forth in paragraph (d) of this section shall be deemed not to be engaged in a distribution of such securities and therefore not to be an underwriter of such securities within the meaning of sections 2(a)(11) and 4(1)of the Act.

Sales by Dealers. Any dealer who offers or sells securities in compliance with the conditions set forth in paragraph (d) of this section shall be deemed not to be a participant in a distribution of such securities within the meaning of section 4(3)(C) of the Act and not to be an underwriter of such securities within the meaning of section 2 (11) of the Act, and such securities shall be deemed not to have been offered to the public within the meaning of section 4(3)(A) of the Act.

Conditions to be met. To qualify for exemption under this section, an offer or sale must meet the following conditions:

The securities are offered or sold only to a qualified institutional buyer or to an offeree or purchaser that the seller and any person acting on behalf of the seller reasonably believe is a qualified institutional buyer. In determining whether a prospective purchaser is a qualified institutional buyer, the seller and any person acting on its behalf shall be entitled to rely upon the following non-exclusive methods of establishing the prospective purchaser's ownership and discretionary investments of securities.

The prospective purchaser's most recent publicly available financial statements, provided that such statements present the information as of a date within 16 months preceding the date of sale of securities under this section in the case of a U.S. purchaser and within 18 months preceding such date of sale for a foreign purchaser.

The most recent publicly available information appearing in documents filed by the prospective purchaser with the Commission or another United States federal, state, or local governmental agency or self-regulatory organization, or with a foreign governmental agency or self-regulatory organization, provided that any such information is as of a date within 16 months preceding the date of sale of securities under this section in the case of a U.S. purchaser and within 18 months preceding such date of sale for a foreign purchaser.

The most recent publicly available information appearing in a recognized securities manual, provided that such information is as of a date within 16 months preceding the date of sale of securities under this section in the case of a U.S. purchaser and within 18 months preceding such date of sale for a foreign purchaser; or a certification by the chief financial officer, a person fulfilling an equivalent function, or other executive officer of the purchaser, specifying the amount of securities owned and invested on a discretionary basis by the purchaser as of a specific date on or since the close of the purchaser's most recent fiscal year, or, in the case of a purchaser that is a member of a family of investment companies, a certification by an executive officer of the investment adviser specifying the amount of securities owned by the family of investment companies as of a specific date on or since the close of the purchaser's most recent fiscal year.

The seller and any person acting on its behalf takes reasonable steps to ensure that the purchaser is aware that the seller may rely on the exemption from the provisions of section 5 of the Act provided by this section.

The securities offered or sold:

Were not, when issued, of the same class as securities listed on a national securities exchange registered under section 6 of the Exchange Act or quoted in a U.S. automated inter-dealer quotation system; provided that securities that are convertible or exchangeable into securities so listed or quoted at the time of issuance and that had an effective conversion premium of less than 10 percent, shall be treated as securities of the class into which they are convertible or exchangeable; and that warrants that may be exercised for securities so listed or quoted at the time of issuance, for a period of less than 3 years from the date of issuance, or that had an effective exercise premium of less than 10 percent, shall be treated as securities of the class to be issued upon exercise; and provided further, that the Commission may from time to time, taking into account then-existing market practices, designate additional securities and classes of securities that will not be deemed of the same class as securities listed on a national securities exchange or quoted in a U.S. automated inter-dealer quotation system; and are not securities of an open-end investment company, unit investment trust or face-amount certificate company that is or is required to be registered under section 8 of the Investment Company Act; and in the case of securities of an issuer that is neither subject to section 13 or 15(d) of the Exchange Act, nor exempt from reporting pursuant to Rule 12g3-2(b) under the Exchange Act, nor a foreign government as defined in Rule 405 eligible to register securities under Schedule B of the Act, the holder and a prospective purchaser designated by the holder have the right to obtain from the issuer, upon request of the holder, and the prospective purchaser has received from the issuer, the seller, or a person acting on either of their behalf, at or prior to the time of sale, upon such prospective purchaser's request to the holder or the issuer, the following information (which shall be reasonably current in relation to the date of resale under this section): a very brief statement of the nature of the business of the issuer and the products and services it offers; and the issuer's most recent balance sheet and profit and loss and retained earnings statements, and similar financial statements for such part of the two preceding fiscal years as the issuer has been in operation (the financial statements should be audited to the extent reasonably available).

The requirement that the information be reasonably current will be presumed to be satisfied if:

The balance sheet is as of a date less than 16 months before the date of resale, the statements of profit and loss and retained earnings are for the 12 months preceding the date of such balance sheet, and if such balance sheet is not as of a date less than 6 months before the date of resale, it shall be accompanied by additional statements of profit and loss and retained earnings for the period from the date of such balance sheet to a date less than 6 months before the date of resale; and The statement of the nature of the issuer's business and its products and services offered is as of a date within 12 months prior to the date of resale; or With regard to foreign private issuers, the required information meets the timing requirements of the issuer's home country or principal trading markets.

Offers and sales of securities pursuant to this section shall be deemed not to affect the availability of any exemption or safe harbor relating to any previous or subsequent offer or sale of such securities by the issuer or any prior or subsequent holder thereof.

PPP (REGULATION D)

A private placement Program is EXEMPT from federal registration. Exemptions have always been available under the Securities Act of 1933 (the Act), but the original exemption provisions (contained in sections 3(b) and 4(2) of the Act) were vague and, therefore, risky for business owners to invoke.

In 1982, the SEC adopted Regulation D, which set forth objectives and quantifiable rules for exemptions from federal registration. Offerings exempt under these rules 504, 505 and 506 have become the most common cost and time saving methods for small and growing businesses to raise capital from private investors.

Rule 506: Provides an exemption for limited offers and sales without regard to the dollar amount of the offering. This exemption does not limit the number of accredited investors, but the number of non-accredited investors may not exceed 35 investors. (An accredited investor is any one investor with a certain net worth and or experience in the financial market) All non-accredited purchasers, either alone or together with a designated representative must be sophisticated enough (i.e., have the knowledge and experience necessary) to evaluate the merits and risks of the investment. (An offering company typically determines the sophistication of its investors with a questionnaire subscription agreement.) Rule 506 requires detailed disclosure of relevant information to potential investors; the extent of disclosure depends on the dollar size of the offering.

Rule 505: Offerings may not exceed $5 million, less the total dollar amount of securities sold during the preceding 12-month period under Rule 504, Rule 505, or Section 3 of the act. This exemption limits the number of non-accredited investors to 35 but has no investor sophistication standards. Rule 505 requires disclosure similar to that required for Rule 506 offerings, under $7.5 million.

Rule 504: Offerings allow a business to raise a maximum of $1 million, less the total dollar amount of securities sold during the preceding 12-month period, under Rule 504, Rule 505, or Section 3 of the act. However, a business can raise only $500,000 by the sale of securities to persons residing in the states of Montana and Alaska, which have no disclosure laws applicable to the offering. For the states that do have disclosure laws, which are 48 out of the 50 states, a business can raise up to $1,000,000. Rule 504 has no prescribed disclosure requirements, no limit on the number of purchasers, and no investor sophistication standards.

Rule 504 is the most commonly used Regulation D exemption. Offerings that are exempt under Rule 504 are relatively simple to prepare, which reduces cost and delay and can generally be underwritten by the offering company (the securities being sold by the company's own officers, directors, and employees).

The USBN World

The USBN World (private placement programs & Managed buy/sell offerings). Historically, when European banks have had temporary liquidity available for investment, they have bought mainly USBNs –unsubordinated senior bank notes- and earned interest income. Likewise, when European banks have needed temporary liquidity, they have sold their own USBNs. In fact, Top 25 World Bank are obligated, under banking legislation, to issue new banking paper.

Such buying and selling of USBNs utilizes or provides liquidity in the same way United States banks buy and sell Federal Funds through the Federal Reserve Bank system (the FED). The major European banking families have always carefully managed and controlled USBN trading.

In recent times, for reasons discussed below, large numbers of USBNs have been sold at a discount to investors, principally by Mandates (The Traders) who operate under contract with the Cutting Houses to issue new USBNs.

As communications improved, USBNs trading has been completed on a "Bank- To-Bank" basis. The buying bank promises to pay for the USBN, and the selling bank promises to deliver its USBN using secure banking codes which authenticate each bank's commitment.

Hard copy of the USBNs are not always "physically cut", especially for bank-to-bank trading to satisfy liquidity requirements. In other circumstances, the hard copy is issued, as in the case of such a USBN being used as a security for a Trading line-of-credit.

Today, the buy/sell trades are accomplished at lightning speed in electronic "closed book" transactions. "Closed book" refers to the fact that when the Trader taps the credit line to buy a USBN, he already has a funds buyer awaiting the instrument. The line-of-credit can only be used for one purpose, to purchase USBNs for resale, period. This is the reason that the trader's credit facility is willing to establish a Trading line-of-credit significantly larger than the credit instrument or cash deposit upon which the line-of-credit is predicated. His bank knows that the credit line they have granted him may not be utilized until proof is obtained that said Bank Instruments have been pre-sold.

This procedure takes place mainly through Euroclear and D.T.C is also used. Euroclear is the mechanism that verifies the institution managing the program (Trader/Program Facilitator) has the funds to purchase the instruments from the Cutting House Mandate. Euroclear also verifies that the end buyer of the USBN(s) has his funds committed for the repurchase. The committed funds of both the Trader and the Buyer show on a Euroclear screen and the transaction moves forward – "closed book".

Several end buyers find the USBNs very attractive, because they have a relatively high interest rate –an annual 5.0%-7.5%-, when compared to other instruments and additionally are purchased at a discount.

Again, the USBNs are only fresh cut after funds are first provided by an end buyer in the secondary market. Mutual Funds, Securities Firms, Pension Funds and Trust Funds have a tremendous appetite for the Primary Market, but are not allowed, by legal imperative, to purchase such until the instruments are registered – registration number, CUSIP number, term of issue, interest rate, etc.

It is the fiduciary responsibility of the fixed income specialists for Mutual Funds, Securities Firms and Banks that typically portfolio these instruments to always protect their investor's principal, and as a result they cannot purchase assets that do not exist yet.

Transacting Banks and their contracted Mandates (the Traders) are not allowed to trade in instruments with their own funds, but are allowed to undertake transactions for bank clients and thus earn fees for their bank services.

CHAPTER 5

THE MACRO'S OF PRIVATE PLACEMENT PROGRAMS.
&
FINANCIAL INSTRUMENTS AND THE SECONDARY MARKET.

FINANCIAL INSTRUMENTS

DEFINITION: Financial Instruments are Financial Assets that are classified within the stock market and their main quality is that their quoted value is based on the price of another asset. They can also be called Derivatives.

In the market there may be several types of financial assets depending on the index

The initial value from which they derive, and these can be Public Debt Bonds (with Treasury Bills of Brazil renegotiated), Historical bonds of Mexico (Duly accepted and recognized by the Department of the Treasury of the country), Chinese bonds (Duly accepted and recognized by the Department of the Treasury of the country), Private Debt Bonds, shares, fixed income, equities, stock indexes, macroeconomic indexes such as the Euribor or interest rates, etc.

Financial instruments or financial derivatives are interesting products that are as familiar to us as other instruments. ***Some of their characteristics can be:***

- They are usually listed on the stock markets, although they may not be.

- The price of the derivative assets always varies with respect to the so-called "Underlying Asset", which is the value to which said derivative is linked.
- It can also be referred to as non-financial or economic products such as raw materials. For example: Wheat, Rice, Metals (gold, nickel, copper), etc.
- Usually the investment to be made is very low compared to a share or a part of the underlying value for which you want to invest.
- Financial derivatives must meet a condition and it is always settled in the future.

In Spain the derivatives are regulated by two governing bodies, mainly MEEF variable income in Madrid and MEEF fixed income in Barcelona. These agencies regulate and manage all purchases and sales on a daily basis through a clearing house of their own that executes settlements between all operations.

These types of financial assets are often interesting because they allow us to play with the future value of the underlying assets without making a large outlay, although their speculative nature is very large because we can not only make normal use of buying and selling Shares, but we can also trade with the rights to buy and sell the assets with the same initial capital playing with the second option rights. So, we can get many more benefits.

Within the financial derivatives we can mention two types:

FUTURES AND OPTIONS

FUTURES: You do not have to pay anything at the time of hiring, but if you have to have a guarantee before payment. The main quality of this type of derivative is that we acquire a payment obligation on the future acquired. The risk is great, but the potential benefits are also great. Futures as a financial product is a commitment to buy or sell an amount preset to the price of financial assets.

For example: I am committed to a person or client that within 3 months I will sell 2000 shares of, say, the company Endesa to € 15, which are currently € 16.80 each. So, I would not be interested in selling them now. But it is possible that within 3 months said action is at € 14. I do not sell them now but I will wait to be able to have a profit margin of 1 euro in the operation.

Within the futures market everything is traded with three underlying assets or base:

Currencies (at a predetermined exchange rate). Interest Rates (lending to that type).

Commodities (cereals, precious metals, etc.).

FUTURE OPERATIONS MORE COMMON

Exchange insurance: consists of hiring today a price and a delivery time within a specified time frame, with quantity and exchange rate not closed but limited to two currencies. Depending on the evolution of the market, the buyer or seller will benefit.

Participatory exchange insurance: it is like exchange insurance but with a firm agreement regarding the concrete time, amount and exchange rate.

The Forward Rate Agreement: a FRA, (as it is commonly called).

It is a contract between two parties whose purpose is to obtain future coverages based on interest rates, as both parties subscribe for a nominal value, and at the time that is wanted to be sold is settled by the difference, and may also leave the possibility that the future is traded indefinitely in the secondary market.

Futures on three-month Euribor: Consists of forecasting the value of Euribor to 3 Months. Being quite risky because it is very dependent on the euro zone interest rate, an initial premium is not required but the minimum guarantees of at least 50% of the operation.

Futures on the Ibex 35: Similar to the previous point but based on the stock index Spanish. It is settled daily by the clearing house of the BME (Spanish stock exchange and markets).

OPTIONS: When hiring an option you must pay a small premium and sometimes also subscribe a guarantee. The good thing about the options is that we are setting a commitment of benefits and losses: if we lose, the limit will always be the value of the previous premium, and instead if we win, the benefits have no ceiling.

It is important to mention that financial derivatives are like insurance against a unexpected fall in the underlying value to which it is referred. Therefore, there are two types of financial derivatives that take the name of "insurance" for the extreme ability to offer such a quality. The types of insurance are the exchange rate and the multiple exchange rate.

In summary, we can say that financial derivatives are a type of assets that they base their value on the future of another, with their risk being very high or more moderate, depending on whether we choose to contract futures or options.

THE SECONDARY MARKET:

The secondary market or trading market is a part of the financial capital market dedicated to the company and sale of securities that have already been issued in a first public or private offering in the so-called primary market.

More generally, the secondary market can refer to any second-hand market, where transactions of all types of used goods are produced, whether financial assets or not.

SECONDARY MARKET FOUNDATION:

Securities, both fixed and variable (stocks, bonds, etc.), are issued by companies in the primary market through different channels. The secondary market begins its function from that moment, taking care of the subsequent sales of those titles between the investors. It behaves like a resale market, in charge of providing liquidity to the securities. In the secondary market securities are bought and sold among different investors. Therefore, an important feature of the secondary market is that it has very high liquidity. Originally, the only way to get this liquidity was for potential buyers and sellers to meet at a fixed location on a regular basis. This is how the stock exchanges originated.

The efficiency of the capital markets in general and of the primary securities market or of the issue in particular depends to a large extent on the proper functioning of the secondary markets. If the secondary market did not exist, investors would be reluctant to buy securities in the issuing market because then they could not get rid of them when they needed money or liquidity.

In the absence of well-organized secondary stock markets, the primary market could only function precariously and companies could not obtain from the financial market the capital needed to finance their long-term investments, which would undoubtedly result in a bottleneck in general economic activity.

DIFFERENT SECONDARY MARKETS:

Stock exchanges are the most important and best organized part of secondary markets.

Although stock exchanges are the most important and most organized part of the secondary markets, they are not the only ones. There are over-the-counter transactions tailored to buyers and sellers of securities. These are the operations called ***"OVER THE COUNTER",*** which are not carried out in an organized market but in a particular way between seller and buyer.

THE STOCK MARKET:

They are the economic institutions in which all kinds of securities are contracted: shares, bonds, public funds, etc. The origin of the name in the Romance and Germanic languages continental comes from Bruges, Belgium, where in the fifteenth century trade in the effects mentioned was developed in the residence of the bankers Van de Bursen, in whose emblem of the facade three bags were sculpted. The bag of Antwerp, heiress of Bruges, was created in 1574. In 1561 was born the London Stock Exchange, which in 1773 acquired its current profile and in 1792 that of New York, today the most important in the world, followed by the Tokyo, London, Paris, Frankfurt, Hong Kong, Singapore, etc.

In operations brokers and dealers act as brokers and daily, and at the end of the session you have the published quotes and stock indexes of the day.

BANK GUARANTEES:

In the present case we are going to treat bank guarantees for international transactions, taking into account initially how a bank guarantee is created from the side of the banker of a business bank or Merchant Bank with Assets or financial assets such as Brazilian national treasury bills duly renegotiated, IBOES (International Bills of Exchange), Mexican debt bonds, metals such as (gold, nickel, silver), and some non-perishable commodities or raw materials such as cereals, rice, sugar, etc., and even movable property such as works of art or real estate such as buildings, Real estate free of charge in general.

The bankization of any of these Assets or financial assets, give rise to the responsibility of the bank and endorsed this "full responsibility" by a first-line bank, so-called Top50 or the 50 most relevant banks in the world, can issue the different bank guarantees that have different classifications according to the risk they cover. For example:

GUARANTEE OF BIDDING

When there is a contract awarding contract (either for the supply of goods or for construction), a guarantee is requested from the bidders. The purpose is to ensure that 13 contestants do not withdraw or modify their offer until the award of the contract.

Otherwise, the beneficiary of the guarantee would be covered by any expenses incurred in examining the offers received.

The amount is usually up to 10% of the value of the offer, and the usual term is limited to the scheduled date of the award, and may be extended if necessary (extension of the bidding period).

Usually these guarantees are issued with the commitment that, if the contract is awarded, a guarantee of compliance or performance will be sent.

WARRANTY OF OPERATION AND/OR COMPLIANCE

This type of guarantee is intended to ensure payment to the buyer in the event that the seller fails to comply with his contractual obligations, either in form or in time. This is why it is possibly the most commonly used type of guarantee in international trade.

The amount is usually set at 10% of the value of the contract, although it can vary between 5 and 20%. Since its function is to secure the interests of the buyer, so that it receives exactly what has been contractually agreed, this type of guarantee may be complementary to the documentary credit, since the latter guarantees the payment to the seller.

Their content can be well established with regard to the delivery of the goods according to the agreed conditions, or extended to other conditions such as installation or repair during the warranty period.

MAINTENANCE GUARANTEE

It is frequent that in the sales of machines and equipment goods when once delivered, that the merchandise establishes a period of time during which the supplier is responsible for its proper functioning. To cover this period, such guarantees are required.

ADVANCE PAY GUARANTEE

These guarantees arise in the event that the seller asks the buyer for a payment anticipated. With this the buyer is guaranteed the return of the anticipated amounts in case the seller does not comply with the contract.

They are issued before making the payment on account, and the guarantee is subject to its entry into force at the time of payment.

The amount of the guarantee coincides with that of the prepayment or account.

PAYMENT GUARANTEE

In the event that guarantees of collection of a sale of goods or provision of services are wanted, the buyer will be required to guarantee payment.

The difference with the documentary credit is that while the credit takes place in the normal way the payment of the same, in the guarantee will only have to make the payment if it fails to comply with the conditions indicated in the contract to which this guarantee refers.

FUND RETENTION GUARANTEE

This guarantee is that a part of each payment made by the buyer is retained until the contract has been completed.

GUARANTEES BEFORE CUSTOMS ENTITIES OR COMMUNITY BODIES

These guarantees are used within the European Union as "Community transit guarantee". With them, the merchandise is allowed to transit through different countries without the need for clearance and settlement of customs duties.

In cases where the goods originate from a country outside the EU bound for a member country, the importation is not released upon entry into the territory of the Community, but is done in the country of final destination.

Likewise, in the case of exports to a country outside the Community, after its export clearance in the country of origin, it freely circulates through the common territory towards the country of destination.

In cases where the merchandise and its transport have origin and destination in countries belonging to the EU, the amount of the guarantee relates to the VAT. On the other hand, we refer to "customs guarantee" as that used to avoid payment of import duties in cases where a temporary importation of goods, such as for a fair machinery is needed. This guarantee is also required when there is a discrepancy between the customs services and the importer regarding the applicable tariff or when it is shipped directly to customs without the intervention of a customs agent.

DOCUMENTARY CREDIT STAND-BY

Its purpose is to guarantee the payment of an obligation of the payer in favor of the beneficiary for concepts, related or not, with commercial operations. They are also called contingent claims.

The main difference with documentary credits is that stand-bys are only used (the exporter would submit documents for collection) if the ordering/importing party fails to fulfill its obligations (it would be like executing an endorsement). As documentation, it is usually requested only as a letter from the beneficiary/exporter stating that the originator/importer has stopped fulfilling his obligations.

They are equivalent to the guarantees, being their main advantage against them that can be well governed by their own rules and uses for documentary stand-by credits (ISP98), or by the rules and uses for documentary credits (UCP500). This characteristic avoids interpretations and problems originated by the different legislations of the countries involved.

MODELS OF BANK GUARANTEES CONCEPTS

The model of issuance of the Bank Guarantee is the one that the Bank deems appropriate according to the conditions that the client prefers, since it is the issuing bank itself that has different types of models for each case. The basic requirements that the Banking Guarantee must have are the following:

1. That the asset is deposited in the account of the client, with full bank responsibility.
2. That the asset is available to the client.
3. That the asset is Assignable, Divisible and Transferable.
4. That the asset can be worked via Swift (MT 760 and MT 700).
5. That the asset can be verified bank-by-bank.

Therefore, within the field of Banking Guarantees, there are different models: the ICC 500, the 458 and the 600, including the 458 with revision 500.

BANK GUARANTEE MODEL 458:

THIS GUARANTEE AT THE OFFICE OF (BANK NAME). FULL ADDRESS SUCH PAYMENT SHALL BE MADE WITHOUT SET

OFF AND SHALL BE UNENCUMBERED FREE AND CLEAR OF ANY DEDUCTIONS, CHARGES, FEES OR WITHHOLDING OF ANY NATURE NOW OR HEREAFTER IMPOSED, LEVIED, COLLECTED, WITHHELD OR ASSESSED BY THE GOVERNMENT OF (----------------), OR ANY POLITICAL SUBDIVISION OR AUTHORITY THEREOF OR THEREIN.

THIS GUARANTEE IS FULL Y CASH BACKED WITH FUNDS ON DEPOSIT THAT ARE GOOD, CLEAN, CLEARED OF NON-CRIMINAL ORIGIN, FREE OF ANY LIENS OR ENCUMBRANCES LEGALLY EARNED BY THE APPLICANT. THIS BANK GUARANTEE IS TRANSFERABLE, ASSIGNABLE, DIVISIBLE AND CONFIRMED WITHOUT PRESENTATION OF IT TO US AND SHALL BE GOVERNED AND CONSTRUED IN ACCORDANCE WITH THE LAWS OF THE (ISSUING COUNTRY) AND THE UNITED KINGDOM.

THIS BANK GUARANTEE IS SUBJECT TO THE UNIFORM CUSTOMS AND PRACTICES FOR BANK GUARANTEE AS SET FORTH BY THE INTERNATIONAL CHAMBER OF COMMERCE - PARIS - FRANCE, LATEST REVISION OF PUBLICATION 458.

INSTRUMENT OF GUARANTEE:

CUSIP NUMBER:

ACCESS CODE:

EXPIRATION DATE:

MATURITY DATE:

CURRENCY: € EURO

AMOUNT: €

FOR AND ON BEHALF OF (BANK NAME)

<FIRST & LAST NAME>	<FIRST & LAST NAME>
BANK OFFICER	BANK OFFICER
CODE NO.	CODE NO.

BANK SEAL

BANK GUARANTEE MODEL 500

LETTER OF GUARANTEE MODEL 600

INTERNAL BANK PROCESS WHEN A BANK RECEIVES A BANK GUARANTEE

When a bank receives a bank guarantee, it always starts with a prior notice Using a Swift MT199, MT 999 or MT799, which are free format messages or the so-called PREADVISE. (Pre-warnings).

In this format, the receiving bank is informed that the issuing bank on behalf of its client, who is the applicant of the guarantee and who on his behalf has deposited and banked the Assets or Financial Assets, is willing and prepared to send a bank guarantee with the bank's responsibility in a MT 760 format in favor of its client (name of company and/or Customer) and its account number where it will receive such guarantee with the condition of receiving an irrevocable corporate purchase order (ICPO), which is the swift that will subsequently be sent to the receiving bank and which guarantees that the customer who will receive the guarantee has an active line of credit to be able to pay the agreement of purchase of the guarantee, or the agreement that has been agreed to in the private contract between the parties.

This process of sending a Swift PREADVISE (MT 199, MT 999 or MT 799) to the bank Receiver does not take much longer than the bank officer takes in formatting the Swift Text and sending it to the banking coordinates of the client of the issuing bank, and can be completed within one hour in normal time. But it can also take 3 to 5 bank days for the international bank office to receive the Swift and verify it from bank to bank to verify its truthfulness. This confirmation process is also done by Swift bank to bank, and by confirmation between bank officials identifying each other with their PIN numbers (code that identifies a bank officer within the bank system). These confirmations are recorded for the safety of the operation.

Once the receiving bank has received and confirmed the veracity of the Swift Preadvise (MT 199, MT 999 or MT 799), it responds as requested in the text of said swift by another Swift MT 799 message, confirming that its customer holder of the account where he will receive the Banking Guarantee will irrevocably pay the amount of the agreed price of the purchase of the bank guarantee or the internal agreement that the parties have, conditioned to receive the Swift MT 760 and mentioning many times in the text that the bank guarantee is TRANSFERRABLE, DIVISIBLE, IRREVOCABLE and CALLABLE at first request.

The time taken for the recipient bank to send the Swift 799 with the irrevocable payment order to the issuing bank in response to the Preadvise (MT 199, MT 999 or MT 799) is between 3 and 5 banking days.

After the fifth day, the issuing bank will receive the Swift MT 799 with the text of the irrevocable payment order of the account holder of the beneficiary's account of the receiver bank, conditioned, logically, to receive the guarantee through Swift MT 760. Likewise, The issuing bank confirms said Swift by telephone communication from bank to bank between bank officers, identifying themselves with PIN codes and recordings of such conversations, and also confirming via Swift the truthfulness of the Swift received.

When the Issuing Bank has received and confirmed the Swift MT 799 with the irrevocable payment order, it proceeds to send the Bank Guarantee through communication protocol MT 760 with the agreed text, and even transcribed many times in the preadvise or the payment order.

This process usually takes between 3 and 5 banking days.

Once the Receiving Bank has received the Bank Guarantee through a protocol of Swift MT 760 communication, the banking officer receives, confirms and conforms the guarantee in favor of its client account holder where the guarantee was sent.

And when it is formed in favor of the beneficiary is when the bank pays the monetization of the guarantee to the account of the customer and in turn, this meets the requirement of the seller of the guarantee to make the payment of the same for the amount or amount agreed by bank transfer to the coordinates given for this purpose.

It is at this time that all participants in the financial operation, charge their fees or management fees.

DIFFERENCES BETWEEN BUYING A BANK GUARANTEE AND RENTING A BANK GUARANTEE.

ADVANTAGES, DISADVANTAGES AND USES

BUYING A BANK GUARANTEE

The purchase of a bank guarantee is an opportunity to raise the financial leverage of the company that does it with the bank where the sale is negotiated or taken as collateral for the financing of a business project. An example:

The company MINERA FORTE SA acquires a bank guarantee of 100 million euros from the DEUTSCHE BANK DE GERMANIA, for the value of 65% on its face value, That is to say that it has really cost him 65 million euros, and with this guarantee that always has an expiration of 1 year and 1 day, the bank that issued it must pay at first demand at maturity to the bank holder or to the investor that has discounted this guarantee.

Said discount is usually no more than 20% of the face value, by the investor or the bank that makes said discount. Therefore, the mining company has increased its cash flow by 15 million euros for only doing this financial operation, since the bank or the investor who has discounted it will charge the first requirement at the expiration of the same. In short, it is to buy money represented in wholesale bank guarantees and sell it at retail.

Usually these operations are usually very synchronized between the seller and the buyer since the emission costs are not cheap.

The margin of maneuver of the bank or investor who has discounted the guarantee and who will charge it at the expiration of 1 year and 1 day is, in this case, 20%.

Note: With a bank guarantee on ownership you can enter into a private investment operation.

RENT A BANK GUARANTEE (LEASING)

A bank guarantee is rented to the applicant company or owner of the same, to serve as collateral of any financial transaction. According to the bank that issues it this way usually cost said Rental or Leasing, which usually ranges from 10% to 20%, depending on the opportunity of the business.

The holder of the rental guarantee, at maturity, is responsible for returning free of charge such bank guarantee when used as collateral of a line of credit for a business project. If this project has its socio-economic viability, let's say 5 years, this guarantee is usually renewed by paying, logically, the cost of renewal that can be in the second, third, fourth and fifth year be 50% less than what you paid the first year.

Note: A bank guarantee for rent cannot participate in private investment operations.

WHAT IS A FRESH CUT GUARANTEE?

A Fresh Cut guarantee is a guarantee that is issued for the first time, and its value will depend on the liquidity in the capital market, and this will depend on the bank that issues it and confirms its full bank responsibility

WHAT IS A SEASONED GUARANTEE?

A Seasoned warranty is a warranty that has already been issued and is on the secondary market for sale. Depending on your issuing bank, that will determine your value in the capital market.

STAND-BY LETTER OF CREDIT (SBLC)

Its purpose is to guarantee the payment of an obligation of the payer in favor of the beneficiary for concepts, related or not, with commercial operations. They are also called contingent claims.

The main difference with documentary credits is that stand-bys are only used (the exporter would submit documents for collection) if the ordering/importing party fails to fulfill its obligations (it would be like executing an endorsement). As documentation, it is usually requested as only a letter from the beneficiary/exporter stating that the originator/importer has stopped fulfilling his obligations.

They are equivalent to the guarantees, being their main advantage against them is that they can be well governed by their own rules and uses for documentary stand-by credits (ISP98), or by the rules and uses for documentary credits (UCP500). This characteristic avoids interpretations and problems originated by the different legislations of the intervening countries.

STANDBY LETTER OF CREDIT TEMPLATE (SBLC)

The SBLC Model will depend on the agreement reached with the beneficiary.

Therefore, depending on the agreement, the issuing Bank issues an SBLC in favor of the beneficiary based on the Asset that the client has contributed.

SBLCs should always be stipulated by the ICC rules Publ. 500/600.

It is important to emphasize that for an SBLC to be issued and used as collateral it must be Assignable, Divisible and Transferable.

STANDBY LETTER OF CREDIT TEMPLATE

STANDBY LETTER OF CREDIT MT 760

FROM ISSUING BANK:
SWIFT:
TO ADVISING BANK:(TO BE ADVISED)
SWIFT:
AT THE REQUEST OF AND FOR THE ACCOUNT OF ……… (THE ACCOUNT PARTY), WE, (ISSUING BANK) HEREBY OPEN AND ISSUE IN FAVOR OF BANK (ADVISING BANK), AN IRREVOCABLE STANDBY LETTER OF CREDIT IN A PRINCIPAL AMOUNT OF USD …000,000 (USD….MILLIONS ONLY) AS A SECURITY FOR YOUR BANKING FACILITIES GRANTED TO COMPANY(THE BORROWER) DRAWING MADE UNDER THIS STANDBY LETTER OF CREDIT MUST BE ACCOMPANIED BY:
1. DRAFT(S) IN RESPECT OF THE AMOUNT TO BE DRAWN UNDER THIS STANDBY LETTER OF CREDIT.
2. SIGNED STATEMENT FROM YOU WHICH CERTIFIES THAT:
A. THE AMOUNT DRAWN SHALL REPRESENT THE UNPAID AMOUNT OF PRINCIPAL, ACCRUED INTEREST AND OTHER CHARGES UNDER THE CREDIT AGREEMENT.
B. SUCH AMOUNT WAS NOT PAID WHEN DUE IN ACCORDANCE TO THE TERMS AND CONDITIONS OF THE CREDIT AGREEMENT.
AND PRESENTED TO US WITH THE FOLLOWING ADDRESS…. FOR THE ATTENTION OF……… ALL PAYMENT UNDER THIS STANDBY LETTER OF CREDIT SHALL BE MADE FREE AND CLEAR OF ANY DEDUCTION OR WITHHOLDING WHATSOEVER

AND SHALL BE PAID IN THE CURRENCY AS SPECIFIED ABOVE.
PARTIAL DRAWING IS PERMITTED.
THE AMOUNT PAYABLE TO YOU UNDER THIS STANDBY LETTER OF CREDIT SHALL BE MADE ON YOUR FIRST DEMAND. WE HEREBY UNDERTAKE TO HONOR YOUR DRAWING WHICH IS AVAILABLE UPON PRESENTATION OF YOUR CLAIM BY AUTHENTICATE SWIFT MESSAGE.
THIS STANDBY LETTER OF CREDIT IS VALID FROM ...2021 UNTIL ....2022 (BEING 365 DAYS OF THE EXPIRY DATE).
ANY CLAIMS UNDER THE STANDBY LETTER OF CREDIT CAN BE PRESENTED WITHIN THE VALIDITY OF THIS STANDBY LETTER OF CREDIT.
THIS STANDBY LETTER OF CREDIT IS SUBJECT TO THE UNIFORM CUSTOMS AND PRACTICES FOR DOCUMENTARY CREDIT, INTERNATIONAL CHAMBER OF COMMERCE PUBLICATION NO.600, ICC PUBLICATION NO.600 AND ANY OF ITS AMENDMENT.
THIS STANDBY LETTER OF CREDIT IS TRANSFERABLE AND ASSIGNABLE BY YOU.
YOUR SIGNED STATEMENT CERTIFYING THAT AMOUNT DRAWN HEREUNDER REPRESENTS AND COVERS THE UNPAID INDEBTEDNESS AND INTEREST THEREON DUE TO YOU ARISING OUT OF YOUR GRANTING GENERAL BANKING FACILITIES TO COMPANY.
INSTRUCTION TO THE ADVISING BANK, UPON YOUR RECEIPT OF THIS CREDIT, PLEASE IMMEDIATELY ADVISE THIS CREDIT TO COMPANY VIA FACSIMILE AND COURIER.
THIS SWIFT CONSTITUTES THE OPERATIVE CREDIT INSTRUMENT AND NO MAIL SHALL FOLLOW.
IN ALL COMMUNICATION PLEASE QUOTE OUR REF NO
Remittance Route (USD)
Bank:
Swift Code: Account:
Further Credit to:
Swift Code:
Bank DD:

Bank Officer:
Beneficiary's Account:
Beneficiary's Name:
Address:
Tel:
Bank Tel:

INTERNAL BANK PROCEDURE

As its purpose is to guarantee a payment by the payer to the beneficiary, and being a document that functions as collateral or as collateral if the payer fails to fulfill his obligations agreed in the contract of import or export to the beneficiary, he will execute without further said guarantee, informing the bank of such default of payment.

The internal banking process when the contracts are issued is by the payer's bank or issuing bank. Under the guarantees of said payer, the SBLC is issued to the beneficiary for the amount and conditions agreed upon in the contract.

According to the expiration, the beneficiary can discount said SBLC, once the conditions of fulfillment of the contract have been fulfilled.

Procedure: The Bank of the payer, after the signing of contracts, issues to the banking coordinates of the Bank of the Beneficiary the SBLC for the amount and conditions agreed in the contract.

The Bank of the Beneficiary, confirms among bank officials the veracity of said SBLC, and deposits it into the securities account of the beneficial owner. By being divisible, transferable and irrevocable, the beneficiary can deduct with his bank the said SBLC (or another) until the expiration of it.

LETTER OF CREDIT

Purpose:

Its purpose is to guarantee payment regardless of the contract that gave rise to the parties that negotiated the agreement. The commonly called international contract of sale has legal support in the rules and uniform uses relating to documentary credits UCP600 of the International Chamber of Commerce (ICC).

With respect to the other payment instruments commonly used in international trade operations, such as collections (UCP522), payment orders or transfers, documentary credits offer greater security in terms of credit risk.

Types of Letters of Credit:

Domestic:

It is the open letter of credit in favor of a beneficiary who has his domicile in the country.

Normally it does not require the intervention of another financial institution. It establishes a triangular relationship between the payer of the instrument, the issuing bank and the selling beneficiary.

Generally, foreign banks intervene as intermediaries to the beneficiary. When opening the letter of credit, the bank sends it to its foreign correspondent to add its confirmation and give notice to the beneficiary, directly or through its own correspondent in the country of destination.

Counter payment:

This type of card can be subdivided in turn into payment on demand and deferred.

- Payment at sight and confirmed by the paying bank. This can't delay payment.

- Deferred (payable to term) and confirmed by the bank. It undertakes against delivery of documents to be paid at maturity.

Counter Acceptance:

The credit is available against presentation of the documents and a bill of exchange released over time against a designated bank, which may be the issuer itself.

Counter Negotiation:

The credit is available against presentation of the documents and a bill of exchange released on demand or against the issuing bank. The negotiating bank "buys" on behalf of the issuer the rights of the beneficiary over the credit. A freely negotiable credit can be negotiated by any bank.

Revocable or Irrevocable:

By default, the letter of credit is considered irrevocable, that is, the commitment issued and accepted by the parties can't be modified without the consent of all parties involved (payer, banks, beneficiary). By express indication a documentary credit can be issued as denominated revocable, in which case it can be modified whenever it has not been used, and will be firm regarding the obligations acquired or in execution of execution.

Commercial or Financial:

Depending on the type of obligation it covers, the letter of credit may be commercial, when the transaction involves a transaction, which may be local or international (import or export), or financial, when it ensures compliance with an obligation of this order (stand by).

Nominative or Negotiable:

The letter of credit that expressly indicates the authorized banks to confirm, warn and negotiate the instrument, and will be freely negotiable those that do not expressly indicate the banks nominated to intervene in its handling.

The letter of credit may be in sight when the payment is made immediately upon presentation of conforming documents; by acceptance, when the payment is made by the acceptance of the bank paying a bill of exchange released over a certain period; for deferred payment, when the payment is established to a certain period after the use of the instrument.

Private Credit Cards:

- **Transferable:** The letter of credit expressly so allows the beneficiary to make available the credit in whole or in part to a third party (second beneficiary), according to the same terms, conditions, obligations and benefits, except the value and price of the goods which may be reduced. The omission of indication implies that it is non-transferable.
- **Revolving:** It includes the immediate restitution of the value of the credit once it is used, allowing its reuse in the same way, amount and original conditions, for a certain period.
- **Advance payment:** Allows the total or partial advance payment against simple receipt and express commitment of presentation of documents (Red Clause) or against a certificate of deposit in authorized warehouse, invoices or other proofs of arrangement previously agreed and identified in the credit (Green Clause).
- **Back to Back:** Established when the bank opens a credit backed by another major credit in favor of the payer.

MODEL CONTRACT BETWEEN THE PARTIES ORIGINATING A POSTERIOR CREDIT CHARTER

Date
Gathered
For one side, Mr ......of age....., domiciled in.......and provided with identification document number.............

And for the other side. MR ....of age, ... domiciled in.......and provided with identification document number.............
SHARE each of them with full legal capacity to be bound in this act in the way they do as they manifest under penalty of falsification in document if it is not true and They intervene,
The first of them in his own name and right (in case of legal entity express the position he holds and the data of the mercantile that the attendant represents) from now on PART A
And the second of them, as sole administrator of the mercantile............., domiciled in.......... and provided with tax identification number................ from now on PART B
Both parties, for themselves and for those who intervene, freely, mutually and reciprocally

MANIFEST

I. PART A Has as ... social .... That habitually develops in the territory of .... called .... Sited in ...... and centralized its management for the purposes of this contract in ......, and at the moment is negotiating the following contract: (transcription of the contract)
II. That for this purpose and as "condition sine aequenon" for the subscription of such contract, it is necessary to guarantee the payment that appears in favor of ... in clause ... of the contract transcribed.
III. That PART B has as social activity, among others, the financial activity aimed at obtaining its own financial instruments that allow to guarantee operations of legal business of any nature within the fair trade and clean source funds of such instruments, at the national level or Internationally due and documented to have effects vis-à-vis third parties and, especially, against the banking/financial entities used for this purpose.

IV. Coinciding those who appear for their own sake, and in the name of the person involved, in joining their wills in an agreement, submit the same to the following.

STIPULATIONS

FIRST. - PART A, with the object and sole purpose of guaranteeing the payment in favor of .... contained in clause ... of the contract transcribed in the first manifestation of the present document, entrusts the PART B the obtaining of a sufficient financial instrument to fulfill the object and the only intended destiny, mentioned above, being this the object of the present contract.

SECOND. In order to perfect the object of the present contract, the parties expressly and expressly agree the following PROCEDURE:

THIRD. The parties recognize that the instrument obtained in the form provided for in the previous stipulation has the function of guaranteeing the payment whose natural, contractual obligation is the responsibility of PART A; Nevertheless, if on the day of payment of this amount, PART A will not make the payment expected, this will be paid by PART B via the instrument object of this contract, and this for the very nature of object and only destination of Said financial instrument agreed between the parties in this act.

FOURTH. In the event that the situation provided for in the previous clause occurred and PART B had to pay the payment provided in the contract transcribed to this document whose obligation corresponds to PART A, it is bound, from now on and for then, to pay PART B the amount paid on its behalf as previously provided. Said payment must be made on the following ... BANK DAYS to the payment made through the timely transfer .. (or other method) From now on and in case of the situation provided for in the previous paragraph, PART A offers to PART B, as a guarantee and in case it could not respond to the payment that would have to pay as planned, Pledge by pledge with registration of the following assets:

-

-

-

FIFTH. Those appearing for themselves and for those who intervene, renouncing their own jurisdiction, if they have it, submit to everything derived from this document, considerations and resolutions of equity that, if necessary,

LETTER OF CREDIT TEMPLATE

44E: PORT OF LOADING: PALUA (VENEZUELA)
44B: FOR TRANSPORTATION TO: MEDITERRANEAN PORT OF BARCELONA
44C: LATEST DATE OF FIRST SHIPMENT 45 DAYS FROM RECEIPT AND ACCEPTANCE OF LC
45A: DESCRIPTION OF GOODS AND I OR SERVICES
COMMODITY: HMS1&2 (80%&20%)
UNIT PRICE: USD 306.00 PER METRIC TON TOTAL QUANTITY: 12.500MT
DELIVERY: CIF BARCELONA PORT. SPAIN SPECIFICATION: GOST 7173-75/GOST 8165-75/ISRI 27-29 PACKING: BULK
46A: DOCUMENTS REQUIRED: THE FOLLOWING DOCUMENTS MUST BE PRESENTED IN DUPLICATE UNLESS OTHERWISE SPECIFIED.
1. ORIGINAL 3 ORIGINAL CLEAN ON-BOARD OCEAN BILLS OF LADING PLUS THREE NON-NEGOTIABLE COPIES SIGNED BY THE OWNER OR MASTER OF THE VESSEL
2. MARKED "FREIGHT PREPAID" AND CONSIGNED TO ORDER AND BLANK ENDORSED WITH NOTIFY PARTY TO BE ADVISED
3. CERTIFICATE ISSUED BY BUREAU VERITAS (OR SIMILAR) AT PORT OF LOADING CONFIRMING THE QUANTITY DETERMINED BY DRAFT SURVEY, SPECIFICATION

(INCLUDING SIZES), OF THE GOODS OF THIS CONTRACT – 3 ORIGINAL AND 1 COPY.
4. CERTIFICATE OF ORIGIN ISSUED BY CHAMBER OF COMMERCE AND INDUSTRY –
3 ORIGINAL AND 1 COPY.
5. CERTIFICATE OF INSURANCE TO COVER 110% OF THE TOTAL INVOICED VALUE OF GOODS SHIPPED: 1 (A) ORIGINAL OR COPY OF + 3 (THREE) COPIES.
6. CERTIFICATE OF QUALITY ISSUED BY SGS, CONFIRMING QUALITY OF THE GOODS – 3 ORIGINAL SETS AND 1 COPY SET.
7. SIGNED COMMERCIAL INVOICES IN FIVE ORIGINALS SHOWING MATERIAL DESCRIPTION, SIZE, QUANTITY OF GOODS, QUALITY, UNIT PRICE AND TOTAL VALUE OF GOODS, AND NAME OF VESSEL; IN ENGLISH LANGUAGE.
8. EXPORT LICENSE.
47A: **ADDITIONAL CONDITIONS**

- TOLERANCE 5 PCT MORE OR LESS ON VALUE AND QUANTITY ACCEPTABLE
- ALL BANK CHARGES IN THE BUYER'S BANK ARE FOR THE BUYER'S ACCOUNT AND ALL BANK CHARGES IN THE SELLER'S BANK ARE FOR THE SELLER'S ACCOUNT.
- ALL DOCUMENTS MUST BE ISSUED IN ENGLISH LANGUAGE
- CHARTER PARTY BILL OF LADING AND THIRD-PARTY DOCUMENTS ARE NOT ACCEPTABLE 71B: CHARGES
- ALL BANKING CHARGES AND COMMISSIONS OTHER THAN THE ISSUING BANK'S CHARGES ARE ON THE BENEFICIARY'S ACCOUNT.

48: PERIOD FOR PRESENTATION WITHIN 14 DAYS OF SHIPMENT DATE.
49: CONFIRMATION INSTRUCTION CONFIRM IF NEEDED
53A: REIMBURSING BANK - BIC TO BE COMPLETED BY ISSUING BANK
78: INSTRUCTIONS TO PAYING/ACCEPTING NEGOTIATING TO BE COMPLETED BY ISSUING BANK 72: SENDER TO RECEIVER

INFORMATION /I KINDLY CONFIRM HAVING NOTIFIED AND CONFIRMED UC TO BENEFICIARIES BY RETURN SWIFT QUOTING YOUR REFERENCE
***MUST BE ISSUED VIA SWIFT ***

INTERNAL BANK PROCEDURE:

As its purpose is to guarantee a payment by the payer to the beneficiary, due to the fulfillment of a contract between the parties (buyer and seller), the beneficiary is guaranteed the payment to the full compliance of its contractual part whatever the agreement with its sending client.

The internal banking process when the contracts are issued is by the payer's bank or issuing bank. Under the guarantees of said payer the LC is issued to the beneficiary, for the amount and conditions agreed upon in the contract.

According to the expiration, the beneficiary can deduct said LC, once the conditions of fulfillment of the contract have been fulfilled.

Procedure: The bank of the orderer after the signing of contracts issues to the bank coordinates of the beneficiary's bank the LC for the amount and conditions in the contract.

Bank of the Beneficiary. It confirms between banking officers the veracity of this LC, and deposits it into the account of the beneficial owner's securities, by demonstrating to the beneficiary who has fulfilled the terms of the contract, that it can discount it with the same bank or other entity depending on the conditions of discount.

PROMISSORY NOTES

A promising note is an informal and signed promise to pay certain amount of money at a predetermined time in the future. Do not use complex legalisms to make a definite promise. However, some details must be considered in order to avoid future legal confusion.

A promissory note should always be written. It should never be just an oral agreement to pay someone a certain amount of money, since it could then be easily reneged. The promissory note must be written in clear language and must include the intentions of repaying a loan after the originally stipulated date.

The promise made on a promissory note has to be unconditional. If conditions apply, creating a promissory note becomes null and void. The writer should also list exactly who will pay the debt later, either the same creator of the note or another person. The promissory note should stipulate that the loan payment will be in legal money and not in other monetary form, such as stocks or bonds.

Anyone who creates a promissory note must sign it with their own name. If someone else will be paying the loan, you must also sign the note. It could have to be signed in the presence of a notary public. The note must also have the date on which it was written or the date on which the payment will take place. It is not essential to validate the promissory note. It could, however, affect how to calculate interest.

In some cases, a promissory note might include the range of interest that one will have to pay on the loan if the loan is paid much later. The loan must be paid with the interest rate mentioned in the note, regardless of whether this range increases after a certain date.

SAMPLE OF AGREEMENT FOR PROMISSORY NOTES:

Gathered on the one hand, ..., of nationality .... Domiciled in ...., for the purposes of this document, and provided with a passport of nationality .... Number ....

And on the other hand, MR ...., of nationality, neighbor of, with Address in ...., Number, and with a passport document .... SHARE each of them with legal capacity to be bound in this act, and INTERVENING, the first of them, in the name and representation of ...., With its registered office in designated expressly for the purposes of this contract; And the second of them as administrator of the mercantile of Spanish nationality called ...., with the same registered office as its representative and provided with tax identification number number ....

In this act, by mutual consent and with the express consent of those appearing for themselves and for whom they represent

MANIFEST

I. .... is a trading company engaged in .... owning the following goods:
   a.
   b.
   c.

II. .... Between its commercial/professional activities the management of assets of any nature for its own account or on behalf of third parties for which it has subscribed documents with banking financial institution XXXX, based in London, UK, hereinafter referred to, Which allow it to use the structure of the same for the Execution of banking financial operations of different types based on and support in assets denominated assets

III. Accordingly, both parties have reached an agreement which they submit to the following

STIPULATIONS

FIRST. ...., from now on, undertakes to issue in favor of, from now on .... based on the assets described in the first manifestation of this document and in accordance with the social agreement that approves and decides it, an instrument called PROMISORY NOTE for the amount of .... Amount that forms the total of the values assigned to the assets described in accordance with the appraisals and insurance contracts issued by the relevant entities and which form an integral part of the documentation that causes the issuance of said instrument

SECOND................ undertakes to deposit said instrument in the house security itself whose use as its own has agreed to be the holders of said deposit the parties appearing in this act and all this with the destination of the operation to be performed on the basis of this instrument

THIRD. Once the deposit has been made, and prior to any planned transaction, the depositors and the financial/banking entity XXXX undertake, from now on, to verify the authenticity and availability for the pre-determined purposes, and once this verification has been made in Form, simultaneously, ..., by itself and through its financial and banking structure, and especially through the company named .... Based in London, UK, shall facilitate the issuance of SWIFT MT 760 FULL RESPONSIBILITY to the banking coordinates designated by ......, either own or third-party customers, with each Swift being sent for a period of ONE YEAR AND ONE DAY, and for the price of ONE PERCENT (1%) of the face value of Swift issued, which will be paid by the recipient of said shipment through the deposit, in the form of a bank check in favor of .... of the amount of the issue and sending the Swift before fifteen banking days of having produced the issue and sending of the Swift in question, deducting the amount of the deposit deposited from the amount allocated to receive the proceeds of the financial transaction to be performed by .... and conform With the provisions of this document, returning the deposited slip to its issuer simultaneously.

FOURTH.................. proposes in this act the realization, by the amount previously established as values of the assets described, of a financial transaction consisting in introducing into financial trading the amount resulting from the monetization of the value assigned to the PROMISORRY NOTE To carry out this type of operations that will be expressly

directed by .... With complete information of each step to follow ...., accompanying the documentation that accredits the operation carried out to this document as an annex to the same that from now and for then parties agree that will be an intrinsic part of this document.
Of the net proceeds of the transaction, the parties agree to a twenty percent (20%) share of the same that will be received .... and eighty percent of the same (80%) that will receive, which will be paid to each of the parties by bank transfer to the bank coordinates designated by each one of the parts for this purpose for each of the transfers duly communicated in a reliable manner.
FIFTH. During the validity of the aforementioned operation and from the signature of this document until the total completion thereof, the assets described in the first manifestation of this document will be available to the object of the This contract will be constituted guarantee of such a situation of provision by means of the creation of the appropriate legal figure agreed upon by the parties appearing, who will extinguish this document once the execution of the object of this contract has been completed.
SIXTH. The parties appearing for themselves and for those involved intervene agree to submit to the jurisdiction of the arbitration tribunals that correspond by reason of territoriality in the fulfillment of the obligations of each one of them, preferably in case of conflict of the Chamber of Trade of Madrid.

CERTIFICATES OF DEPOSIT

The Certificate of Deposit known or identified as a CD is a financial document that certifies the ownership of goods, money or goods deposited in the warehouse that issues it. Based on the General Law of Credit Institutions, banking institutions in Mexico and the General Deposit Stores registered and audited by the National Banking and Securities Commission are authorized to issue these securities.

The certificates, receipts or certificates issued by other persons or institutions to accredit the deposit of goods or merchandise, will not produce effects as securities.

This document can be transmitted through an endorsement, and grants the holder of the same rights over the merchandise covered by the document.

MODEL OF A CD IN MONEY

BANK COMFORT LETTER FOR CERTIFICATE OF DEPOSIT SAMPLE:

This Certificate of Deposit does not allow for any corrections.

Upon maturity of this Certificate of Deposit (Bank Name) promises to pay the holder the total amount of this Certificate of Deposit with no protest or notice, against the presentation of this Certificate of Deposit, without delay, free of any deduction or compensation, charges, costs or withholdings of any current or future nature emerging or imposed by the (Bank's country) Government, properly endorsed at the counter of (Bank Name and address). This Certificate of Deposit is subject to the laws forthcoming from the competent authorities of (Bank's country) and is governed by the Uniform Customs and Practice for Documentary Credits, international Chamber of Commerce, Paris, France, publication 500-600, latest revision.

This Certificate of Deposit is issued with full bank responsibility and is an operative unconditional, irrevocable, fully confirmed and recorded negotiable instrument and is transferable, assignable and callable and may be verified on a bank-to-bank basis.

Verifiable through (Bank Name and address)

For and on behalf of

(Bank Name and address)

(Bank's Seal)
(Officer's Name and position)

USUAL DOCUMENTS

FUNDS TEST:

It is a financial document, usually a statement or a letter, showing one of the parties to record that there is financial capacity and/or funds available to complete a particular transaction. It is often provided by the bank of the account holder in the form of a specific bank letter for the transaction in question. The bank letter assists the stakeholder, with the confidence that there are cash funds available, which can be obtained and are legitimate.

The Proof of Funds, POF, can also be used in the preliminary stages of credit enhancement when applying for funding, or when attempting to conduct a multi-purpose operation, including acquisitions of companies, materials, equipment, automobiles, real estate, OER, as well as banking instruments and financial instruments.

The Proof of Funds is based more on the statements of the Funds in a cash account, or funds in a cash bank account backed by requiring verification of the account.

The Proof of Funds letter is not commonly used in consumer products for purchase and financing.

A POF chart usually does not need to show the starting balance, current balance, or average balance. It also does not need to show the transaction history, nor give details of whether the account holder in a particular bank has outstanding loans, credit cards or savings accounts. Instead, a proof of funds letter issued by the bank holding an account simply has a language designed to verify that the funds are legitimate for a specific transaction in the account, without going into details of the history, balances, etc. The origin of the funds must be credited by letter of Proof of Funds they are clear, clean and transparent of non-criminal origin. This may or may not be a requirement of the interested party.

The supply of the POF can be done in several ways: by letter by fax, email, sending from one bank to another via telex, by mail printed copy, or delivered in hand by the account holder directly. In trade finance, project finance, global finance, or asset financing is also commonly issued by the banking protocol, called Swift.

SWIFT messages have a variety of message types assigned to various financial transactions. The series of electronic messages delivered through the SWIFT corresponding to the Proof of Funds is often done by a bank with the SWIFT MT103 conditional or through the types of unformatted messages, such as SWIFT MT799, and less frequently SWIFT MT999.

PROOF OF FUNDS BANK COMFORT LETTER SAMPLE:

PROOF OF FUNDS LETTER
RE:
ACCOUNT NAME: XXXXXXXXXXXXXXXXXXXXXXXXXX
ACCOUNT NUMBER: XXXXXXXXXXXXXXXXXX (USD A/C)
DATE: XXXXXX XX, 2021
WE, XXXXXXXXXXXXXX BANK XXXXXXXXXXXXXXXX., LOCATED AT XXXXXXXXXXXXXX, XXXXXXXXXXXXXX, XXXXXXX, DO HEREBY CONFIRM WITH FULL BANK RESPONSIBILITY, THAT WE IRREVOCABLY HOLD FOR OUR CLIENT XXXXXXXXXXXXXXX, REPRESENTED BY ITS PRESIDENT, MR XXXXXXXXXXXXXXXX (ACCOUNT SIGNATORY), UNDER ACCOUNT NUMBER XXXXXXXXXXXX (USD A/C), CASH FUNDS IN THE AMOUNT OF (AMOUNT IN NUMBERS AND LETTERS), ... IN ... (CURRENCY – USD/EURO/GBP) ...IN THE LAWFUL CURRENCY OF ... (THE UNITED STATES OF AMERICA)/(THE EUROPEAN ECONOMIC COMMUNITY)/(UNITED KINGDOM OF GREAT BRITAIN), PRESENTLY HELD UNDER CUSTODY WITH

OUR BANK AND IMMEDIATELY CALLABLE UPON FIRST DEMAND.
WE FURTHERMORE CONFIRM THAT:
- THESE FUNDS ARE FREELY TRANSFERABLE AT OUR CLIENT'S DIRECTIONS, AND THAT OUR CLIENT'S ACCOUNT IS IN GOOD STANDING WITH OUR BANK AND THAT
- THESE FUNDS TO BE GOOD, CLEAN, AND CLEARED FUNDS OF NON-CRIMINAL AND NON- TERRORIST ORIGIN, AND ARE FREE FROM ANY AND ALL LIENS AND ENCUMBRANCES AND THAT

SIGNED BY:	BANK SEAL SIGNED BY:
BANK OFFICER	BANK OFFICER
PIN & TITLE	PIN & TITLE

RWA:

Document of bank ratification and essential in the final process of the processing.

With this document, the bank confirms:

* The asset is good, clear, clean and of non-criminal origin
* The Asset does not have any type of external load
* Asset can be worked via SWIFT MT799 - MT760

It must be signed by two bank officials and stamped by the bank itself. With this document, the bank undertakes to issue the Swift MT-760 when the client orders it and at the coordinates it indicates.

RWA LETTER MODEL ISSUED BY THE BANK

RWA LETTER
TO: PROGRAM MANAGER
RE:
ACCOUNT NAME: XXXXXXXXXXXXXXXXXXXXXXXXXX
ACCOUNT NUMBER: XXXXXXXXXXXXXXXXXX
(EUR)

DATE: XXXXXX XX, 2021
WE, XXXXXXXXXXXXXX BANK XXXXXXXXXXXXXXXX., LOCATED AT XXXXXXXXXXXXXX, XXXXXXXXXXXXXX, XXXXXXX, DO HEREBY CONFIRM WITH FULL BANK RESPONSIBILITY, THAT WE IRREVOCABLY HOLD FOR OUR CLIENT XXXXXXXXXXXXXXX, REPRESENTED BY ITS PRESIDENT, MR XXXXXXXXXXXXXXXX (ACCOUNT SIGNATORY), UNDER ACCOUNT NUMBER XXXXXXXXXXXX CASH FUNDS THE AMOUNT OF XXXXXXXXXXXXXXX MILLION EURO (€ XXX,000,000.00), THE LAWFUL CURRENCY OF THE EUROPEAN ECONOMIC COMMUNITY, PRESENTLY HELD UNDER CUSTODY WITH OUR BANK AND IMMEDIATELY CALLABLE UPON FIRST DEMAND.
WE FURTHERMORE CONFIRM THAT:
- THE AFOREMENTIONED BG/SBLC/CD IS ASSIGNABLE, DIVISIBLE, NEGOTIABLE AND FREELY TRANSFERABLE AT OUR CLIENT'S DIRECTIONS, AND THAT OUR CLIENT'S ACCOUNT IS IN GOOD STANDING WITH OUR BANK AND THAT
- THESE FUNDS TO BE GOOD, CLEAN, AND CLEARED FUNDS OF NON-CRIMINAL AND NON- TERRORIST ORIGIN, AND ARE FREE FROM ANY AND ALL LIENS AND ENCUMBRANCES AND THAT
- WE ARE READY TO BLOCK AND RESERVE THE AFOREMENTIONED CASH FUNDS VIA A PREADVISE S.W.I.F.T. MT-799 FOLLOWED BY A BINDING, CALLABLE AND AUTHENTICATED
S.W.I.F.T. MT-760 UPON FIRST DEMAND OF OUR CLIENT XXXXXXXXXXX TO BANK COORDINATES AS DESIGNATED BY OUR CLIENT.
- WE ALSO CONFIRM THAT THE ABOVE-MENTIONED INSTRUMENT IS AUTHENTIC, LEGAL AND VALID, AND IT CAN BE VERIFIED AND CONFIRMED THROUGH THE FOLLOWING BANK COORDINATES:
Bank Name:
Bank Address:
Telephone Number:

SWIFT code:
Bank Officer:
SIGNED BY: BANK SEAL SIGNED BY:
BANK OFFICER: BANK OFFICER: PIN & TITLE: PIN & TITLE:

LOI (LETTER OF INTENT)

LOI, also known as the Letter of Intent, is a formal document through which the client expresses his intention to participate in a Private Placement Program.

MODEL OF CORPORATE LOI

LETTER OF INTENT

DATE:

TO: Trade Authority/Program Manager

RE: Participation in Structured Private Financial Opportunity INVESTOR TRANSACTION CODE:

Dear Sir,

I, (NAME), the undersigned, hereby confirm under penalty of perjury, my full commitment and agreement to participate in an investment opportunity, subject to my acceptance of the terms, conditions and procedures that shall be outlined in the Private Placement Program.

Furthermore, I hereby warrant and represent that I have available for placement into the proposed investment, the sum of (SPELL AMOUNT) Euro/United States Dollars (€/$, 000,000.00) of clean, clear funds, free of any levy, liens or encumbrances and of non-criminal origin, and herewith attach documentary evidence of same. I hereby warrant and represent that the Rule of Full-disclosure has established these funds were legally obtained from non-criminal business or actions. I further confirm that I am the beneficial owner of these cash funds that I have full signatory authority and control thereof, and that such funds are available for immediate placement at my sole discretion.

I confirm and acknowledge, with full responsibility, that neither your company nor anyone working on your behalf has solicited me; that the documents that I shall receive shall not be deemed to be a solicitation of funds in connection with an investment program; and, that I am approaching you voluntarily for the purpose of securing participation in a bona fide Secure Private Placement Program.

I am prepared to instruct my bank to act upon the funds as required pursuant to the specifics of this program. In the case of Blocked Funds, it is my understanding the funds will be blocked and or reserved) in the account and they will remain, at all times, noncallable.

I hereby request information from you covering the terms, condition and procedures of a secured investment and look forward to commencing the transaction, upon my acceptance of the agreement.

Email, facsimile copies or photocopies of documents or agreements pertaining to this subject are declared and regarded as valid and equal to the original, provided they are represented by proper signatories. Originals may be obtained upon request.

I, (NAME), hereby swear under penalty of perjury, that the information provided herein is accurate and true as of this date:

For and on behalf of (NAME OF COMPANY)

Signature: SEAL OF COMPANY Name/Title:
Company: Passport Number: Date of Issue: Date of Expiry:
Country of Issuance:

AUTHORIZATION TO VERIFY:

This authorization is assigned to PROGRAM MANAGER so that the verification of the Asset is carried out successfully.

Such verification will ALWAYS be performed BANK TO BANK as required by banking operations.

In order for an authorization of this type to be properly completed, it must include names, surnames and telephones of the bank officers in addition to their identification number. You must also send COPIA to these bank officials so that they themselves are aware of the moment in which the verification by the bank of the trader takes place.

LETTER OF AUTHORIZATION TO VERIFY:

AUTHORIZATION TO VERIFY AND AUTHENTICATE

DATE:
TO: Trade Authority/Program Manager
RE: Authorization to Verify

INVESTOR TRANSACTION CODE:
Know all men, by these that I, (NAME), at the address shown above, give you clear notice that you have my direct permission and full authority to do all matters necessary to confirm, verify, and authenticate my beneficially owned cash funds and/or application asset(s) and its associated good standing account status, in an amount of (SPELL AMOUNT) Euro/United States Dollars (€/$,000,000.00) on a bank to bank basis. The below stated beneficially owned account is of good, clean, and cleared cash funds obtained via legal means, and is currently available at the bank coordinates below:
Cash Amount: (€/$,000,000.00)
Bank Name: (NAME OF THE BANK)
Bank Address: (ADDRESS OF BANK)
Account Name: (ACCOUNT NAME)
Account Number: (ACCOUNT NUMBER)
Account Signatory: (ACCOUNT SIGNATORY)
Bank Officer & Title: (BANK OFFICER/TITLE)

COPY OF THIS AUTHORIZATION WILL BE LODGED AND PRESENTED TO MY BANK OFFICER.
In witness hereof I, (NAME), hereby swear under penalty of perjury, that the information provided herein is accurate and true as of this date:
For and on behalf of (NAME OF COMPANY)
Signature: OF COMPANY
Name/Title:
Company:
Passport Number:
C.C.: (NAME OF BANK AND BANK OFFICER)
SEAL

CIS (CLIENT INFORMATION SHEET)

Known as CIS, the Client Information Sheet is the document that identifies the Inverter with all its data.

This document will be essential to be able to present the transaction in the office of the trader and thus initiate a process of "Due Diligence".

CIS MODEL (CUSTOMER INFORMATION SHEET)

CLIENT INFORMATION SHEET

Directions: This document should be completed in full. If a line item does not pertain then insert the term: "N/A" (non-applicable).
Corporate Information
Full Name of Corporation:
Date of Incorporation:
Incorporated in (City/State/Country):
Registration Number:
Board of Directors (Name & Title):

Officers (Name & Title):
Shareholders:
Location of Address:
Registered Address (Corporation)
Full Name of Corporation:
Street Address:
City:
State:
Country:
Postal Code:
Location of Address:
Mailing Address (Corporation)
Full Name of Corporation:
Street Address: City:
State:
Country:
Postal Code:
Contact Information (Corporation)
Telephone Number:
Fax Number:
Mobile Number:
Email Address:
Languages/Translator Languages:
Does the Signatory speak English?:
If No, Name of Translator:
Tel Number:
Email Address:
Legal Advisor Full Name:
Company:
Address:
City:
State:
Country:
Postal Code:
Telephone Number:
Fax Number:

Email Address:

Bank Information (Corporate)
Bank Name (where funds are currently on deposit):
Street Address:
City:
State:
Country:
Postal Code:
Account Name:
Account Number:
Sort Code ABA No.:
SWIFT Code:
Account Signatory (1):
Account Signatory (2):
Bank Officer # 1 Name:
Bank Officer # 2 Name:
Telephone Number:
Fax Number:

Client Account where Profits to be paid Bank Name:
Street Address:
City:
State:
Country:
Postal Code:
Account Name:
Account Number:
Sort Code ABA No.:
SWIFT Code:
Bank Officer Name:
Telephone Number:
Fax Number:

Personal Information of the Transactional Signatory Authorized by Corporation

(Please attach copy of the corporate resolution adopted by the Board of Directors appointing and authorizing said officer(s) below to represent and legally bind the corporation)
First Name:
Middle Name:
Last Name:
Gender:
Date of Birth:
Social Security Number:
Country of Citizenship:
Languages:
Passport Information of Officers(s) of Corporation
*Please attach copy of photo and signature page of passport
Passport Number:
Date of Issue:
Date of Expiry:
Issuing Authority:
Location of Address: Home-Legal Residence (Officer of Corporation)
Full Name of Officer:
Street Address:
City:
State:
Country:
Postal Code:
(You may duplicate the section above for each Director involved in transaction)

Investment
Funds available for this transaction:
Type of currency:
Origin of funds:
Are these funds free and clear of all liens, encumbrances and third party interests:

I, (NAME), hereby swear under penalty of perjury, that the information provided herein is accurate and true as of this date:

Today according to the financial possibilities that an investor possesses a financial instrument or any asset that can be banked using the financial engineering, we could use it as financial leverage and therefore to work it in the Secondary market.

There are many possibilities for generating cash to be used in the financing of projects in the real economy, if adequate banking channels are known and ways of using financial instruments.

Asian banks are now well aware of the dynamics of the collateralization of financial instruments, the monetization of them and their trading in the secondary cash market.

THE BANKING OF FINANCIAL INSTRUMENTS AND/OR ASSETS FURNISHED OR REAL ESTATE

WHAT IS BANKING?

Banking is to get our financial asset also called Assets, of which we can mention among others the Bonds, Treasury Bills, IBOES or our movable or real estate assets like works of art, buildings, land, products called commodity (rice, sugar, soy, gold, nickel, iron etc.), be taken as guarantees by Business Banks to increase their balance sheets and these in turn back with "full bank responsibility" the issuance of bank guarantees or SBLC (stand by letters of credit) in favor of its depositors, being thus an applicant of such instruments that are issued by means of interbank communication protocols (Swifts MT 799 and Swift MT 760), either directly or indirectly with other banks of better rating for their solvency and rating, to be able to do operations of trading in the secondary market.

While these instruments are being traded on the secondary market, Assets or property or property guarantees remain as collateral until the intended transaction is completed.

BANKING PROCEDURE

Banking any type of asset and depending on its nature, has in each case its particular procedure.

For example:

1. To Banking Movable Assets (Bonds, Treasury Bills Recharged from Brazil, American IBOES, etc.), the following documentation must be provided:
   A. CIS and Passport of the holder of Assets.
   B. KYC of the Asset holder. (Complete information on how the client acquired the Assets and source of funds that I use for this purpose)
   C. Experimentation of the Assets. (Such experimentation must be in original and made by expert recognized for such purpose).
   D. Financial valuation of Assets issued by a recognized expert for this purpose.
   E. Pay the costs of Banking and the Costs of Deposit and Custody in a Security House that, generally, are linked to the banks of businesses that do the banking. These costs usually vary depending on the bank that does so, because of the rating and solvency of the bank's full bank liability.
2. To Banking Assets (Works of Art, Commodity, Gold, Nickel, Copper, Aluminum, etc.), the following documentation must be provided:
   A. CIS and Passport of the holder of Assets.
   B. KYC of the Asset holder. (Complete information on how the client acquired the Assets and source of funds that I use for this purpose)

C. Experimentation of Assets. (This experimentation must be in original and made by recognized expert for this purpose).
D. Financial valuation of the Assets issued by an expert recognized for this purpose.
E. Pay the costs of Banking and the Costs of Deposit and Custody in a Security House that, generally, are linked to the banks of businesses that do the banking. These costs usually vary depending on the bank that does so because of the rating and solvency of the full bank issuing bank liability. These banking costs include the deposit and custody of the asset, the power to issue with the backing of the full bank responsibility of the bank that makes the bank guarantees and/or SBLC (standby letter of credit), through SWIFT interbank communication protocols MT 799 and MT 760, to be later monetized through credit lines and converted into cash these guarantees to operate in the secondary market by trading.

3. Para Bancarizar Activos Inmobiliarios (Edificios, Terrenos) se debe aportar la siguiente documentación:
   A. CIS and Passport of the holder of Assets.
   B. KYC of the Asset holder. (Complete information on how the client acquired the Assets and source of funds that I use for this purpose).
   C. Valuation of Assets. (This assessment must be in original and made by an expert recognized for this purpose, authorized by the competent authorities that regulate the Professional appraisers in each country).
   D. Be free of charges. (Do not have mortgages that affect the asset).

E. Pay the costs of Banking and the Costs of Deposit and Custody in a Security House that, generally are linked to the banks of businesses that do the banking. These costs usually vary depending on the bank that does so because of the rating and solvency of the bank's full bank liability.

BANKING COSTS

As we have already mentioned, the cost of banking will depend on the bank that does it and the "full bank responsibility" that can be confirmed by the first-line correspondent bank, either European or Asian.

This bank responsibility is assumed by these banks with the payment of a significant percentage at the time of issuance of the BANK GUARANTEE or SBLC for subsequent discount or monetization.

Usually, these bank costs that cover insurance and reinsurance range from 10% to 15% on the face value of the issued guarantee, and are paid when a monetizing bank discounts the guarantee. What is paid prior to the time of banking these assets are the costs of deposit, custody and banking of the asset, which usually are around 600,000 euros including the costs of issuing bank swifts MT 799 and MT 760 backed by the bank that has made the banking possible.

The guarantee issued, not to be sent to the collection at maturity, is returned free of charge at the end of the year, reimbursing the line of credit with interest included.

In these cases only the financial returns obtained in trading operations in the secondary market are available, which is really the reason for these types of financial transactions.

MERCHANT BANKS

The Merchant Banks are growing at a dizzying pace, taking advantage of the need for financing that exists in the market, since traditional banking is not currently providing the required credit to companies and/or projects that are socioeconomically viable.

That is why the business model of these types of banks is very attractive for both the banker and the entrepreneur, because the guarantees that are constituted to return the capital are usually based on the joint administration of the important projects to develop, and flowing synergies that are beneficial to the parties.

Acquiring a business bank is simple. By means of law firms in Switzerland you can buy these type of bank licenses authorized by the central bank of the country where they are issued.

By using these banks, financial instruments can be acquired for themselves or in trust administration, to be banked and later to constitute bank guarantees to be able to operate in the secondary market.

ESCROW:

Definition: It is a formal legal agreement voluntarily created and financed by a person (trustor) who directs another person (the trustee) to assume a legal title and control of the property donated by the trustor, to be used and administered for the benefit of a one or more persons designated by the settlor (the beneficiaries). The beneficiary of a trust receives from this income or distributions of assets and owns the equitable and forced ownership of the benefits, but does not control the assets of the trust or manage the operation of the trust.

THE HOUSES OF DEPOSIT AND CUSTODY OF FINANCIAL INSTRUMENTS (HOUSE SECURITY)

House Security are usually offices with special security and designed for the custody of valuable documents and are authorized for this purpose, complying with the standards required by the Icontec custody, not only documents but also currency.

These House Security offices are almost always directly linked to the business banks and/or are part of the same business group.

DIFFERENCES BETWEEN SKR DEPOSIT IN CUSTODY OF SECURITIES, AND BANK INSTRUMENTS, ACTIVE MOVEMENT OR REAL ESTATE

The custodial deposit SKR that issues securities via a security house is the certificate issued by said security house due to the deposit in custody that has been left to the depositor client's safe deposit. These types of contracts are also often used to give representation and power to the security house to represent the owner of the security or depositor of the same in any transaction of purchase and sale of the asset.

Banking of a financial instrument or movable or immovable asset is the responsibility that the custodian bank takes directly from the assets deposited in the house security and takes them for itself, in its balance sheet, to be able to issue a bank guarantee or SBLC with "full Bank Responsibility" in association with first-rate banks that have better solvency and bank rating, so that they can be monetized and/or discounted in the secondary market.

BANKING OF MOVABLE PROPERTY (WORKS OF ART)

EXPERTISE AND INSURANCE

It is said that works of art are banked when they have complied with the protocol of deposit and custody in a house security, contributing the experience of the originality of the work and its respective insurance against all risks that must have while it is in the dependencies of the safe house.

From these times and according to the price for which the custodian bank or bank, which is usually taken at a price of between 40% or 50% of its current valuation, is issued the certificate of banking of the same but already on the part of the bank.

This certificate gives rise to a bank guarantee that can work together between the custodian bank or Merchant Bank and the depositary client AND by means of confirmation from the bank, since such guarantee is confirmed by the Swift MT 799 interbank communication protocol and MT 760, the guarantee can be monetized in the secondary market through owned or third-party credit lines.

BANKING OF FINANCIAL ASSETS (HISTORICAL BONDS, LTNS OR NATIONAL LETTERS OF THE TREASURY OF BRAZIL). EXPERTIZACION, CETIP, CODIP, DOCUMENTATION, CERTIFICATE OF REPACTUATION, VERIFICATION IN THE CENTRAL BANK OF BRAZIL AND THE NATIONAL TREASURY, VERIFICATION AND HIGH IN BOVESPA (BOLSA DE BRASIL)

With the national treasury bills of Brazil (LTNs), there has always been a lot of speculation and much fraud about the instruments, since there are many CARECAS letters in the market, as they are called in Brazil to letters that are not REPACTED AND/Validated and accepted by the Government of Brazil as Treasury Debt.

In the Brazilian market there are many CARECAS LTNs, whose authenticity is only guaranteed by an expert report, made by an expert specialized in Brazil to attest to the experience of these titles. This experience of the letter is accompanied by the sealing inside a PLASTIC BAG with security tape of the numbered letter or LACRE SEALED. This identification number is referred to in the same EXPERT REPORT. Such sealing can't be violated because the expert's report and therefore the AUTHENTICITY OF THE EXPERTISE OF THE LETTER would be of no value.

The letters CARECAS only accompany a Certificate of the National Treasury and a Guide of Receipt. In some cases, some have a DOMAIN CHAIN, where the previous owners of the title are shown, as well as a Deed of Assignment signed at a notary's office in Brazil.

Trading with these letters in Brazil is very common in an informal market, but they are not accepted by any bank as a guarantee because they lack the PROCESS OF RE-AGREE: This process, as I have already mentioned, is the Validation and Acceptance made by the National Treasury of Brazil as public debt.

Currently the National Treasury and the Central Bank of Brazil do not make official confirmations to give the authenticity of these CERTIFICATES OF REPACTUATION ISSUED BY THE NATIONAL TREASURY, but the Brazilian stock exchange, Bovespa, has internal mechanisms to verify this authenticity. That is why when it is intended to Bancarizar this type of instruments are asked to be discharged on the Brazilian Stock Exchange to have the convenience of being electronically verified by the banks that will make the instrument bankable.

DEFINITIONS

CODIP/ CETIP: It is a codification given by the Brazilian Ministry of Public Treasury to the public debt assets that have been recognized as authentic, and of course up to that point have canceled the taxes of the declaration of tenure of this debt.

CURRENT FACIAL VALUE: The current face value of the security is given by the value that the National Treasury has recognized the title in mention, and usually this value refers to the value of the one that expresses the title as a bond.

Example: A PURPLE LTN THAT HAS A VALUE IN THE TITLE OF 1.2 BILLION CRUISERS. This value to the change in dollars is more or less equivalent to about 600 million dollars, although the treasury has recognized in its moment of renegotiation that at the end of the next 30 years costs 8.4 billion. This current face value can be taken as the benchmark for bankroll.

VALUE OF REPACTUATION OR FUTURE VALUE: This value is the amount that the Government of Brazil, through the Ministry of Finance, has accepted as liquidable debt at future value within 30 years. Usually in PURPLE LETTERS or H series, they have values equivalent to 8.4 Billion Cruises.

TITULARITY OF A LTN OF BRAZIL:

It is important to know that to hold the title of a Brazilian Treasury Letter, if you are not a Brazilian citizen you should choose to found a partnership in Brazil, and this logically happens to have a Brazilian partner. These instruments can be traded or collateralized by means of notary powers where they are authorized to carry out any type of financial operation. But the time comes when you must transfer the ownership of the instrument if you want to sell, and you will have to turn to the one who bought it so you can make the transfer to the Brazilian Ministry of Finance.

BANKING OF REAL ESTATE (BUILDINGS, HOTELS, COMMERCIAL CENTERS)

Banking of real estate such as buildings, hotels, shopping malls or housing packages in excess of 20 million euros, can be Banked by the following procedure:

Each and every real estate asset must be free of charges. In addition the asset must be generating rent yield. From this moment an Insurance Policy is issued to wrap the whole package of real estate so that it is the insurance policy that is banked or used as collateral to be deposited in the bank. The bank can then issue a bank guarantee with full bank liability, confirmed by swift communication protocol MT 799 and MT 760, to be discounted in the secondary market.

BANKING OF COMMODITIES NOT PERMISSIBLE (RICE, SUGAR, SOY, WINE, HAM, ETC.)

In the same way as a work of art or property is banked, we can bank non-perishable raw materials such as rice, sugar, soy, wine, ham, etc. The only difference is that instead of being deposited or stored in a Security House in safes (as the documents are kept), it is made in industrial buildings with similar security, and logically insured against all types of risk while the operation of trading is executed.

The banking procedure is the same as for the previous ones.

BANKING OF METALS (GOLD, COPPER, NICKEL, ETC.)

One of the main advantages of Banking an asset is to be able to work in the secondary market, to make profitability and to continue owning the asset.

That is why the holders of this type of precious metal assets, prefer to bank them to continue generating wealth, because they work for its owner.

The banking procedure is the same as that described for the other movable and immovable assets.

THE WARRANTS

DEFINITION, THE PARTIES, DISCOUNT IN THE SECONDARY MARKET.

DEFINITION:

The warrant is a contract or derivative financial instrument that gives the buyer the right, but not the obligation, to buy/sell an underlying asset (futures, etc.) at a given price at a future date also determined. In terms of operation, warrants are included within the options category. If a warrant is a purchase, it is called a warrant, and if it is a sale, it will be a put warrant. The warrant, as well as the options, give the holder the possibility of making or not the associated transaction (purchase or sale, as appropriate) and the other party the obligation to carry it out. The fact of making the transaction is called "exercising the warrant".

DISCOUNT IN THE SECONDARY MARKET:

These types of derivatives can be sold in the secondary market without banking them because by its nature of being a derivative financial instrument, any investor can buy the warrant to carry out the operation, since one of the main characteristics is that they have a lot of liquidity, and they have a limited life from 1 to 2 years.

The entire process of banking financial instruments will always depend on the payment of the costs involved. Banking an asset or financial instrument means being able to market it in the secondary market by means of guarantees or bank guarantees that can be issued by banks with the full responsibility of banks.

In short, to make money, you have to invest money.

COLLATERALIZATION OF FINANCIAL INSTRUMENTS OR ASSETS FURNISHED OR REAL ESTATE

WHAT IS THE COLLATERALIZATION OF ASSETS?

Collateralising a financial asset, furniture, or real estate means that after being banked the bank uses it for itself and adheres to its balance as its own to issue a bank guarantee on its behalf, backed by the assets we have banked.

PERCENTAGE OF COLLATERALIZATION OF AN ACTIVE:

When a bank takes in a financial asset, furniture or real estate, the percentage of the collateral by which it is taken almost never exceeds 50% of its current market value.

MARGIN OF MANEUVER AND MEASURING THE RISK AND VALUE FOR WHICH AN ACTIVE INSTRUMENT SUCH AS A GUARANTEE IS TAKEN

When the bank collateralizes a movable or immovable asset or takes it as collateral, it leaves a margin of maneuver of 40% or 50%, to cover in this type of business any possible contingency related to the associated risk in the event that they do not return the guarantees which have been issued based on these assets being free of charges at the end of the year.

INSURANCE AND REINSURANCE:

The bank that collateralizes our assets always establishes insurance of the operation and in turn reinsurance of policies of Credit Risk, to assure the risk of the operation.

The quality of the asset we give as collateral to the bank, is always linked to the percentage by which the bank takes it as collateral. It is not the same to give in deposit for guarantee the Gold, the Copper or the Nickel, other than a Shopping center for example. Most liquid assets are taken at more percentage of their market value as collateral.

GREY SCREEN OPERATIONS

In the world of Macro banking you hear a lot about Grey Screen operations.

They are operations that are usually very high amounts, and are carried out through direct communication protocols through the mechanism "server to server" (communication between computer servers), disclosing between the parties some access codes, and logically with the permission of bank officials.

"Server to server" operations, for their important amounts, are reserved for governments, foundations, banks, and millionaires of any sector that are aware of this fund-raising system. Generally, one of the reasons of the use of this form of transfer of funds, is that they do not appear registered in the financial system in the sight of the inspection agencies, and after the discharge do not leave electronic traces.

These operations, when made or downloaded from computer systems, must be authorized by the Currency Control Department of the country where the funds are entered and are usually used to make significant payments of raw materials and/or any type of commodity, for example oil, coal, etc.

The bank procedure always has to be based on the knowledge and authorization of the issuing bank or the sending bank, through its banking officer, and the bank must authorize this discharge to the receiving bank by means of a corporate acknowledgement and telephone verification and/or mail between bank officials.

If this situation does not happen, that is, the issuing bank does not authorize the discharge in either case: either by mail or by telephone, we are incurring a felony bank fraud, and therefore the funds may be blocked by the receiving bank if there is no authorization from the issuing bank, without mentioning the legal problems in which we may be involved.

When the funds are blocked from the screen of the gray screen of the bank where these funds are deposited, in order to monetize them it is necessary that the company that makes them available to use them as collateral has an active line of credit, and the blocking of funds is done by exchanging access codes between servers.

The documentation that is requested to be able to initiate the process of an operation of this type are:

1. CIS AND PASSPORT OF THE FUND HOLDER.
2. KYC OF THE FUND HOLDER.
3. SERVER ACCESS CODES.
4. AUTHORIZATION TO VERIFY THE BANK OFFICER OF THE BANK WHERE THESE FUNDS ARE DEPOSITED, WHICH WILL AUTHORIZE THE CONFIRMATION OF DISCHARGE BY MAIL OR AS BY TELEPHONE.
5. SIGNATURE OF CONTRACT.
6. AUTHORIZATION OF THE DEPARTMENT OF CONTROL OF THE FUNDS OF THE COUNTRY WHERE THE FUNDS WILL BE DOWNLOADED OR COLLATERALIZED AND MONITORED.
7. EXECUTION OF THE OPERATION.

OPENING COMPANIES IN FISCAL HAVENS

The opening of companies and the consequent bank accounts that are opened in tax havens, are very necessary to be able to operate in the world of Macro banking.

Whatever your business purpose, this type of business and banking structure allows you to operate at lower costs and have a presence in important financial countries like Hong Kong, Singapore or Dubai, among others.

Hong Kong's ability to open a company and its bank accounts in prime banks such as HSBC, BANCO DE CHINA, STANDARD CHARTERED BANK or DBS BANK, among others, should be highlighted.

The costs of opening a company in this country can amount to 6000 euros with all the costs of opening bank accounts included and with virtual office.

Annually for the renewal of this company the fees paid are typically 1,450 euros. Otherwise the taxes that are paid there are zero.

OPENING OF AN ASSET MANAGEMENT COMPANY

A company, such as an Asset Management Company, is responsible for the responsible management of capital and corporate guarantees such as bonds and shares by managing institutions like banks to achieve the greatest benefits to investors.

Unlike financial advice, asset management is not only a way of having investment advice, but it is also a relevant activity of asset management institutions, which must make decisions about the management of investments.

The center of this type of commercial banking business is the management of assets from private companies and national or foreign companies whose assets can be presented in the form of shares, pension funds, real estate and liquid assets.

The objective of asset management is present in the management of clients' investment portfolios taking into account their risk situation.

In Switzerland, we can open an Asset Management company, and at the same time, the bank license that allows us to establish an offshore bank with all banking services, including the founding of a House Security, and trust company. Costs of the banking license with the company Asset Management Group are around 200,000 Euros. For this, I would like to recommend a very experienced and serious person in the field of acquiring offshore banking licenses called Andrea Paredes Von Roth, Expert Chilean Elite Sportsman and Guru of Finance, Owner and CEO of the company Moneda Management LLC. http://www.monedamanagement.com

THE ISSUANCE OF BANK SWIFTS

When a bank Swift is issued, it is made against the guarantee of an Asset or Asset that supports the Swift.

These assets can be:

Cash: when the guarantee is Cash backed.

LTNs or bonds: when the guarantee is the blocking of a bond or LTN whose authenticity is verified and endorsed by the issuing bank.

Example of a Swift text when the guarantee is a Brazilian LTN and the bank confirms its blocking by Swift MT 760.

Example of a Swift text, when the guarantee is Cash Backed.

Text of the Swift Mt 799: Notice sent by the Bank Issuer to the Recipient Bank.

Swift Text Icpo: Response sent by the receiving bank, committing itself to the Monetization and irrevocable payment agreed in the previous contract, conditioned to receipt of the MT 760.

Text of Swift MT 760: Sending of the Guarantee by the issuing bank to the receiving bank usually with a maturity of collection at 1 year and one day. This guarantee must be transferable, divisible, irrevocable, with payment at first demand and confirmable between banks through their banking officers.

Text of a BCL: (BANK CONFIRMATION LETTER), is a bank confirmation letter where, prior to sending the Swift MT 799 and MT 760, the bank issuing the guarantee confirms that it is ready and ready to issue said Swift in favor of their client and that the funds are clear, clean and transparent as well as the willingness to verify from bank to bank among bank officials the veracity of the same.

THE APPLICANT AND THE BENEFICIARY ON A BANK GUARANTEE

THE APPLICANT:

The applicant in a Bank guarantee or in a SBLC (Stand by Letter of Credit), is really the owner or owner of the guarantee, for which the issuing bank is supporting its issuance.

For this, and previously, this owner has had to constitute to the bank issuing the same the necessary and sufficient guarantees for the bank to assume in his name such responsibility.

THE BENEFICIARY:

The beneficiary in a Bank Guarantee or in a SBLC (Stand By Letter of Credit) is the natural person, legal entity or Bank that will make the discount of said guarantee, and that therefore has available an Active Credit Line to be able to execute the Discount and at the end of the year send it to the collection.

TRANSIT OF A BANK SWIFT

The transit of a bank Swift depends on whether the issuing bank is accepted by the receiving bank as a solid bank with an acceptable rating or is one of the 50 best banks in the world, called TOP 50. If it is not so and the bank needs to rely on a correspondent bank of these characteristics, then the bank will finally transmit through the bank that reconfirms that guarantee with the end-bank's endorsement.

FULL BANK RESPONSIBILITY

It is the payment responsibility assumed by the issuing bank that confirms a bank guarantee, SBLC, Letter of Credit, or any type of guarantee on behalf of its client, which in turn has had to deposit the necessary guarantees for it.

Many times this banking responsibility is shared by the banks that are at that moment associated with the transaction assuming the responsibility of this guarantee.

SWIFT 199/SWIFT INFORMATION OR PRE-WARNING

They are Swifts with free message format, or Swifts of informative messages. They are used in this case to inform the receiving bank that the issuing bank is willing and ready to send a bank guarantee through the Swift MT 760 communication protocol, and that therefore the receiving bank needs to reply that it is willing to receive the Bank guarantee and monetize it.

The model of this type of Swift also applies in the Swift MT 799, since both are Swift formats of free message.

SWIFT 999:

Like the Swift 199, it has exactly the same usage and definition, since they are Swifts with free message formats.

The difference with a Swift 799 is actually the lower bank cost of issuance.

SWIFT MT 799:

It is a Swift format of free message just like a MT 199 or MT 999, but it has more relevance with respect to the information it transmits as a free message pre-notice.

SWIFT MT 760:

It is a Swift guarantee. It is used to send a bank guarantee or a SBLC to the receiving bank, where it needs to be taken as collateral and discounted in the secondary market.

It is very important that before initiating any interbank communication by issuing Bank Swifts, to ensure that the issuing bank will send the corresponding Swift MT 799 and MT 760 guarantee, we require that the issuing bank first issue a bank confirmation letter or BCL signed by two banking officers, where they are informed that they are willing to issue a bank guarantee for a certain amount in favor of their client, and that this letter is confirmed between banking officers from bank to bank.

BANK GUARANTEES THAT ARE ONLY CONFIRMED BY DTC OR EUROCLEAR

The fact that a bank takes as collateral financial instruments that are only confirmed by DTC and/or Euroclear has its limitations, since the blockages made by Euroclear and DTC are made by Screen or Windows Time, which is the blockage that can be made in a determined moment in time on an open screen, in common agreement between the banking officers.

EUROCLEAR DEFINITION:

Euroclear: is the financial services company, based in Belgium, specializing in the liquidation and custody of securities. It was founded in 1968 as part of JP Morgan & Co, to settle operations in the Eurobond market and then to develop them.

Euroclear liquidates national and international securities transactions, including bonds, derivatives, shares and mutual funds.

Euroclear provides financial services to more than 90 countries worldwide, as well as being a principal depository of securities.

From 1968 to 2000, the Euroclear system was managed by JP Morgan Guaranty Trust, a New York company that was part of JP Morgan & Co. In 2001 the company MGT transferred the company to Euroclear Bank.

DTC DEFINITION:

The DTC's subsidiary, the Depository Trust Company (DTC), established in 1973, was created to reduce costs and provide clearing and settlement of efficiency by immobilizing the securities and making "scriptural" changes to ownership of securities. DTC provides securities movements for the NSCC net settlement and liquidation of institutional transactions (which generally involve money and securities transfers between custodian banks and agents/distributors) as well as money market instruments.

In 2009, transactions worth more than $299 billion were established in DTC, and 299,500,000 entries were processed. In addition to settlement services, DTC brings efficiency to the securities industry by retaining custody of more than 3.5 million securities worth nearly $34 billion, including securities issued in the US and more than 120 foreign countries and territories.

PROCEDURE FOR ISSUANCE AND CONFIRMATION OF A BANK GUARANTEE BY DTC WITH THE INTERNAL COMMUNICATION PROTOCOL MT 799 AND MT 760

When a bank guarantee is issued by the DTC system, an internal database that is accessed electronically between banks to be verified and blocked by a Windows time. It is necessary that in real time, access is made by the two bank officials of both the issuing bank and of the bank that is interested in taking the guarantee, and blocking is done to be able to discount or monetize.

Swift model that is sent by DTC:

To:

Attn:

Subject:

We, (…), located at (…), do hereby confirm with full legal and bank responsibility that, on the date of this letter, your good self, (…), represented by Mr. (…), holder of (…) Passport Number: (…), as authorized account holder and signatory maintains and currently has on cash deposit with us € 500,000,000.00 (Five Hundred Million Euros) in the account (…).

Such funds are unconditionally and irrevocably blocked, at the transmission date of this SWIFT Message, for a period of One (1) year and One (1) month for investment purposes in favor of (…). Also, we confirm hereto that the fore captioned blocked fund in our Bank custody will not be changed, altered, amended or pledged for a period of One (1) year and One (1) month commencing from the date of this SWIFT or until completion of the above investment, if less than the aforementioned One (1) year and One (1) month.

We further confirm, that this Cash deposit is known to us and has been legally acquired, clean, clear, of non-criminal origin and though various trade related businesses, and are free of any liens and encumbrances and are freely transferable upon the instructions of the authorized signatory.

This is an OPERATIVE BANKING INSTRUMENT and this SWIFT message may only be confirmed on Euroclear & DTCC screens.

Kindly acknowledge receipt of this SWIFT within twelve (12) hours of receipt hereof.

Thanks for your co-operation. ACCEPTANCE ACKNOWLEDGEMENT:

Sincerely,

BANKING SWIFTS ISSUANCE COSTS:

As we have discussed during the course development, the costs of issuing a bank Swift depend on what is sent. For example if you send a Swift MT 199, MT 999 or MT 799, which are informational Swifts, these Swifts really have the cost that the bank wishes to charge the customer as a service more than just the transmission of data, and can be about 100 Euros.

The cost of issuing a bank guarantee issued in a Swift MT 760 interbank communication format usually costs between 0.5% and 5% of the total face value of the guarantee, and its cost will fluctuate according to the rating and solvency of the issuing bank.

Leverage through bank guarantees is the most used in the secondary market to obtain the liquidity that is invested in the real economy to companies.

Unfortunately, there are many opportunists in the market who claim to issue these types of instruments when they do not, but when it is done with the right and serious ways, it is a real opportunity to develop business and humanitarian growth.

ISSUING BANKS AND THEIR CORRESPONDENTS

When a second-order issuing bank issues a bank Swift with "Full Bank Responsibility" and needs to reinforce this responsibility by a first- class bank, it is necessary to establish an internal agreement between banks for the responsibility to be shared and endorsed. In this way the monetizing bank has cleared the operation of its monetization or discount.

Usually banks collaborate with each other to provide a more efficient service to the client. Therefore they establish agreements by correspondence, even to endorse a full bank responsibility of a Swift MT 760. In this way the conditions of risks are covered and they can do it without a problem.

When establishing an agreement between banks for the correspondence of products and banking services, the main responsibility is given by the first issuing bank to the correspondent bank. This is the one that has to form internally the necessary guarantees for the correspondent bank, if it is going to use it as guarantor in an operation of emission of bank guarantees.

MONETIZATION AND/OR DISCOUNT OF A BANK SWIFT

The process of monetization and/or discount of a bank Swift is simple provided that the necessary steps are rigorously followed.

In the first place, the company that has an active credit line and which will handle the discount of the Banking Guarantee or Stand by Letter of Credit by sending a communication protocol MT 760 by the issuing bank, will require the company (BCL), which is a bank confirmation letter, where the issuing bank is confirming that with the "full bank liability of the bank" they are prepared and ready to issue an SBLC or a BG for a certain value in euros or dollars, in favor of his client, with his name and with his account number, in favor of the company that will make the discount, i.e. the beneficiary of the BG or SBLC, which is the company that discounts or monetizes it.

Secondly, once the bank officials have confirmed that the BCL (Bank Confirmation Letter) is correct and true, a contract is signed between the parties (investor and monetizer) to initiate the interbank communication protocol through Swift MT 760, preceded by a MT 799 notice. When the advance notice of the receiving bank is sent, an ICPO (irrevocable payment order conditioned to receive the guarantee by means of Swift MT 760) must be answered in order for the receiving bank to monetize the guarantee according to the terms of the contract.

The percentage of monetization of a bank guarantee or SBLC, sent through the Swift MT 760 communication protocol, will depend on the rating and the solvency of the issuing bank, and said monetization according to this rating will be deducted between the percentages of 50% to 90%.

INVESTMENTS IN PRIVATE INVESTMENT PROGRAMS (PPP)

Participation in private investment programs, so-called PPPs, usually comes from the monetization of a financial instrument (BG or SBLC). With the monetization percentage of said instrument, a first-rate bank is signed when it is made directly (HSBC, STANDARD CHARTERED BANK, BANK OF CHINA, etc.), and in the commercial office of these banks through a trader, to Participate jointly with the bank in investments in the secondary market. The yields obtained are usually distributed as 50% between the investor and the trader.

These investments in the secondary market are usually made in the purchase and sale of financial instruments (MTNs, BGs, SBLCs, shares ...), and also in the purchase and sale of commodities by trust companies (rice, sugar, soy, petroleum, precious metals, nickel, copper, etc.).

The financial returns that are obtained in the commercialization (purchase and sale) are those that are invested in the real economy for the financing of business and humanitarian projects.

PROCEDURE FOR SIGNING WITH A BANK A PRIVATE INVESTMENT PROGRAM THROUGH A TRADER

When we already have the monetization of a financial instrument (i.e. cash), we sign with the Trader a JV (joint venture), or investment agreement for the purchase of commodities or financial instruments in the secondary market. The Trader offers us a moderate minimum yield of 50% of monthly financial returns on the investment we have made with cash. It is important to mention and clarify that these percentages of financial returns will depend on the amount of cash with which we are participating. This 50% would correspond to an investment of at least 100 million euros. Financial returns are payable month by month, and when we sign a 40-week program, financial returns are liquidable according to the agreement with the bank, but as we have said, the minimum is usually 50% monthly.

When you participate in Spots (specific operations of some purchase and sale of oil and/or derivatives thereof), yields are generally higher and shorter participation in investments.

ACCOUNTS OPENING:

When participating in private investment programs with first-order banks with the above procedure, the bank performs the respective opening of bank accounts to the participants in the trading operation, i.e. those that have to do with the financial transaction. Among them are the applicant of the guarantee, the monetizer of the guarantee, and in special cases the one that has participated like a contributor in the financial leverage in payment of the emission of the bank Swift MT 799 and MT 760 charges.

The documentation that is necessary to provide for the opening of any bank account in any of these banks of the first order are:

For a company:

1. A notarized copy of the company's articles of incorporation.
2. CIS notarized documents of the company.
3. Notary copy of the legal representative's passport.
4. Copy of the notarized CIS of the legal representative.
5. Copy notarized of proof of address or habitual residence.
6. Sworn translation in English of all previous documentation, approved by the consulate of the country of origin of the legal representative, at the place where the account will be opened, and/or apostille of the documents.

For a Physical Person:

1. Copy of notarized passport.
2. Notary copy of the proof of residence or habitual residence (can be a receipt of the light, telephone or gas of your residence).
3. Sworn translation in English of the previous documents.

When opening any of the account types, whether of company or personal, it is advisable to make a deposit of at least 1000 Euros.

Asian banks are charged for access to the electronic banking service, and this cost can range from about 30 or 50 euros per month.

FINANCIAL INCOME IN THE PARTICIPATION IN A PRIVATE INVESTMENT PROGRAM

With respect to the financial returns obtained in the participation in a program of private investment (PPP), much is speculated with respect to the percentage of the same. There is talk of yields of 100%, 200% and 300%, when in reality the financial performance will depend on the opportunity of the market that exists for the trading bank at that time, with respect to the investment of the buy and sell.

It is true that in a timely operation of oil or its derivatives and/or in any other type of commodity, you can earn very important percentages. But that opportunity is not constant. It is therefore more convenient to speak of moderate returns, in the environment of historically 50% monthly, which in any case is not bad.

HOW IS THAT 50% MONTHLY?

This 50% monthly historic return is generated from the average of each and every one of the purchases and sales made by the trading bank participating in operations in the secondary market.

HOW IS THIS MONTHLY PERFORMANCE DISTRIBUTED WHEN RECEIVED?

This leaves the liquidity that is offered to inject liquidity into the real economy.

When signing the participation contracts or JV (joint venture), this percentage of 50% monthly financial income is distributed to 50% between the owner of the line of Credit and the owner of the financial instrument that has collateralized the line of credit.

That is, each group is given yields of 25% per month.

And of that 25% of the side of the one who has put the financial instrument, usually if there is an investor in the leverage of the Swift bank issue, this yield is granted as a loan to finance a business or humanitarian project.

TIMES THAT ARE MANAGED TO RECEIVE SUCH FINANCIAL INCOME

When the issuance of a bank guarantee through the Swift MT 760 communication protocol preceded by a MT 799, followed by the response of the receiving bank of an ICPO, and subsequent monetization of the guarantee, it is generally established for a period of 15 days to obtain such monetization. Subsequently, the financial returns are received as a result of the investment of this cash obtained in the monetization of the financial instrument (BG/SBLC). From this moment forward the financial returns are received month by month.

FINANCIAL INCOME PAID BY PAY ORDER IN THE FOLLOWING 3 DAYS?

This practice of issuing "pay order" or post-dated payment orders to pay for future income is quite delicate and usually is not done. By banking regulations, banks do not do this, but they are usually issued by the foundations that operate as financial platforms and have lines of credit to monetize instruments supporting humanitarian projects.

These pay orders are corporate, they are not bank pay orders. It is equivalent to saying that I issue you a promissory note from my company when you cover the monetization of the bank guarantee. The advantage at least of having a corporate "pay order" is that it generates tranquility in the sense that it is going to charge the agreed upon.

In any case, having a corporate pay order from the foundation that is currently acting as a financial platform in the trading operation gives the opportunity to negotiate a discount of the same in the secondary market.

INVESTMENT IN THE REAL ECONOMY WITH CASH OR FINANCIAL INSTRUMENTS

As we have seen before, we are aware of where the cash used to invest in business and/or humanitarian projects comes from.

But when you can invest in the real economy by directly using financial instruments in business or humanitarian projects, these instruments are used as guarantees or guarantees for a bank to provide us with financing in a given time and in accordance with the socio-economic feasibility of the project.

The use of these financial instruments as collateral for the attainment of bank credit implies making clear in the financial cost of the company that the cost of rent or financial leverage is necessary to take this service.

Usually taking this service has an annual cost which is between 12% to 15%, depending on our supplier of guarantees to be used to free the line of credit and finance the project. As a business project normally is not recoverable from the investment in the first year, it becomes necessary for the bank to renew this guarantee, and therefore we have to make a financial projection of this cost for at least the next 4 years.

The cost of continuing to obtain this guarantee for the following years will decrease more or less in the following percentages:

First year: 15% on the face value of the guarantee or credit that is guaranteed.

Second year: 12% of the face value of the guarantee or credit that is guaranteed.

Third year: 10% on the face value of the guarantee or credit that is guaranteed.

Fourth year: 9% on the face value of the guarantee or credit that is guaranteed.

Fifth year: 8% on the face value of the guarantee or credit that is guaranteed.

COUNTER GUARANTEES:

When issuing these guarantees that guarantee business and/or humanitarian projects, the issuer of the guarantee may request a counter-guarantee from the guarantee it is providing.

Usually it is the pledge of the shares and/or the asset acquired in the society with the cash that is being endorsed.

WHAT RESPONSIBILITY DOES THE ASSISTANT OR OWNER OF THE BANK GUARANTEE ACCRUING THE CREDIT FOR THE BUSINESS AND/OR HUMANITARIAN PROJECT HAVE?

The responsibility is total, since at the moment that the company that receives the credit stops paying the bank the fees of the same, the bank will collect the bank guarantee that is backing the credit. That is why banks today prefer liquid guarantees, such as a bank guarantee, because by making the guarantee effective it can be charged at first requirement without going through a lengthy and expensive legal process.

For this reason the Financial Professional that acts in the consultancy of the companies that require these endorsements to obtain financing of business projects, must ensure that these projects comply with all the socio-economic feasibility standards to avoid that they subsequently fail, since with this they can drag in the same way many actors of the process.

There are many benefits that can be obtained from the secondary market, and in particular on this point on bank guarantees. Therefore we must know how to make good use of them. With the bad banking practices many are doing we are discrediting the sector of specialized financial advisors in Macrobanca, and at the same time we are responsible for the bad effects that happen economically to banks and investors who own bank guarantees. By winning a major commission now we do not have to sell our soul to anyone. The consequences can be dire.

WHAT IS DUE DILIGENCE?

The term "Due Diligence" is used for concepts that imply the investigation of a company or person prior to the signing of a contract or a law involving careful diligence. It may be a legal obligation, but the term is more commonly applicable to voluntary investigations.

An example: Due diligence on an industry or company is the process by which a potential buyer evaluates an industry or target company, or its assets, for a later acquisition.

In our case it would be the evaluation process that is done to a potential investor when it wishes to participate in a Private Investment Program (PPP), either with cash or by providing a financial instrument such as a Bank Guarantee (BG) or a SBLC (Stand by Letter of Credit) to be discounted in the secondary market through an active line of credit.

WHY A DUE DILIGENCE?

The capital movement that exists in the Macrobanca business is very susceptible to auditing or voluntary investigations, not only for the amounts that are moved but also for compliance with the US Patriot Act that the US government demands for control of the financing of terrorism in the world.

We must be aware that European and Asian banks cooperate with this control of capital in the world, and that is why every time we allow our data to be consulted or investigated this information goes back to the secret agencies of the United States and others such as INTERPOL or the FBI.

PATRIOT LAW

The US PATRIOT Act is an American legal text promulgated on October 26, 2001. It was approved by an overwhelming majority by both the House of Representatives and the US Senate after the attacks of 11 September of the year 2001. The purpose of this law is to expand the State's control capacity to combat terrorism by improving the ability of the various US security agencies to coordinate and provide them with surveillance against terrorist offenses. The law also promulgated new crimes and hardened the penalties for crimes of terrorism. The Patriotic law has been harshly criticized by various human rights organizations and organizations because of the restriction of constitutional freedoms and guarantees it has meant for citizens of both the United States and foreigners.

In a "Due Diligence" review in our field, what is investigated is the origin of the funds that gave rise to being able to issue a bank guarantee (BG) or SBLC. That is why it should be clear in the client's KYC, that the applicant of a bank guarantee clearly explains where the funds went to constitute this type of collateral or banking collateral.

CONFIDENTIALITY AGREEMENT:

The NON-DISCLOSURE AGREEMENT (NDA) is a legal agreement between at least two parties to share confidential material or knowledge for certain purposes, but restricting its public use. An NDA creates a relationship of confidentiality between participants to protect any trade secret. Therefore an NDA can protect information from a private company. NDAs are usually signed when two companies or individuals who agree on a business relationship and need to understand the processes used in the other company for the purpose of assessing the interest of that relationship. Confidentiality agreements may be mutual, so that both parties have restrictions on the use of the information provided, or may affect only one party.

For our case in the MACROBANCA business, confidentiality contracts are usually signed very frequently, because either party requests that their professional secrets, or proof of funds, or client funds, or financial capacity of the companies will be been protected by such contracts. It is of special relevance in this business not to reveal the sources or contacts for the execution of the financial operations.

MODEL OF A CONFIDENTIALITY CONTRACT

This Agreement, attempt, directly or indirectly, to contact the others' business and professional sources or contacts (including banks, investors, sources of funds, etc.) ("Business Sources"), or negotiate with any of the other Parties' Business Sources, except through the relevant other Party, or with the express written consent of the other Party as to each such Business Source is simply not permitted.

For the avoidance of doubt, this means that the Parties shall not contact, deal with or enter into business transactions with any Business Source provided by another Party unless written permission has been obtained from the other relevant Party disclosing the same.

The restrictions stated above shall not apply when one Party had a previous active business relationship with the relevant other Party's Business Source in the previous 2 (two) years. Should either party be introduced through an independent source to any contact already engaged with either party, the opposite party must go through the parties governed by this agreement, or get written permission to engage with that contact.

2. The Parties agree not to disclose any of each others Confidential Information to anyone else, unless specifically authorized in writing by the relevant other Party. For the purposes of this NCND, "Confidential Information" shall mean any kind of clearly private, sensitive or confidential information including (without limitation), unofficial or highly personal information relating to any of the Parties, and information of

whatever nature regarding the business arrangements of any of the Parties themselves or their employees, clients and associates, including business workings, plans, fee agreements, contracts, banking and account information and/or literary works such as manuscripts, screenplays, treatments and synopses.

The requirements of this NCND as regards to Confidential Information shall not apply to any information which has been legally put into the public domain, or when a Party legitimately learns of the Confidential Information in question by a wholly independent third party in good faith at some point in the future.

3. The Parties agree to use all reasonable endeavors to ensure that, in matters relating to fee sharing on the Mutual Transactions, a suitable fee protection agreement is negotiated in good faith between the Parties and entered into accordingly, so that all Parties are appropriately remunerated.

4. The Parties herewith irrevocably agree that, unless otherwise specifically stated in writing at some point in the future, they do not assume any responsibility for the Mutual Transactions they enter into, and shall not hold each other liable for any reason associated with them.

5. Electronic and/or faxed and/or postal and/or courier signature and transmission of this NCND shall all be fully valid, legally binding and enforceable in respect of all of its provisions.

6. This NCND shall be governed by, and construed in accordance with English law in the U.K. - and the Parties hereby submit to the exclusive jurisdiction of the U.K courts.

7. Nothing in this NCND shall be construed as creating any form of partnership or employee/employer relationship between the Parties.

8. Except as otherwise provided and/or supplemented by the terms of this NCND, the relationship of the Parties shall be governed by the terms of the International Chamber of Commerce's Publication No. 619 (which deals among other things with non-circumvention issues).

9. Unless otherwise agreed between the Parties in writing at some point in the future, each of the Parties shall be responsible for covering its own expenses incurred in respect of the Mutual Transactions.

ACKNOWLEDGED AND ACCEPTED BY:

....

Name: Mr. xxxxxxxx
Passport Number/Nationality:
US Passport No. xxxxx (Copy attached)
Company Name: xxxxxxxxxxxxxxxxxxxxxxxxx
Address: xxxxxxxxxxxxxxxxxxxxxxxxxxxx Hong Kong
Date:
Phone: US (xxx) xxxxx HK (xxx) xxxxxxx
E-Mail: rooss@xxxxxxxx.com
AND

....

Name: xxxxxxxxxxxxx
Passport Number/Nationality: xxxxxxxxxxxxxx
Company Name [or personally]:
Address: xxxxxxxxxxxxxx
Position: Phone: xxxxxxxxxxxxxx
E-Mail: xxxxxxxxxxxxxx
Signed Date:
Company Seal & Signature:

....

And

....

Name: Mr. xxxxxxxx
Passport Number/Nationality: xxxxxxx/xxxxxxxx
Company Name [or personally]:
Address: xxxxxxxxxxxxxxxxxxxxxxxxx
Position: Phone: + xxxxxxxxxxxx
E-Mail: xxxxxxxxxxxxx

Signed Date:
Company Seal & Signature:

……………………………………………

And

………………………………………………………………

Name: Mr xxxxxxxxxxxxxxxxxx
Passport Number/Nationality: xxxxxxxxx
Company Name [or personally]: xxxxxxxx
Address: xxxxxxxx.
Position: xxxxxxxxxxxx
Phone: xxxxxxxxxxxxxxxxxxxxxx
E-Mail:
Signed Date:
Company Seal & Signature:

Confidentiality agreements are frequently used in business relationships to safeguard the disclosure of unauthorized information that is likely to cause any kind of economic or moral harm to companies or individuals. Confidentiality agreements signed through the internet through use of an electronic signature have the same validity as if they were signed in person.

JOINT VENTURE CONTRACT

It is understood as a "joint venture", and is a type of long-term joint venture investment agreement between two or more parties (usually legal entities). A Joint Venture does not have to constitute a separate company or legal entity. In Castilian, joint venture literally means "joint venture". However, in the legal sphere, this meaning is not used. Terms such as "strategic alliance" or "commercial alliance" are used, or even the term itself in English. The joint venture is also known as "joint venture," when two or more companies come together to form a new one in which a protocol is used taking into account the best tactics in the market. The objective of a "joint venture" can be very varied, from the production of goods or the provision of services to the search for new markets or mutual support in different links in the chain of a product. It will be developed for a limited time in order to obtain economic benefits for the parties.

To achieve the common objective, two or more companies agree to make various contributions to this common business. The contribution of the parties may consist of raw material, capital, technology, market knowledge, sales and distribution channels, personnel, financing, in short: capital, resources or the simple know-how. Such an alliance shall not imply loss of identity as a legal person of each party.

CHARACTERISTICS OF THE JOINT VENTURE

The principle of wanting to form a Joint Venture is to unite knowledge, skills and resources in turn sharing profits and risks. There are no requirements on how to act together. Companies can sign a collaboration agreement, set up a UTE (recognized by Spanish and Argentine law), or even found a company in which the parties participate.

These types of partnerships are generally established in the medium or long term, since the objectives they seek are not simple to achieve and require a lot of planning and execution, so doing so in the short term would represent too many difficult costs.

It is a distinctive feature of a joint venture, which its members (called "ventures") maintain their identity and independence for the joint venture, as well as for the other Venturers. There is no merger or absorption to implement the joint venture. It can also happen in the case of venturers joining only for very specific things, such as the creation of a new product or the streamlining of an assembly line.

The difference between a joint venture with a new company, and a merger between two, is that in the case of the joint venture, companies A and B come together to create a company C. There are now three companies. This modality is identified as a joint or corporate joint venture. Instead, in a merger (merger), company A (merged) merges with company B (merger) and the result is now a single company, the merged company.

In a "joint venture" the partners continue to operate their businesses or companies independently. The joint venture is a business whose profits or losses will be reported in the profit and loss account of each party, depending on the legal form with which the joint venture itself has been structured.

It should be clarified whether the Joint Venture involves only the strategic partnership between private companies or whether the concept is applicable to private companies in conjunction with national, provincial or municipal public administration organizations. If this is possible, the integration of private capital with public investment would bring great benefits to States, especially when these joint actions take place in the area of science and technology.

JOINT VENTURE CONTRACT MODEL FOR ASSETS AND ISSUANCE DEPOSIT OF BANK SWIFTS MT 760

Date..................

TOGETHER

On the one hand, Mr xxxxxxxx, of nationality xxxxxx domiciled at xxxxxxxxxxx

CP: xxxxxx, for the purposes of this document, and provided with a nationality passport Xxxxxxx number xxxxxxx.

And Mr xxxxxxx, of nationality xxxxxx domiciled at xxxxx, for the purposes of this document, and provided with nationality passport xxxxxxx number xxxxxxxxx

And on the other hand, Mr xxxxxxx, of nationality xxxxx, neighbor of xxxxxx, domiciled at xxxxxxx, number xxxxxx, and provided with passport document No. xxxxxxxxxxxxxxx

SHARE each of them with legal capacity to be bound in this act, and INTERVENE, the first of them, in the name and representation of PLC xxxxxxxxx and the second as president of the company with registration number xxxxxx and registered at xxxxxxxx No. xxxxxxxx CP: xxxxxxx City xxxxxxx Country xxxxxxx, designated expressly for the purposes of this contract; And the second of them as administrator of the mercantile nationality xxxxxxx denominated xxxxxxxxx, with the same registered address as its representative and provided with tax identification number number xxxxxxxxxxxx.
In this act, by mutual consent and with the express consent of those who appear for themselves and for whom they represent

MANIFEST

I. XXXXXXX is a trading company dedicated to all kinds of financial and banking matters, as it is public and notorious, whose commercial turn is international in scope and is, therefore, subject to its own law that is territorial application as it is Provided for such purposes.

II. Xxxxxxxx counts among its commercial/professional activities the management of assets of any nature for their own account or on behalf of third parties.

III. Accordingly, both parties have reached an agreement which they submit to the following.

STIPULATIONS

FIRST. xxxxxxxxxxxx PLC, form now on xxxxx, agrees to facilitate the use of its own house security for the deposit of assets of any nature: LTN, BONDS, MORTGAGES, DERIVATIVES, CASH, etc. ..., to XXXXXXXX., form now on xxxxxx, designated by said company, own or third parties, with the purpose of being used in designated financial transactions and agreed by both parties.

SECOND. Each and every one of the assets deposited and prior to any planned operation, both parties undertake to verify the authenticity and availability for the pre-marked purposes of each of the deposits, and once this verification has been done in a positive way, xxxxxxx shall issue in favor of xxxxx or of the individual or legal entity designated for such purpose a bank draft for a period of validity of ninety days in order to be used as payment of the assets deposited for the purpose of their change of ownership from xxxxxx, being the responsibility of this xxxxxxx, the content of the shipment made for all obligatory effects against the issuer xxxxxxx.

THIRD. Simultaneously with the positive verification of each of the assets deposited in the form described above, xxxxxx, by itself and through its financial and banking structure, and especially through the company named XXXXXXX based in xxxxxx, UK, will facilitate the issuance of SWIFT MT 760 FULL RESPONSIBILITY to the banking coordinates designated by xxxxxxx, either their own or their own third party clients, each Swift being set for a period of ONE YEAR AND ONE DAY, and for the price of xx PERCENT (Xx%) of the face value of EVERY Swift issued, to be paid by xxxxx to xxxxx. THE USE OF THE FINANCIAL STRUCTURE OF THE xxxx, through the recipient of said shipment, shall be paid within fifteen banking days of having produced the issue and the shipment of the Swift in question.

Xxxxxx, SHALL PAY FOR THE SWIFT MT 760 ISSUANCE IN ADVANCE, BY BANKING DRAFT AT A NOTARIAL EVENT AND THEN FOLLOWING 5 BANK DAYS MAXIMUM THE xxxxx THROUGH ITS PARTNER xxxxxx ISSUING THE SWIFT MT 760 AGAINST THE GUARANTEES OF THE OWNED DEPOSITED GUARANTEES OF xxxx.

FOURTH. CONFIDENTIALITY: The parties agree confidentiality and absolute respect in all matters concerning each and every one of the operations, persons that mutually present themselves and stages of the procedure in which they could be involved, in each case, formally undertaking not to do business Direct in the absence of prior knowledge, management and approval, whose consensus will result from mandatory mutual observation. To this end, the parties assume the establishment and unconditional fulfillment of a penalty for breach of this clause, in the unavoidable suffrage they would incur, in case of non-compliance. Should this occur, the parties agree to fix the establishment of compensation in the unavoidable, irrevocable and irrevocable payment of an amount of xxxxxx. €000.000.00.

FIFTH. In the presence of any case of litigation, controversy or legal discussion, the parties agree to submit, for all that may be derived from the foregoing and concerning the celebration and fulfillment of the spirit and letter of this contract, to the legal jurisdiction of the Paris Chamber of Commerce, given the nature of this document and its content, freely, expressly and voluntarily waiving any privileges of its own, if any of them had it.

And with nothing more to add, those appearing in this act, by themselves and by those who represent them, ratify this document, signing the same in two original copies that each party holds for itself, at the place and at the date that are cited in the heading of the same.

Signature.

There are many Joint Venture models that we can write based on the specific objective of the agreement between the participating parties. But the most important thing is that it should never be forgotten that not only is everyone interested in joint participation of the benefits in a JV, but also of the risks that are involved.

A TYPICAL SCENARIO OF A PRIVATE BUY/SELL TRADING PROGRAM

a. The Trader's Bank communicates with the Issuing Bank as well as with the Exit Buyer's Bank, obtaining a detailed agreement with the Issuing Bank Officer and with the Exit Buyer's Bank that they are both prepared to commence the contracted series of Transactions. The Exit Buyer's Bank forwards a POF to the Trader's Bank for the amount of the first purchase of a $100M (Note - When a POF has been issued for the Exit Buyer and forwarded to the Trader's Bank, there is a legal Funding Commitment to complete that Transaction, which may NOT be revoked while the transaction is taking place).

b. The Trader's Bank forwards to the Issuing Bank a POF in the name of the Trader and requests that a MTN be issued in the name of the Trader, along with an Invoice at a discounted price, say for example only $97M, payable in 8 Hours.

c. A copy of the Note and an invoice at $97M, is forwarded to the Trader's Bank, which authenticates signatures and the MTN terms to verify compliance with the Purchase Contract.

d. The Trader's Bank then forwards the copy of the MTN, along with a Conditional Assignment of the MTN, to the Exit Buyer's Bank, along with an Invoice at the Exit Buyer's Purchase Contract Price, $100M for example purposes, payable in 4 hours.

e. The Exit Buyer's Bank authenticates signatures, verifies compliance with the Purchase Contract, and pays the $100M Invoice price to the Trader's Bank for credit to Trader's account, within the 4-hour limit.

f. The Trader's Bank pays the Issuing Bank's Invoice for \$97M within the 8-hour limit, along with instructions for the Original MTN to be sent to the Exit buyer's Bank by courier.
g. The Trader's Bank debits the Trader a Bank Fee (1/4% for example purposes) for their Services Rendered, and forwards the balance, \$100M minus \$97M minus 1/4 %, to the Trader, who pays the Trader's 'Associate' for their Service Rendered.
h. The Procedure used for this example, typically takes place 4 times each day of a 4-business day week, and repeats until the Trader's Purchase Contract is completed. Using this formula, the weekly payments to the 'Associate', would be equal to 22% of their POF amount. (3% per transaction x 4 per day x 4 days per week = 48% - 4% as Bank Fee = 44%/2 = 22% = \$22M per week)

Note: The Operation described above is a very conservative one. There are other MTN Trade Operations, of the same MTN basis but involving a resale of the MTNs by the 'Exit Buyer', which have a higher Rate of Return to the Trader involved, and therefore an even higher payment to the 'Associate' involved.

An experienced Associate can safely state that with the listed procedure and controls for the Transactions, the only reason for a Transaction failing, once commenced, would be for the Exit Buyer's Bank to default on completing a contracted purchase of a Note, which would result in a jeopardy to their Bank Charter.

Should any default take place, it would be quite simple for the Trader to make the required Payment, using their own Funds, to complete their purchase of the Instrument, and to immediately sell it to a different contracted Exit Buyer. This action by the Trader eliminates any risk of loss by the Buyers and Exit Buyers and 'Associate'.

BULLET TRADING PROGRAM

This program is exclusive for Private and Corporate/ Institutional Clients as well as Asset Managers.

GENERAL DESCRIPTION (Cash Clients):

Trading transactions are arranged on the Swiss Banking Platform.

We accept fund amounts from USD $2m (1.5m Euro) or more. (Other major currencies are welcomed). Special consideration will be made for others amounts, but please contact us specifically for your request.

We instruct clients to transfer funds to a Top-rated Swiss Bank, into a new account in the name of the client only with complete control and sole signatory ability. We do not accept any transfer, SWIFT or otherwise on the capital side required.

There is no blocked funds during the period of trading.

Clients can have trading stop in certain cases and with prior notice. The client can also make withdrawal of his funds. Profits can be paid weekly or monthly, and can be written in as requested in the trading contract. Monthly is preferred.

The trading time period is 12 months, and can be renewed with prior notice and requests for Multiple accounts for parallel trading are allowed upon request. Profits are historically around 40% per month and higher and based on the best effort from the trader.

GENERAL PROCEDURE:

Step 1: Forms and Documentation needed:
Client Information Sheet (CIS), only on required format
Clients Passport copy (color copy preferred)
Letter of Request/Intent (LOI)
Proof of Funds- Bank Statement/Tear Sheet
Step 2: Due Diligence

Full Due Diligence will be performed on the Client and Funds presented

This may include a compliance call between the Client and the trader`s representative.

Step 3: Account, Banking, and Trading Begins

The Trading Manager will provide and detail a prospectus of the trading fund.

The Trading Manager will provide to the client a clear Trading Contract.

Once the Trading contract is reviewed and signed, a new Bank account will be opened for the Client.

The Client then transfers funds to his "own account" and within 3 normal banking/business days of notification the trading program then starts approximately 7-10 days after the funds are received in the new account and the first profit payment is made in approximately 4 weeks.

CHAPTER 6

THE TIER 1 TRADING PLATFORM

HOW TO CORRECTLY APPROACH A TIER 1 TRADE PLATFORM AND AVOID REJECTION:

Are You Truly Ready, Willing and Able? - A Matter of the Right Attitude & Sophistication!

Being on the receiving end of dozens of submissions that come in on a daily basis, we find most of which come from people who do not understand the proper etiquette to successfully be invited into a trade program as many times a capital provider/potential client has a pre-conceived notion about how to approach a platform and sees trading as a 'right'. They want to do things their way.

However, those pre-conceived procedures they would like to follow do not fit with the actual way a Tier 1 platform must operate, by banking rules, federal, as well as financial legislation, financial regulatory, Tier 1 bound regulations to begin the process, and not even being aware that banks themselves can NOT trade on this level by law!

The client/capital provider who insists on this 'tail wagging the dog' is declined even the chance to be considered and not even heard or considered in a 100% secured Tier 1 trade arena.

Think of it like this; you know that there is a party being held where the guests are all participating in very lucrative trade programs. They took the correct approach, followed the orders and instructions of the trade platform principals/program director to conform to the financing and trading rules. The people who are inside having a grand time while they multiply their assets and receive proceeds by the platform every trading week renewed; some already for years in ongoing huge project financings.

Now..., you were not invited to this party, but you really would like to attend. If you were going to try to barge in and crash the party, you know you would be automatically resolutely rejected and most likely banned from ever showing up again in the future! None of the participants nor the organizers of this particular party are actually really looking forward to any new-comers, all based on the fear that someone new could well spoil the party's pleasant, secured ambiance and existence in time! Pretty severe, is it not? Yet many times capital providers think they can push their way in, which is hardly the way to get in or to be ever invited at all!

To make yourself attractive for an invitation to the party, you must 'dress up' by providing the documents that start the invitation process handed to you by the Program Director of the Tier 1 platform. Those are commonly the bank letter (BCL/RWA as is prewritten on purpose!), passport and client information sheet of the client/signatory (CIS), a bank tear sheet no older than 5 days, and some other necessary documents. There is also the matter of your personal manner. Are you cooperative? Have you disclosed everything? Will you act like a partner who has a pleasing personality with whom the platform can work?

No matter how rich you are, remember you are dealing here with the owners of every USD, Euro, or other legal currency on the planet, which will have to approve your Tier 1 trade entry!

Listed here are just a few things that you as the client/capital provider need to be prepared to do.

The next step is presenting your documents to the designated Program Director of the platform. This is how you make the request to come to the party. After a brief time making sure that you and the monies you want to put up for trade are clean and clear as well as owned in full by you or your company! You have now passed through the first doorway in joining the party.

The due-diligence is mandated by the Know Your Customer rules! This is also the ONLY correct way for the relationship to begin. You, as the client/capital provider, have to take the first step and introduce yourself. Your documents are your introduction. If all the necessary paperwork is presented and you are cleared to enter the next door, you will be dealing directly with the principal(s) of the platform.

This is the point where you must pay close attention to the instructions that the platform will give you. They are required to follow ever-changing rules and requirements to invite you through the last door, which is the entry to the party itself.

This, the Trading Contract which binds you and the platform in a legal relationship for the duration of the mutually agreed trade program, it's rules and possible extensions (evergreens) as well as to accelerated trade possibilities (bullet trades) when they occur. Because of the enormous amount of fraud and misrepresentation in the market that has resulted in extremely muddy waters for a potential capital provider, each step is taken as rapidly as possible, but very carefully, to make sure that all of the 'i's are dotted and 't's crossed at each step by the authorities, legislators and regulators supervising these Tier 1 trades.

If you have the right attitude (Willing), the right presentation of yourself through your documents, and are truly RWA to follow the required laws in order to let you in to the party, then success is likely - assuming you are dealing with someone who truly IS connected to one of the real few performing trade groups there are in this world and that number is very, very small. Beware!

Never underestimate what the trading entities know about you and your efforts to get into a trade scenario. Failure to disclose or cooperate in all stages of the DD followed by the intake will disqualify you resulting in a 'NON-PERFORMANCE' status.

These programs are aimed to finance commercially approved projects or humanitarian natured projects on an 80/20 basis, not to solve just a personal financial gain or to generate money to make some individuals richer on the planet!

The minimum Proof of Funds is 100 Million Euro in Cash ONLY, proved to be owned in FULL by a prospective client! This minimum entry level for Tier 1 trades is set per the G20 meeting in Cannes, France in 2011 by the trade regulators and legislators. The rest is unimportant as the actual trade will only come per complied and passed Due Diligence in full, as well as is by Invitation Only, having passed the compliance part in full!

Please do not take this process lightly as it goes well beyond the detail you will initially think it will. The process is very deep and strict! Tier 1 Trades are the ONLY asset enhancement mechanisms where traders as well as the client both are 100% under total supervision by all global financial legislator and regulatory bodies.

As such, Tier 1 trading is the only safe way of asset trading, where both parties are protected from fraud and any illegal steps at all times! The Tier 1 platform principals set procedure at all times.

PROTOCOL FOR ENTRY INTO A TIER 1 TRADE PROGRAM

There is a certain protocol, or order, in which the client is brought into the program. These are mandated by the trade platform and the government agencies which require these.

Our Consultants are here to assist you so please do not hesitate to contact us. We will make sure that everything is done to make your access as smooth as possible.

STEP 1

The Client first provides his documentation as requested. This is the "Request for an Invitation" and is to be considered by the Platform's Program Director.

- Client Information Sheet CIS and Passport of Account Holder/Signatory
- Board Resolution (if a corporation) and Authorization to Verify (ATV)
- Current Bank statement, by BCL/RWA Letter + Latest Tear Sheet
- Letter of Non-Solicitation
- A Detailed History of how the Funds presented as Proof of Funds were earned.

The above-mentioned documents have a certain lay out, on purpose and ONLY being handed these templates and using them as they were handed to you (to the letter) will provide you the chance to get into a DD process! As these documents are written in a legal language which banks cannot sign if the situation of your Proof of Funds provided is in any which way not coherent to the desired status as it should be. Please Do NOT take this lightly!

With every prospects of any type (large or small, personal or company), make sure you know UPFRONT... before you get to the Program Director that you may and/or can NOT vet the Principals on the Platform side because it violates the trade commission's prohibition against solicitation and the banks "know your customer laws" (KYC), in order to engage IN ANY WAY with a client UNTIL they have passed Compliance, signed an agreement with us, have successfully sent funds, and are "in a legal business relation" with the platform.

The potential new participant needs to know immediately that he cannot vet any of us and will get no information until HE performs first in passing compliance. If he does not trust us and/or they are not comfortable with these circumstances then do not waste any time at all with them..., because nothing else will matter! These rules are deadly serious - written in stone - and, as the gate-keeper of the platform, the Program Director, whose main job is to mitigate potential liabilities to the Platform ONLY can pass you an invitation and guide you in.

There is NO NEED for a face to face meeting. Everything is done electronically till DD has been passed successfully.

STEP 2

After successfully passing through the mandatory compliance Due-Diligences by all involved in a Tier 1 trade, you will receive a Trading Contract, which is where you will formally enter the legal relationship officially, along with all the other terms and agreements.

STEP 3

When the funds have been correctly blocked in your own bank account (CASH ONLY in a Tier 1 Trade!!), the principal platform will establish a line of credit by the platforms' own funds which will be used for the trade. So, your money is NEVER at risk!!

STEP 4

In mutual consent or per your request, the platform will also advise how to set up an account for you to receive the proceeds from the trading, after all, you are now an official guest in the party...!!

It is not a complicated process. It is made complicated by brokers and naive intermediaries, but the real program is simple when you follow the above steps, in the correct order. After submitting the correct paperwork, you are working now with the Program Director directly, which means you are working with the platform directly. He is here to guide you and assist you, but it is up to you to produce the needed documents that he must have by law, in order to start and for you to get invited.

Never forget: "Only the small secrets of the Fractional Reserve Trading System need protection. The big ones are kept secret by public disbelief and/or the crap around it in the published information and the spook stories about it!"

If you never participated in a trade before – You can NOT know how it is all functioning, as all is different from what 99.9% of the brokers do tell you, as they themselves, ignoring the dreaded exception here, our fixed liaisons in this market, never produced a single trade participant which made it into a Tier 1 trade!.. and we ...? We trade happily ever after in the meantime, week after week, year after year, with our existing 'club members', financing the worlds' biggest commercially approved projects and projects of a humanitarian nature, being careful as to whom we will let have access to the exclusive party here.., the participation again, is by INVITATION ONLY.., never forget that, as non-solicitation laws prohibit the marketing, shopping or soliciting of these programs in any which way, shape or format under an increasingly more difficult global banking system, where we will accept only the compliance of the above, IN FULL!!

Shopping for a trade entry at multiple trading parties will result in an immediate rejection for a Tier 1 trade! Through our global bank intelligence, we will know so, as every time you try to get in a trade, you will leave a footprint in the financial legislative system!

NB: AGAIN;

Tier 1 Trades are the ONLY programs where the trading platform as well as the client both are 100% under total supervision by all global financial legislator and regulatory bodies and need their joint approvals. - As such Tier 1 is the only safe way of asset trading, where both parties are protected from fraud and any illegal steps at all times!

40 WEEK TRADE VS PERSONAL MTN TRADE PROGRAMS

A 40 Week Private Placement Trade Program is where the investor's funds are blocked, by their banker, from being used for any other purpose than for the trader's own Buy/Sell Program. Typically this type of program lasts for a 40 week period where historic returns for the investor have run 50% to 100% per month.

The investor's funds are not used for any other purpose but to allow the trader to activate its own credit line of 10 to 20 times the amount of the investor's funds. (Explanation: $100 Million to $5 Billion from Investor x 10 to 20 = Up to a $100 Billion for the trader).

With those amounts of a credit line and the trader making 20% to 30% Gross Profits on each trade, with up to say 4 trades a day, it is easy to see how the trader can afford to pay the investor such high returns for the investor's involvement. Keep in mind, the trader NEEDS investor funds in order to activate the trader's own credit line. With arbitrage type trading, the trader does not actually use the funds from its own credit line; the borrowed funds, the trader's credit line, need only be in place.

Most problems and horror stories stem from the use of SWIFTS, a wire transfer via MT760 and the like. The trader can make his own credit line available easily enough via an Administration Hold wherein the investor's bank agrees not to allow movement or use of the investor's funds. A typical Administration Hold will last for One year and a Day.

Most seasoned investors believe these types of returns are impossible to achieve, or they simply do not have the contacts to make it happen. This business, as are many, is not so much about what you know, but whom you know. How many of you have made excellent returns through the use of a Wall Street broker and have very little idea of how it all works? Just ask my next door neighbor, the one with the low IQ.

A very peculiar and noteworthy financial event took place in 1913 in the USA. President Woodrow Wilson signed into law the Federal Reserve Act, which formulated the cartel that is now in charge of orchestrating money. The absolute power that the Federal Reserve System has over the economy and individuals is immense.

Actually, very few people know how money is created, and even fewer know how the Federal Reserve System was created and what it does. A very famous media guru, philosopher and communication theorist called Marshall McLuhan said, "Only the small secrets of the Federal Reserve System need to be protected. The big ones are kept secret by public disbelief."

Later after WW II, the British suggested to leverage on the Marshal Plan's help in Asia and Europe, to institutionalize programs where could be created for humanitarian as well commercially approved projects in the form of trading derivatives. These programs grew out to be the Private Placement Programs as we know them today.

While commercial projects with vocational aspects get funded as well as humanitarian projects, the here coming in the system opens the route for the ECB and the FED to print new Euros as well as new Dollars without inflation hitting these currencies.

A clear mark was set as of which these programs were to be classified, as well as to be executed under all the regulatory supervising financial authorities and which placed these trades under the most stringent supervision with full protection for the participants of 100M Euro minimum per a G20 meeting in Cannes, France, November 2011.

FED/ ECB/ IMF/ WORLD BANK ARE ACTING AS REGULATORY AUTHORITIES ON ALL LEGAL TIER 1

TRADE PLATFORMS, THOUGH THEY ARE NOT PARTICIPATING THEMSELVES.

Moving on, A PERSONAL MTN BUY/ SELL PROGRAM, my terminology, is orchestrated by a licensed trader wherein the trader arranges the purchase and sale of Mid Term Notes (MTNS) in the investor's name utilizing the investor's funds. With this program, the investor can gross up to 20% on each trade, up to 4 times each trading day. (That's a gross of up to 80% per trade day), and instead of the trader making outrageous sums of proceeds, this program gives the opportunity to the investor.

The investor becomes a link in the Buy/Sell chain that runs from the newly issued MTN contract to the pension fund, hedge fund, foundation, and to the end buyer.

The nice thing is that it does not make a difference where the investor falls in the Buy/Sell chain, the returns are the same. Example: Buy at 30% of the face amount of the MTN and sell, normally within a few hours at 50% of face. Buy at 50% and sell for 70%. These contracts are all pre-sold and the investor's contract is one of them.

Typically, these $50 Billion Buy/Sell contracts can be secured for $150 Million to $500 Million, and more than one contract at a time can be secured. These programs have no time limits such as the 40-week trade does, therefore they can be renewed endlessly or as long as the paper is there to be bought and sold.

Cash trade program

Small cap

Best Small Caps – Mid/ Large/Instruments – PPP Programs

A.1 New 1mm+ Small cap

$1M+ USD OR EURO TEAR SHEET PRIVATE PLACEMENT INVESTMENT TRADE PROGRAM

STRICTLY CONFIDENTIAL & PRIVATE APPLICATION BY INVITATION ONLY

LONDON REGULATED TRADE PLATFORM PRIVATE PLACEMENT INVESTMENT TRADE PROGRAM

10 X return in 45-60 days less 10% fees

Ability to re enter the program multiple times

Minimum Entry is $1 Million USD or Euro Equivalent

No Maximum Entry

NO UP-FRONT FEES OR OTHER FEES OF ANY KIND

No Swifts, No Blocks, Client's accounts are monitored through pings and TEAR SHEETS.

There is no risk to Client's funds because they stay in their account under their control!

Client simply agrees to leave the committed amount in their designated account for the duration of the program. If account balance drops below the committed amount their trade will be stopped with no payout of further profits.

Pay Out of Profits Generated: lump sum at the end of the 45-60 day program to the Client's Bank of choice.

This is a program that can be re-entered multiple times.

A.2 SMALL CAP TEAR SHEET PRIVATE PLACEMENT PROGRAM – $/€/£1m+

SMALL CAP TEAR SHEET PRIVATE PLACEMENT PROGRAM – $/€/£1m+

BRIEF SUMMARY

CASH FUNDS ONLY – TWO STAGE PROGRAM – HIGH YIELDS

FOR COMPLIANCE APPROVED FUNDS IN MAJOR INTERNATIONAL BANKS IN MAJOR COUNTRIES

TEAR SHEET ONLY – NO TRANSFER – NO BLOCK

INDICATIVE STRUCTURE – SUBJECT TO AVAILABILITY ETC.

DESCRIPTION Tear Sheet Only – 13 Months – see details

ASSET TYPE Transactable Verifiable Transferable Clean Free and Clear Cash

Funds without Liens or Encumbrances – only

CURRENCY USD/Euros/Sterling

ACCEPTABLE CLIENT Clients with acceptable funds on Current Account in any major

International Bank – in a major acceptable Country.

Subject to due diligence & Compliance.

DURATION Total Term – 13 Months (approx)

Transaction #1: Two (2) Weeks

Transaction #2: Forty (40) Weeks in a Year

PROFIT/YIELD Indicative Yields (subject to contract):

Transaction #1: 15x Contracted Investment Funds – at the end of 2 weeks

Transaction #2: 40% per week x 40 weeks

Normally all yields are Gross to the Investor.

Transaction Fees (10%) payable to Introducers paid separately by the Investor via Paymaster.

CONTRACT After full Compliance/Due Diligence – the Investor signs the contract with the Trade Platform.

The Contract contains all terms etc.

TRANSACTION PROCEDURES

The Client provides an Initial CURRENT Tear Sheet/Bank

Statement/ Proof of Cash Funds/Internet Screen Full Print Out showing the FULL DETAILS OF THE BANK/ACCOUNT NAME/

NUMBER/FUNDS/BALANCE ETC. with Transactable Verifiable

Transferable Clean Free and Clear Cash Funds without Liens or Encumbrances – as requested for both Transaction #1 and Transaction #2.

Funds or a part of Funds from Transaction #1 are normally rolled over into Transaction #2 by agreement between the Parties.

The Account balance must be readily verifiable Bank to Bank –

Day to Day – Week to Week.

APPLICATION DOCUMENTATION

The Client as Applicant must provide the required format of KYC

+ Current Bank Statement etc.

TRANSACTION FEES. The Client as Applicant/Investor will sign a Fee Protection

Agreement for a Fee of 10% of Client Yield to be paid to

Introducers via a Paymaster.

This will cover ALL Introducers who do not have any Fee arrangements with the Investor.

It will be split fairly between the parties by arrangement.

SMALL CAP 3 MILLION + PROGRAMS:

TOP RECOMMENDED!!
CLIENT SAFELY INVESTS €1 MILLION EUR PRIVATELY UNDER A "NO-SWIFTS" ACCOUNT MONITORING/RESERVING BANK PROTOCOL (EG, "TEARSHEET", "INTERNAL BLOCK" OR "ADMINISTRATIVE HOLD") CONFIRMED INTERNALLY AT THE CLIENT'S OWN BANK, IN A 40 TRADE-WEEK HIGH-YIELD LEVERAGING PROGRAM HAVING A MINIMUM HISTORICAL TRADE ROI RATE OF 100% GROSS PER TRADE MONTH OF A 10 MONTH TRADING YEAR, DELIVERING ROI TRADE WEEKLY AND WITH A 5-DAY BULLET PRELUDE RETURNING 100% AT THE OUTSET. FROM PROCEEDS OF THIS LEVERAGING PROGRAM SOME €2 MILLION EUR IS DIVERTED FOR ROLLING-IN TO A SEPARATE AND EXCEPTIONALLY LUCRATIVE 40 WEEK BOOSTER

PROGRAM WHICH HAS AN UNDERLYING GROSS TRADE ROI RATE OF 25% PER TRADE WEEK HISTORICALLY, COMPOUNDS WEEKLY AND PAYS WEEKLY. AGAIN, THE ROLLED-IN FUNDS ARE PLACED IN THE CLIENT'S OWN BANK ACCOUNT, THERE TO BE HELD UNDER "INTERNAL BLOCK" ACCOUNT MONITORING PROTOCOL WITHIN THE CLIENT'S OWN HOLDING BANK FOR THE DURATION OF TRADE. THE TWO PROGRAMS ARE LAUNCHED ABOUT TWO CALENDAR MONTHS APART AND CONTINUE BEING TRADED CONCURRENTLY IN PARALLEL. WHEN PERFORMED WITH BOOSTER UNDER THE COMPOUNDING SCHEMA ILLUSTRATED HEREUNDER, THIS PIO POTENTIALLY GENERATES AN ALL UP HISTORICAL ROI AGGREGATE NET TO THE CLIENT OF OVER €228 MILLION EURO. ALL PROCEEDS ARE DELIVERED ON AN ENTIRELY NON-RECOURSE BASIS AND THE CLIENT'S FUNDS NEVER LEAVE THE CLIENT'S OWN BANK ACCOUNTS. ROLLOVERS & EXTENSIONS ARE PERMISSIBLE:

As regards to Small CAP prospects for Euro 3m plus, we are accepting compliance filings from clients who have accepted our respective FCOs and will be taking proceeds to take into trade groups in groups of 5 individual applicants who each shall have passed compliance…

Small CAP prospects must immediately file their preliminary KYCs with POF so that we can issue appropriate FCOs in the first instance.

USD +10M SBLC MONETIZATION OFFER

GENERAL OVERVIEW:

The $10M does not have to leave the account if the bank is a Top 100 bank.

The minimum amount is 10M in US$, Euro or GBP. If it's not a top 100 Bank, client can send funds to attorney escrow.

Returns are generated by the issuance and monetization with Non-recourse Loan of an SBLC.

An SBLC of 80M is issued and monetized for every 10M.

Overall the cash funds in the client account is used only as a POF and the Provider will lock their own account on their end and secure the SBLC issuance.

– The SBLC will be monetized with Non-Recourse Loan to pay cost and expenses of the transaction and the client´s returns. The process from start to finish takes 30 days. On the first round after all issuance and monetization costs the client would receive minimum $20M less fee for every 10M, the client would take the minimum $18M NET and the process again but we would get a higher amount SBLC, for example like $160M. After 30 days the Client would receive about $40M less fees. The process continues until you reach upward of $100M.

The cost and expenses of the transaction on the provider and monetizer side that are paid before the clients get their 200% less (10%) fee on the first round. All these cost and expenses are taken out before the Client gets their payment so they don´t have to worry about paying this.

PROCEDURE:

1. - Client sends the KYC and POF (Standard KYC and online bank statement is good enough).
2. - Intake Officer calls the client to confirm he knows and understands the proposal and to answer any question the client may have.
3. - We send Fee agreement for the client to sign and return signed.
4. - Platform sends engagement agreement for the client to review and return signed.
5. - Platform sends the monetization contract for the client to review and return signed.
6. - Issuance of the SBLC and monetization process begins.
7. - After 30 days the client will receive his profits in a paymaster account.

8. - The client may repeat this process with the initial funds plus his profits until the client gets 100M.

SUMMARY:

The process takes 30 days.

Once the first round is done we do a second round which takes another 30 days but it would be higher amount SBLCs used over the course of the 3 months so higher pay-outs every 30 days.

The ultimate objective is: to get each client to 100M USD so they can enter a Tier 1 trade program, which returns historically 100% or more per month.

DOCUMENTS REQUIRED:

Update KYC and POF (no more than three days old) with a copy of the banker's business card(s).

(Attached KYC and online bank statement are good enough).

SMALL CAP TRADE PROGRAM 10M+

This program has been performing for about 15 years. Century Capitol UK is direct to the assistant of the program manager.

European Trade Program

Admin Hold/Tear Sheet Trade

1. For clients who have $10M and above to enter a trading program from top world banks.
2. 40-week program with either Admin Hold and/or Tear Sheet method.
3. The trade earn will 100% or better per month with a weekly, bi-weekly or monthly payout.
4. 70/30 profit sharing (on the 100% or better historically) between Client (70%) and Platform (30%).
5. Possibility of enhanced programs to be offered, then rolling into a 40-week program.
6. In order to move forward the client needs to submit the following Documents:

a. KYC
b. POF
c. Photo screenshot of Client Account online and a video of his account online to match the screenshot.
d. 2 Client bankers' business cards.
e. A statement of from where the funds are originating.
f. It is essential that all requested documents are submitted.

LARGE CAP TEARSHEET TRADE PROGRAM

VERY SECURE BANK TRADE AS THE FUNDS WILL NEVER BE ENCUMBERED OR USED AS COLLATERAL, NO SWIFT, NO BLOCK.

TEARSHEET TRADE PROGRAM

The transaction will be carried out only by means of evidence of funds (POF) in the Client's Bank Account (without Block).

Funds have to be free and clear and unblocked. Funds stay in the client's account. The platform deals ONLY with top banks.

SUMMARY:

Description: Multi-Step program with evidence of funds via Bank to Bank communication, the funds of the Client remain within their existing Bank Account and are not moving or blocked.

Asset type: CASH ONLY, top banks within the USA, Canada, Europe, Hong Kong, and Singapore.

Currency: $ USD, € Euro, and £ Pound Sterling.

Twelve (12) Month Trade Duration: evidence of funds via Bank to Bank communication initially and weekly thereafter.

Returns: Historical around 100% monthly with Bullets to be determined according to availability.

Trade amount: Usually 100M+ but currently the Platform can put in the trade from 10M+ Introductory Proof of Funds Tearsheet Trades to qualified Clients.

Smaller amounts ($1M – $9M) The client has to open a Trade Account with platform assistance, in his name, to proceed. The platform also has a Private Trust for this as well. In this case, historical returns will be between 50 to 80% (This Can be Varied upon financial Market Movement from time to time) monthly.

Payment Schedule to the Client is monthly within the Contract Duration.

TRADE PROCEDURE SUMMARY:

Bank to Bank POF to be delivered as instructed in the Trade Contract; after verification, the Trade commences.

The Client does not transfer the funds to the Trader; the funds stay in the client's bank accounts for the full duration of the investment.

The Client is the only Owner/Holder and Signatory on the Bank Account. The Bank Account does not have any Sub-Account created.

The key requirement is for the Client to accept and agree to keep the level of funds in the Bank Account for the duration of the program (12 months).

TO GET STARTED IS REQUIRED:

1. - UPDATED KYC.
2. - Bank Account Statement showing funds signed and stamped by two (2) Bank Officers (No older than 3 bank days).
3. - Copy of Banker's Business Card (Scan Front and Back of Card).

Attached Platforms KYC either for KYC Corporate for a Company, or KYC Individual for an individual name, please fulfill the below instructions:

KYC Corporate (To be completed & signed, page 4 (INDEMNITY AFFIDAVIT REQUESTING INFORMATION) & page 18 (SOURCE OF FUNDS AFFIDAVIT) to be notarized, page 23 Bank Tear Sheet Signed by 2 Bank Officers, page 24 front & back of the 2 Bank Officers Business Cards).

KYC Individual (To be completed & signed, page 14 (SOURCE OF FUNDS AFFIDAVIT) to be notarized, page 19 Bank Tear Sheet Signed by 2 Bank Officers, page 21 front & back of the 2 Bank Officers Business Cards, page 24 Bank Statement Signed by the Account Holder).

After the Client, based upon the provided information, is accepted and funds are verified and confirmed between the banks, the trade contract will be issued signed and the transaction commences.

LARGE CAP TEARSHEET TRADE PROGRAM

PROGRAM OVERVIEW

DESCRIPTION: Tear Sheet Trade Program with a five (5) day/300% bullet and 40 weeks with historical returns of 50% weekly. This trade requires NO SWIFT; NO BLOCK Funds remain in client's account only KYC, POF and BCL sent via email.

LOCATION: The Trade Group has two platforms where this trade can be conducted in HSBC London or DBS Singapore.

REQUIREMENTS: MINIMUM 100M USD – EUR in Top 100 world banks preferably located in Europe North America Australia Singapore. Others considered case by case.

CONTRACT: Contract signed with the Trader for Bullet and 40 Week Trade. The contract can be evergreened for 3/5 years.

RETURNS: One 5 Day Bullet 300% of gross and +40 weeks based on historical returns 50% per week.

COMMISSIONS: 20% Commission to Lawyers and Consultants.

DOCUMENTS REQUIRED: KYC, Passport, Bank Account Statement, and a Bank Confirmation Letter to be sent via email ("BCL") signed by bank officers in wet blue ink, two banker's business cards.

To pass compliance the client will need to send via email the Bank Statement and the Bank Confirmation Letter (attached) to the platform representative with the email tracking showing that the client has received these documents directly from his bank officer.

Once the client pass compliance the trader will ask the client to send the BCL (attached) via email between the account holder's banker and the trader's transaction account banker.

5 Day Bullet Plus 40 Week Up To 5 Year PPP

LARGE CAP EUB 100M

Program Overview: Tear Sheet Trade Program with a five (5) day bullet x 3 (300% profit), then you can put as much or as little of the money you made into the Trade Platforms 40 Week or more program.

Payments are guaranteed via Fixed Term Contract directly with the Trader with a minimum 100% but averaging 200% plus profit per month. Trades are normally conducted in HSBC London.

Trade Limitations: minimum 100 Million Euro or equivalent USD to maximum 5 Billion Euro. Multiple contracts at one time are permitted. Example: 5 x 5B=25B. This is a EUB program for European Corporations with their funds in Top European Banks.

NOTE: This Primary Platforms has other excellent options for highly qualified clients with 100M Euro or more that do not have a European Corporation. Please discuss with your representative.

Length of Program: Starts with (1) 5 Day Bullet, your next choice of 40 weeks, 3 year or 5 year PPP.

Limited Requirements: This trade requires no SWIFT and funds are not blocked and remain in the investors' bank account throughout the entire program. It is similar to a tear sheet trade as it utilizes the bank account statement and a Bank Comfort Letter with confirmation. The BCL is sent via email between the account holder's banker and the trader's transaction account banker.

ZERO PERCENT RISK!!!

Investors Banks With Whom We Workk: Top world banks preferably located in Europe, North America, Australia, Singapore. Others considered case by case.

Documents Needed To Start The Process: KYC, Passport, Bank Account Statement, ("BCL") signed by bank officers in wet blue ink, two banker's business cards.

ADDITIONAL INFORMATION

Account holder submits required documents for due diligence (KYC, BCL, Account Statement, Banker business cards) to consultants for review and submission.

Account holder signs consulting profit participation agreement (FPA) 5-20% for platform – includes consultant fees.

Application submitted to the trade group.

Trade Groups conducts due diligence 3 to 5 days.

Upon approval a contract is offered. The contract is reviewed and direct communication with trade platform and trader begins.

Contract signed and returned.

Emails exchanged between the account holder's banker and the trader's banker as needed.

Trading commences the following Monday.

Profit receiving accounts established as needed and agreed.

CHAPTER 7

MID TERM NOTE MONETIZATION (MTN)

MTN - MEDIUM TERM NOTE

It is a Medium-Term Note, usually due in one to ten years. Business notes continuously offered by a company to investors through a reseller. Investors can choose between different maturities, ranging from nine months to thirty years.

They range in maturity from one to ten years. Knowing that a note is medium term, investors have an idea of its maturity by comparing its price with that of other fixed income securities. "Ceteris Paribus", the medium-term notes coupon rate will be higher than those obtained in short-term notes.

This type of debt program is used by a company to have constant cash flows from its debt issue; it allows a company to tailor its debt issue to meet the financing needs. Medium-term notes allow a company to register with the SEC only once, rather than several times, for different maturities.

Instrument & Service Description:

Complete Non-Recourse Monetization of Mid Term Notes (MTNs)

We offer 3 Monetization settlement methods:

1/ Bank SWIFT – We use the Bank SWIFT Network to have the Mid Term Note (MTN) delivered Bank to Bank using a SWIFT MT799 followed by a SWIFT MT760.

2/ Euroclear – We use the Euroclear Network because the Euroclear settlement process is fast, transparent and uses the Free Euroclear Delivery process so Clients DO NOT incur any SWIFTING FEES or Delays. Euroclear is a well-established European financial transaction settlement network that was founded in 1968 by JP Morgan and continues to operate successfully employing over 3500 people today.

3/ DTCC – On some deals we now also accept delivery of the Mid Term Note (MTN) by DTC also known as DTCC (The Depository Trust & Clearing Corporation). The advantage of DTC is that clients using this process to deliver a Mid Term Note (MTN) DO NOT incur bank SWIFTING FEES. DTC is a well-established International business that was founded in 1999 and in 2015 was recorded as settling 1.5 Quadrillion Worldwide making it the highest value securities settlement processor in the world.

Intellifinance, and their Monetization services are ideal for clients looking to Discount, Monetize, or create an immediate Non-Recourse loan against a Mid Term Note (MTN) that they own. The Monetization process for Mid Term Note (MTN) issues Non-Recourse funds to the Client shortly after the Mid Term Note (MTN) is delivered to the Monetizer.

Important: Our contracts also include the monetizer returning the Mid Term Note (MTN) to the original owner or Issuing bank 15 days prior to the Mid Term Note (MTN) expiration or after 1 calendar year (whichever the client prefers). We can also complete the Mid Term Note (MTN) transaction using Screen, Block and Pay on the Euroclear or SWIFT Networks if requested by the client.

Monetization LTV:

- Mid Term Note (MTN) – 60% to 80% Non-Recourse
  Estimated Completion Time:

- 7 to 14 Days after all documents are signed and verified or 3 to 4 Days After Instrument Delivery on the SWIFT or Euroclear Networks.
- Sometimes because of the size of Mid Term Notes (MTN) the Monetizer will give clients two options:

o A one off 60% LTV Non-Recourse Payment on delivery of the Mid Term Notes (MTN), OR

o 3 Split Payments Totaling an 80% LTV over a 6- or 8-week period

Closing Process – SWIFT

1. After execution of the monetization contract by both parties the Client will instruct his bank to send a SWIFT MT799 to the bank coordinates provided by the Monetizer.
2. The Monetizer's bank on receipt of the SWIFT MT799 from the clients' bank will reply with a SWIFT MT799.
3. On receipt of the Monetizer's bank SWIFT MT799 the Client's bank will deliver the Mid Term Note (MTN) by SWIFT MT760 to the Monetizer's bank.
4. Upon receipt, confirmation, and delivery of the SWIFT MT760 the Monetizer will within maximum four (4) banking days grant a Non-Recourse Loan for the LTV as agreed from its nominated bank to the Client.
5. The Monetizer agrees to return the Mid Term Note (MTN) unencumbered fifteen (15) calendar days before the 1-year anniversary of the signed contract between the parties.

Closing Process – Euroclear:

1. After execution of the monetization contract by both parties the Client will instruct his bank to assign the Mid Term Note (MTN) using FREE Euroclear Delivery to the bank coordinates provided by the Monetizer.

2. The Client's Banker shall immediately email a certified Euroclear execution receipt of the Mid Term Note (MTN) delivery to the Monetizer.
3. Upon receipt and confirmation of the Euroclear assignment and delivery, the Monetizer will within maximum three (3) banking days grant a Non-Recourse Loan for the LTV as agreed from its nominated bank to the Client.
4. The Monetizer agrees to return the Mid Term Note (MTN) unencumbered fifteen (15) calendar days before the 1-year anniversary of the signed contract between the parties.

Example:

The Mid Term Note (MTN) is issued with a Value of: $100,000,000,000.

The Mid Term Note (MTN) is Monetized Non-Recourse at 80% LTV being: $80,000,000,000.

The Client is paid $80,000,000,000.

MULTI-STEP BULLET TRADE PROGRAMS FOR CASH FUNDS & BANK INSTRUMENTS

The Multi-Step trade program is a flexible trade that consists of multiple programs in which the approved client can choose to participate in some or all in the series:

1. 10–days bullet trade program,
2. then second 10–days bullet trade program,
3. then 30–days bullet trade program,
4. then second 30–days bullet trade program,
5. then 40-weeks long term trade program,
6. then the option to enter a 3-5 year evergreen trade program.

PROTOCOL OPTIONS:

Swift MT -103: cash funds transfer only

Swift MT -760: cash funds or bank instruments Swift MT - 542: bank instruments only

Swift MT -799: for heritage funds or interest on heritage funds or special bank instruments (fed trade program only)

Small Cap Trade Program: Cash funds or bank instruments only Mainland China Trade: Swift MT-103, MT-760, MT -799 only

SPECIAL ADMINISTRATIVE HOLD PROGRAMS (NO SWIFTS REQUIRED)

(#1) 200M-900M CASH, HSBC-LONDON (#2) 200M-900M CASH, HSBC-HONG KONG

(#3) 200M-2B CASH, TOP 25 WORLD EUROPEAN BANKS

(#4) 1B-5B CASH, MAJOR BANKS, TABLE-TOP MEETING REQUIRED

Cash funds only (no instruments, no CD, BG, etc.)

Minimum amount: two hundred million (200M) to two billion (2B)

DAILY TEAR SHEET TRADE PROGRAM (NO ADMIN HOLD AND NO SWIFT NECESSARY)

Minimum amount: two million (2M) to five billion (5b+)

Cash funds only (no heritage funds or interest on heritage funds are accepted) Cash funds at HSBC Hong Kong & Standard Chartered Bank Hong Kong clients only).

NO PROOF OF FUNDS PROGRAM

For clients with MT 799 ICBPOS or MT 103/23 can immediately participate in this no proof of funds managed buy/sell transaction of 500M with rolls & extensions.

Client completes "letter of intent/contract" document.

EURO CLEAR ACCOUNT/MANAGED BUY-SELL PROGRAM

For clients with Cash funds on Euro clear the trade platform can perform a special managed trade on Euro clear; cash funds only.

Client must have or can open a Euro clear account at his bank for the trade platform to perform the managed buy/sell trade directly from the Euro clear account with the client and the trader as joint signatories on the account

WEB LINK AND SERVER-TO-SERVER TRANSACTIONS

Web link account receiver immediately available for genuine web link transfer

Server-to-server (funds provider) transaction can close immediately with genuine receiver (service provider) via server-to-server protocol

Receiver is ready to review and approve these transactions immediately and can execute the activity within 24 hours

A special services paymaster and enhanced services available for transfer clients

FED TRADE PROGRAM (HERITAGE FUNDS & SWIFT MT 799)

HERITAGE FUNDS & SWIFT MT-799 CLIENTS (FED TRADE PROGRAM ONLY):

This is a highly selective and fed registered trader program; a swift MT-799 is mandatorily required.

Because of the senior regulatory oversight with such cases, no client will be considered unless they produce a current letter from their bank confirming they are RWA to send a Swift MT-799, along with current KYC package of account signatory and account statement; this trade program is for clients that can only send a swift MT-799 or for clients with Heritage Funds.

All major banks worldwide accepted.

Forty (40) weeks trade program;

Profits: 40% monthly (historical),

Paid out on a weekly basis directly by fed.

Minimum amount: one hundred million to fifty billion (100M to 50B+), Larger amounts are considered on a case by case basis.

If client can send MT 760 - then this would be a bullet trade

MONETIZATION AND TRADING OF ALL TYPES OF BANK INSTRUMENTS

SWIFT MT-760 OR MT-542

Is required for monetization and trading of all types of bank instruments (e.g. bank guarantee; certificate of deposit, standby letter of credit, medium term note, government treasuries, bank draft, etc).

Pre-advise swift MT-199 or MT-799 or MT-999 is required prior to sending the swift MT-760, but no pre-advise is needed if sending MT-542.

Note: if a pre-advise swift MT-199 or MT-799 or MT-999 is not sent before MT-760, then after the swift MT-760 is sent, then the platform bank will require that the client meets the trade platform in Zurich with the copy of the Swift that was sent by the issuing bank.

Loan-to-Value (LTV): 75 - 85% loan - value (LTV) depending on the ratings of the bank issuing the bank instrument. Monetization can take place within five (5) banking days of bank-to-bank verification of bank instrument validity.

MULTI-STEP PROGRAM

PLEASE NOTE THE REQUIREMENTS FOR THE SMALL CAP PROGRAM WITH MINIMUM 10M. SWIFT TO BLOCK OR CONFIRM FUNDS REQUIRED MT103, 542., OR 760. ADVANCE FEE AFTER BANK TO BANK CONFIRMATION OF THE SWIFT. COMPOUNDING IS ALLOWED.

EXAMPLE; 50M WOULD EARN 3X OR 150M IN 30 DAYS. THEN OPTION TO ENTER THE 40 WEEK AT 25-50% PER WEEK.

GENERAL PROFIT GUIDELINES:

Profit (1): advance (3% of the face value received, paid in 72 hours after swift receipt/verification) Profit (2): 10-day bullet trade program (2x the face value received, historical) Profit (3): 10-day bullet trade program (2x the face value of received, historical) Profit (4): 30–day bullet trade program (8x the face value received, historical) Profit (5): second 30–day bullet trade program (8x the face value received, historical) Profit (6): 40-weeks long-term trade program (1x the face value received, historical) Profit (7): option to enter 3-5 years evergreen trade program (1x the face value received, historical)

All profits are paid out on a weekly basis; the profit structure is spelled out in full detail in the trade agreement. Further, although not necessary, the client has the option to re-invest a portion of his profits (compounding) into the next step of the multi-step program, as may be agreed.

This option can greatly increase trade profits; also, assistance with new profit receiving account(s) and additional services are available to the trading client(s).

UNDERSTANDING AND USING LETTERS OF CREDIT

Letters of credit are commonly used to reduce credit risk to sellers in both domestic and international sales arrangements. By having a bank issue, a letter of credit, in essence, one is substituting the bank's credit worthiness for that of the customer.

The parties involved:

Buyer (who makes the request);
Bank of the buyer (the issuer);
Beneficiary (the seller);

Bank of the beneficiary (teller and confirmatory);

Types

There are two basic forms of letters of credit: Standby and Documentary. Documentary letters of credit can be either Revocable or Irrevocable, although the first is extremely rare. Irrevocable letters of credit can be Confirmed or Not Confirmed. Each type of credit has advantages and disadvantages for the buyer and for the seller, which this information will review below. Charges for each type will also vary. However, the more the banks assume risk by guaranteeing payment, the more they will charge for providing the service.

Documentary Revocable Letter of Credit

Revocable credits may be modified or even canceled by the buyer without notice to the seller. Therefore, they are generally unacceptable to the seller.

Documentary Irrevocable Letter of Credit

This is the most common form of credit used in international trade. Irrevocable credits may not be modified or canceled by the buyer. The buyer's issuing bank must follow through with payment to the seller so long as the seller complies with the conditions listed in the letter of credit. Changes in the credit must be approved by both the buyer and the seller. If the documentary letter of credit does not mention whether it is revocable or irrevocable, it automatically defaults to irrevocable. See Credit Administration, Sample Procedure for Administration of a Documentary Irrevocable Letters of Credit for a systematic procedure for establishing an irrevocable letter of credit.

The debit contracted with such a letter, in its simplest form, is between the agent and the principal; although it may also be possible to charge a debtor against the person provided by the trustee.

When the letter is bought with money by the person who wishes the credit abroad, or is given as a result of a check in his checking account or obtained by the credit of guarantees presented by the person granting it, or in payment of money owed by him to the creditor, the letter is, in effect, similar to an exchange note issued against an outside trader. The payment of money by a person to whom the letter is granted raises a debt or goes into the account between him and the issuer of the letter; but does not raise any debts to the person paying the letter, against whom the money is paid.

When it is not purchased but an accommodation is made to raise a debt, the commitment is usually to pay any advances made to it or to guarantee any accepted draw or discounted note. In this case, the agreement with the agent generates a debit, both against the issuer of the letter and against the person accredited. The holder of the letter of credit is not considered obliged to receive the money; he can use the card as he pleases and he hires an obligation only when he receives the money.

There are two forms of irrevocable credits:

Unconfirmed credit (the irrevocable credit not confirmed by the advising bank).

In an unconfirmed credit, the buyer's bank issuing the credit is the only party responsible for payment to the seller. The seller's advising bank pays only after receiving payment from the issuing bank. The seller's advising bank merely acts on behalf of the issuing bank and, therefore, incurs no risk.

Confirmed credit (the irrevocable confirmed credit).

In a confirmed credit, the advising bank adds its guarantee to pay the seller to that of the buyer's issuing bank. Once the advising bank reviews and confirms that all documentary requirements are met, it will pay the seller. The advising bank will then look to the issuing bank for payment. Confirmed Irrevocable letters of credit are used when trading in a high-risk area where war or social, political, or financial instability are real threats. Also, common when the seller is unfamiliar with the bank issuing the letter of credit or when the seller needs to use the confirmed letter of credit to obtain financing its bank to fill the order. A confirmed credit is more expensive because the bank has added liability.

STANDBY LETTER OF CREDIT

This credit is a payment or performance guarantee used primarily in the United States. They are often called non-performing letters of credit because they are only used as a backup should the buyer fail to pay as agreed. Thus, a stand-by letter of credit allows the customer to establish a rapport with the seller by showing that it can fulfill its payment commitments. Standby letters of credit are used, for example, to guarantee repayment of loans, to ensure fulfillment of a contract, and to secure payment for goods delivered by third parties. The beneficiary to a standby letter of credit can cash it on demand. Stand-by letters of credit are generally less complicated and involve far less documentation requirements than irrevocable letters of credit. See Credit Administration, Sample Procedure for Administration of a Standby Letter of Credit for a systematic procedure for establishing a standby letter of credit.

Special Letters of Credit

The following is a brief description of some special letters of credit.

Back-to-Back Letter of Credit

This is a new letter of credit opened based on an already existing, nontransferable credit used as collateral. Traders often use back-to-back arrangements to pay the ultimate supplier. A trader receives a letter of credit from the buyer and then opens another letter of credit in favor of the supplier. The first letter of credit serves as collateral for the second credit.

Deferred Payment (Usance) Letter of Credit

In Deferred Payment Letters of Credit, the buyer accepts the documents related to the letter of credit and agrees to pay the issuing bank after a fixed period. This credit gives the buyer a grace period for payment.

Red Clause Letter of Credit

Red Clause Letters of Credit provide the seller with cash prior to shipment to finance production of the goods. The buyer's issuing bank may advance some or all of the funds. The buyer, in essence, extends financing to the seller and incurs the risk for all advanced credits.

Revolving Letter of Credit

With a Revolving Letter of Credit, the issuing bank restores the credit to its original amount once it has been used or drawn down. Usually, these arrangements limit the number of times the buyer may draw down its line over a predetermined period.

Transferable Letter of Credit

This type of credit allows the seller to transfer all or part of the proceeds of the original letter of credit to a second beneficiary, usually the ultimate supplier of the goods. The letter of credit must clearly state that it is transferable for its to be considered as such. This is a common financing tactic for middlemen and is common in East Asia.

Assignment of Proceeds

The beneficiary of a letter of credit may assign all or part of the proceeds under a credit to a third party (the assignee). However, unlike a transferred credit, the beneficiary maintains sole rights to the credit and is solely responsible for complying with its terms and conditions. For the assignee, an assignment only means that the paying bank, once it receives notice of the assignment, undertakes to follow the assignment instructions, if and when payment is made. The assignee is dependent upon the beneficiary for compliance, and thus this arrangement is riskier than a transferred credit. Before agreeing to an assignment of proceeds arrangement, the assignee should carefully review the original letter of credit.

Common Problems with Letters of Credit

Most problems result from the seller's inability to fulfill obligations stated in the letter of credit. The seller may find these terms difficult or impossible to fulfill and, either tries to fulfill them and fails, or asks the buyer to amend to the letter of credit. As most letters of credit are irrevocable, amendments may at times be difficult since both the buyer and the seller must agree.

Sellers may have one or more of the following problems:

- The shipment schedule cannot be met;
- The stipulations concerning freight costs are unacceptable;
- The price becomes too low due to exchange rates fluctuations;
- The quantity of product ordered is not the expected amount;
- The description of product is either insufficient or too detailed; and,
- The stipulated documents are difficult or impossible to obtain.

Even when sellers accept the terms of a letter of credit, problems often arise late in the process. When this occurs, the buyer's and seller's banks will try to negotiate any differences. In some cases, the seller can correct the documents and present them within the time specified in the letter of credit. If the documents cannot be corrected, the advising bank will ask the issuing bank to accept the documents despite the discrepancies found. It is important to note that, if the documents are not in accord with the specifications of the letter of credit, the buyer's issuing bank is no longer obligated to pay.

Basic Procedures for Establishing a Letter of Credit

The letter of credit process has been standardized by a set of rules published by the International Chamber of Commerce (ICC). These rules are called the Uniform Customs and Practice for Documentary Credits (UCP) and are contained in ICC Publication No. 500. The following is the basic set of steps used in a letter of credit transaction. Specific letter of credit transactions follows somewhat different procedures.

1. After the buyer and seller agree on the terms of a sale, the buyer arranges for his bank to open a letter of credit in favor of the seller. Note: The buyer will need to have a line of credit established at the bank or provide cash collateral for the amount of the letter of credit.
2. The buyer's issuing bank prepares the letter of credit, including all of the buyer's instructions to the seller concerning shipment and required documentation.
3. The buyer's bank sends the letter of credit to the seller's advising bank.
4. The seller's advising bank forwards the letter of credit to the seller.
5. The seller carefully reviews all conditions stipulated in the letter of credit. If the seller cannot comply with any of the provisions, it will ask the buyer to amend the letter of credit.
6. After final terms are agreed upon, the seller ships the goods to the appropriate port or location.
7. After shipping the goods, the seller obtains the required documents. Please note that the seller may have to obtain some documents prior to shipment.
8. The seller presents the documents to its advising bank along with a draft for payment.
9. The seller's advising bank reviews the documents. If they are in order, it will forward them to the buyer's issuing

bank. If a confirmed letter of credit, the advising bank will pay the seller (cash or a bankers' acceptance).

10. Once the buyer's issuing bank receives and reviews the documents, it either (1) pays if there are no discrepancies; or (2) forwards the documents to the buyer if there are discrepancies for its review and approval.

Opening a Letter of Credit

Level of Detail

The wording in a letter of credit should be simple, but specific. The more detailed a L/C is, the more likely the seller will reject it as too difficult to fulfil. At the same time, the buyer will wish to define in detail what it is paying for.

Type of Credit

Letters of credit used in trade are usually either irrevocable unconfirmed credits or irrevocable confirmed credits. In choosing which type to open both the seller and the buyer should consider the generally accepted payment processes in each country, the value and demand for the goods, and the reputation of the buyer and seller.

Documents

In specifying required documents, it is very important to include those required for customs and those reflecting the agreement reached between the buyer and the seller. Required documents usually include the bill of lading, a commercial and/or consular invoice, the bill of exchange, the certificate of origin, and the insurance document. Other documents required may be an inspection certificate, copies of a cable sent to the buyer with shipping information, a confirmation from the shipping company of the state of its ship, and a confirmation from the forwarder that the goods are accompanied by a certificate of origin. Prices should be stated in the currency of the letter of credit and documents should in the same language as the letter of credit.

The Letter of Credit Application

The following information should be addressed when establishing a letter of credit.

1. Beneficiary

The seller should provide to the buyer its full corporate name and correct address. A simple mistake here may translate to inconsistent or improper documentation at the other end.

2. Amount

The seller should state the actual amount of the letter of credit. One can request a maximum amount when there is doubt as to the actual count or quantity of the goods. Another option is to use words like "approximate", "circa", or "about" to indicate an acceptable 10 % plus or minus from the stated amount. For consistency, if you use this wording you will need to use it also in connection with the quantity.

3. Validity

The seller will need time to ship and to prepare all the necessary documents. Therefore, the seller should ensure that the validity and period for document presentation after the shipment of the goods is long enough.

4. Seller's Bank

The seller should list its advising bank as well as a reimbursing bank if applicable. The reimbursing bank is the local bank appointed by the issuing bank as the disbursing bank.

5. Type of Payment Availability

The buyer and seller may agree to use sight drafts, time drafts, or some sort of deferred payment mechanism.

6. Desired Documents

The buyer specifies the necessary documents. Buyers can list, for example, a bill of lading, a commercial invoice, a certificate of origin, certificates of analysis, etc. The seller must agree to all documentary requirements or suggest an amendment to the letter of credit.

7. Notify Address

This is the address to notify upon the imminent arrival of goods at the port or airport of destination. A notification listing damaged goods is also sent to this address, if applicable.

8. Description of Goods

The seller should provide a short and precise description of the goods as well as the quantity involved. Note the comments in step #2 above concerning approximate amounts.

9. Confirmation Order

With international arrangements, the seller may wish to confirm the letter of credit with a bank in its country.

Amendment of a Letter of Credit

For the seller to change the terms noted on an irrevocable letter of credit, it must request an amendment from the buyer. The amendment process is as follows:

1. The seller requests a modification or amendment of questionable terms in the letter of credit;
2. If the buyer and issuing bank agree to the changes, the issuing bank will change the letter of credit;
3. The buyer's issuing bank notifies the seller's advising bank of the amendment; and
4. The seller's advising bank notifies the seller of the amendment. Tips for Buyers and Sellers:

Seller

1. Before signing a sales contract, the seller should make inquiries about the buyer's creditworthiness and business practices. The seller's bank will generally assist in this investigation.
2. In many cases, the issuing bank will specify the advising and/or confirming bank. These designations are usually based on the issuing bank's established correspondent

relationships. The seller should ensure that the advising/ confirming bank is a financially sound institution.

3. The seller should confirm the good standing of the buyer's issuing bank if the letter of credit is unconfirmed.
4. For confirmed letters of credit, the seller's advising bank should be willing to confirm the letter of credit issued by the buyer's bank. If the advising bank refuses to do so, the seller should request another issuing bank as the current bank may be or is in the process of becoming insolvent.
5. The seller should carefully review the letter of credit to ensure its conditions can be met. All documents must conform to the terms of the letter of credit. The seller must comply with every detail of the letter of credit specifications; otherwise the security given by the credit is lost.
6. The seller should ensure that the letter of credit is irrevocable.
7. If amendments are necessary, the seller should contact the buyer immediately so that the buyer can instruct the issuing bank to make the necessary changes quickly. The seller should keep the letter of credit's expiration date in mind throughout the amendment process.
8. The seller should confirm with the insurance company that it can provide the coverage specified in the letter of credit and that insurance charges listed in the letter of credit are correct. Typical insurance coverage is for CIF (cost, insurance, and freight) often the value of the goods plus about 10 percent.
9. The seller must ensure that the goods match the description in the letter of credit and the invoice description.
10. The seller should be familiar with foreign exchange limitations in the buyer's country that could hinder payment procedures.

Buyer

1. When choosing the type of letter of credit, the buyer should consider the standard payment methods in the seller's country.
2. The buyer should keep the details of the purchase short and concise.
3. The buyer should be prepared to amend or re-negotiate terms of the letter of credit with the seller. This is a common procedure in international trade. With irrevocable letters of credit, the most common type, all parties must agree to amend the document.
4. The buyer can reduce the foreign exchange risk by buying forward currency contracts.
5. The buyer should use a bank experienced in foreign trade as its issuing bank.
6. The validation time stated on the letter of credit should give the seller ample time to produce the goods or to pull them out of stock.
7. A letter of credit is not fail-safe. Banks are only responsible for the documents exchanged and not the goods shipped. Documents in conformity with the letter of credit specifications cannot be rejected on grounds that the goods were not delivered as specified in the contract. The goods shipped may not in fact be the goods ordered and paid for.
8. Purchase contracts and other agreements pertaining to the sale between the buyer and seller are not the concern of the issuing bank. Only the letter of credit terms is binding on the bank.
9. Documents specified in the letter of credit should include those the buyer requires for customs clearance.

REGULATED PRIVATE PLACEMENT PROGRAM (RPP)

Where the World's Wealthiest Companies & Individuals Store their Money

1. ELIGIBILITY DECLARATION

I ______________________ (Insert First and Last Name) residing at address:
____City__________
_State:_________Country: _______hereby confirm the following:
Neither I or any person or company I represent is in ANY of the following categories that Secure Platform Funding will NOT provide service to:
We DO NOT provide ANY services to Passport holders or Businesses from the following countries:

- Afghanistan
- Libya
- North Korea
- Sudan
- Syria
- Yemen

I, (INSERT YOUR NAME), hereby declare with full personal and corporate responsibility under penalty of perjury that the information given here is true and correct, genuine, and accurate and I am not in any of the categories or groups listed above.
By: (INSERT YOUR NAME)
Signed________________________
Date____/____/____
Title__________________________
Passport Number _______________
Correct Document Completion: Electronic Photos of Clients Initials and Signature should be inserted into this document. Text initials and Signature are not accepted.

2. CLIENT INFORMATION SHEET

In accordance with Articles 2 through 5 of the Due Diligence Convention and the Federal Banking Commission Circular of December 1998, and under the US Patriot Act of 2002, as amended in February 2003 concerning the prevention of money laundering and 305 of the Swiss Criminal Code and Anti Money Laundering Act, the following information may be supplied to banks and/or other financial institutions for purposes of verification of identity and activities of the Client described below, and the nature and origin of the funds which are to be utilized. The foregoing is subject to agreement by all parties to whom this information is provided that they are obligated to respect the privacy rights of the Client and all individuals described herein, as well as the generally accepted professional standards relating to the maintenance of confidential information, and to take all appropriate precautions to protect the confidentiality of the information contained herein, This legal obligation shall remain in full force indefinitely without restriction.

I ____________(Insert First and Last Name) residing at address: ____City____________

State_______Country:________hereby confirm the following:

A. Program Confirmation

I would like to apply for enrolment and acceptance into the Regulated Private Placement Program:

[_] I would like to invest: €__________________ EURO

$__________________ USD

I, (INSERT YOUR NAME), hereby declare with full personal and corporate responsibility under penalty of perjury that the information given here is true and correct, genuine, and accurate.

By: (INSERT YOUR NAME)

Signed__________________________

Date____/____/____

Title___________________________

Passport Number ________________

TO: Regulated Private Placement Program Manager
RE: Participation in Regulated Private Placement Program
Attn: Compliance Department DATE:
In accordance with Articles 2 to 5 of the Due Diligence Convention and the Federal Banking Commission Circular of December 1998, and under the US Patriot Act of 2002, as amended in February 2003 concerning the prevention of money laundering and 305 of the Swiss Criminal Code, the following information may be supplied to banks and/or other financial institutions for purposes of verification of identity and activities of the Client described below, and the nature and origin of the funds which are to be utilized. The foregoing is subject to agreement by all parties to whom this information is provided that they are obligated to respect the privacy rights of the Client and all individuals described herein, as well as the generally accepted professional standards relating to the maintenance of confidential information, and to take all appropriate precautions to protect the confidentiality of the information contained herein, This legal obligation shall remain in full force indefinitely without restriction. - All Questions must be completed in English.
Individuals Information
Full Name
Address 1
Address 2
City, Country, Post (Zip) Code
Passport Number & Country of Issue
Date of Issue of the Passport
Expiry Date of the Passport
Telephone Number
Mobile/Cellphone Number
Email
Skype ID
Company Information (If Applicable)
Full Name of Corporate Institution
Registration Number

Date of Registration
Domicile/Jurisdiction
Postal Address
Registration Address
Physical Address
(if different from Registration Address)
Business Telephone Number
E-mail Address
Skype ID
Languages
Do you speak English? [ ] Yes [ ] No
If NO, what language/s do you speak?
Translator's Name
Translator's Phone Number/s
Translator's Facsimile Number
Translator's E-mail Address
Clients Bank Account – Program Deposit will be Paid from:
Bank Name
Bank Address
Bank Swift Code
Account Name
Account Number
Account Signatory Name and Title
Bank Officer Name and Title
Bank Officer Phone Number
Bank Officer E-Mail Address
Clients Bank Account – Program Returns/Profits will be Paid to:
Bank Name
Bank Address
Bank Swift Code
Account Name
Account Number
Account Signatory Name and Title
Bank Officer Name and Title
Bank Officer Phone Number

Bank Officer E-Mail Address
Investment Experience
How many years have you been investing? [ ] Less than 1 [ ] 1 to 3 years [ ] 3 to 5 years [ ] 5+ years

SOURCE OF FUNDS

A. Describe Corporate Activity:
(nature of the business, years involved in industry)
B. Describe how the Funds were earned or obtained by you or the corporate entity you represent?
C. Are the Cash funds beneficially owned by the undersigned?
[ ] Yes [ ] No
D. Are the cash funds free and clear with no liens or encumbrances or governing restrictions? [ ] Yes [ ] No
E. I, (NAME) OR (NAME, FOR AND ON BEHALF OF CORPORATION) as authorized signatory and beneficial owner/trustee, hereby grant the TRANSACTING PRINCIPALS including their Compliance Department full permission and authority as part of the compliance and verification process in assessing my/our submission, to verify, confirm, and reconfirm said information presented in my submission. This includes but is not limited to verification of account information with/by bank officers, verify cash funds by email, phone on a bank-to-bank basis, conduct standard background checks of the cash funds and the corporate entity owning such.
F. I (NAME) OR (NAME, FOR AND ON BEHALF OF CORPORATION) warrant and attest that I have not authorized any other party to place these cash funds and/or asset(s) into a Trade or Buy/Sell program.
G. NON-SOLICITATION STATEMENT
I, (NAME) OR (NAME, FOR AND ON BEHALF OF CORPORATION), the undersigned, hereby confirm that I have requested of you and your organization specific confidential information on behalf of ourselves regarding a Private Placement program.

I hereby declare that I am fully aware of the information received from you is in direct response to my request, and is not in any way considered or intended to be a solicitation of funds of any sort, or any type of offering, and is intended for our general knowledge only. I hereby affirm under penalty of perjury that you have not solicited in any way. I understand that the contemplated transaction is strictly one of private placement, and is in no way relying on or related to the United States Securities Act of 1933, as amended or related regulations, and does not involve the sale of securities.
That affiant makes this affidavit knowing that the recipients will rely on the contents hereof, and agrees to indemnify and hold-harmless all recipients and all other parties -- including intermediaries -- against any and all claims resulting from any applicant misrepresentation of a material fact or any loss of asset value or any act (legal or not) of a bank or other financial institution, governing authority or agency, the Federal Reserve or an official or other insider of any such entity.
Further, I hereby declare we are not licensed brokers or government employees, and understand that neither are you or your organization. We mutually agree that this private placement transaction is exempt from the Securities Act, and not intended for the general public, and all materials are for private use only.
I, (NAME) OR (NAME, FOR AND ON BEHALF OF CORPORATION), warrant and attest, with full personal and corporate responsibility that as the beneficial owner/trustee/authorized signatory, I have full legal title and authority with no governing restrictions over the herein described cash funds and am also acknowledged as such by my secure depository/financial institution.
I declare under penalty of perjury that the information given above is accurate and true to the best of my knowledge.
I, (INSERT YOUR NAME), hereby declare with full personal and corporate responsibility under penalty of perjury that the information given here is true and correct, genuine, and

accurate and I am not in any of the categories or groups listed above.
By: (INSERT YOUR NAME)
Signed_______________________
Date___/___/___
Title______________________________
Passport Number _______________

3. BOARD OF DIRECTORS CORPORATE RESOLUTION

All of the directors of (COMPANY NAME) below listed were in attendance, in person or by telephone conference. General discussion was then held concerning the issue, and all aspects of the same, were fully explained in detail to the satisfaction of the board members.

DIRECTOR Name/Title:
Passport No.:
DIRECTOR Name/Title:
Passport No.:
DIRECTOR Name/Title:
Passport No.:
The Board of Directors of (COMPANY NAME) an International Business Company incorporated on (DATE) in (LOCATION) in (COUNTRY), with Registered Offices at (ADDRESS) in a meeting held on this the (Day) Day of (MONTH), (YEAR), adopted the following resolutions.

RESOLUTION 1:

It is resolved that the Board of Directors of (COMPANY NAME) hereby authorizes: (NAME) holder of Passport Number (NUMBER) issued on (DATE).
As our Managing Member, as the (President-CEO etc.) who assigned authority, on our behalf stay and name, to instruct, negotiate, arrange, monitor, execute, manage, and sign any and all agreements and/or necessary contracts with third parties

pertinent to all financial transactions with bank instruments and Private Placement Program. (securities/derivatives)

RESOLUTION 2:

It is resolved that at this meeting of the Board of Directors that our Managing Member and in fact (NAME) acts for (COMPANY NAME) with regards to the aforesaid financial investment.

RESOLUTION 3:

It is resolved that (NAME) is hereby authorized to act as our Financial Director for afore said purpose.

RESOLUTION 4:

It is resolved the Board of Directors of (COMPANY NAME) hereby authorized (NAME) to assume all authority, powers, duties, signatory rights, and responsibilities on our behalf.

RESOLUTION 5:

It is resolved that (NAME) is hereby authorized to open a personal, corporate, trading, trust and/or custodial account in any bank, domestic or foreign and to sign such resolutions as may be required by such bank to accomplish the objective(s) as stated herein and to give irrevocable instructions to said bank(s) on our behalf.

I, (NAME), hereby swear under penalty of perjury, that the information provided herein is accurate and true as of this date

Signed and sealed this date of ___/___/___

Signature: ____________________

Full Legal Name: ________________

Title: ________________________

Passport: _____________________

Passport Issuing Country: _________

4. DECLARATION OF NON-SOLICITATION AND FUNDS OWNERSHIP

I, (INSERT YOUR NAME) warrant and attest, with full personal and corporate responsibility that as the beneficial owner; I have full legal title and authority with no governing restrictions over the herein described Bank Funds.
We hereby grant THE TRANSACTING PRINCIPALS and/or Secure Platform Funding full permission and authority to verify, confirm, and reconfirm said collateral and/or assets on a bank-to-bank basis and conduct standard background checks of the collateral and/or assets, and the corporate entity owning such.
I warrant and attest that I have not authorized or offered to any other party, consultant, broker, or investor the placement of the collateral and/or assets defined herein nor have I shopped the collateral and/or assets to any other financial broker, consultant, or company in the last 8 weeks.
I certify and attest that at no time has your organization or any agent and/or appointee on your behalf made any offer or solicitation.
I, (INSERT YOUR NAME) attest and warrant with full responsibility under the penalty of perjury that:
a) The available Bank Funds listed in this Application are from good, clean, cleared sources, free and clear of security interests or similar interests of any kind or nature whatsoever.
b) I or the company I act for are the full owner or beneficiary of the Bank Funds.
c) The Bank Funds has been legitimately earned and obtained from non-criminal & non terrorist origins.
d) The Bank Funds is free and clear of any liens or encumbrances and the Bank Funds are under my control, immediately available and freely transferable without consent of any third party.
e) The Bank Funds are legally earned, taxed, and include no independent third-party interests.

f) The Bank Funds owner and beneficiary are not a party to a lawsuit or pending adverse legal action, further, there are no pending contracts existing, or about to exist, that could affect the said Bank Funds.

g) All information supplied in the documentation submitted with this Application and the Bank Funds involved, are not in violation of the Patriot Act of October 26, 2001, and amendments thereto, with its related financial crimes counterparts however interpreted, defined, and enacted, whether within the United States or any other international jurisdiction.

I, (INSERT YOUR NAME), as Account Holder and duly Authorized Signatory, do hereby confirm that I have requested of you and your organization, specific confidential information, and documentation on behalf of myself regarding currently available Private Financial Opportunities to serve only my interest, education, and not for further distribution.

I hereby agree that all information received from you is in direct response to my request, and is not in any way considered or intended to be a solicitation of any sort, or any type of offering, and for my general knowledge only. I hereby affirm under penalty of perjury, that I have requested this information from you and your organization of my choice and free will and further, and that you have not solicited me in any way.

I hereby represent that I am not an informant, nor am I associated with any government agency of the United States of America, or any other country, such as the Secret Service, Internal Revenue Service, Federal Bureau of Investigation, Central Intelligence Agency, Securities and Exchange Commission, Banking Commission, Interpol, any countries Financial Market Authority, nor any agency whose purpose is to gather information regarding such transactions or offerings.

I understand that any contemplated transaction is strictly one of a private nature, and is in no way relying upon, or relating to, the United States Securities Act of 1933, as amended, or related regulations, and does not involve the sale of public securities.

Further, I hereby declare that you have disclosed that you are not a licensed security trader, attorney, bank officer, certified public accountant, or financial planner. Any information, work or service conducted hereunder is that of a private individual and that this is a project funding transaction that is exempt from the Securities Act and not intended for the general public but Private Use only.

I acknowledge that submission of this application is no guarantee of acceptance, that no reason for being declined needs to be given, nor do I have a right to appeal any decision. I agree that regardless of the outcome with my application I will not to make any negative public or private statement either in writing or verbally to any other party, website, media company or person.

The electronic or facsimile transmission of these documents shall be considered a binding and enforceable instrument, treated as original copy. Original may be obtained upon request.

I, (INSERT YOUR NAME), hereby declare with full personal and corporate responsibility under penalty of perjury that the information given within this application true and correct, genuine, and accurate, that I have had the opportunity to consult appropriate professional accounting and legal advice and that I have read and voluntarily agree to all statements in this documentation without reservation or hesitation.

By: (INSERT YOUR NAME)

Signed________________________

Date____/____/____

Title____________________________

Passport Number _______________

5. COLOR PASSPORT PHOTO

Provide Full Color Photo of Passport Photo

Insert Full Color Photo of your Passport

I, (INSERT YOUR NAME), hereby declare with full personal and corporate responsibility under penalty of perjury that the

Passport above is mine and is true and correct, genuine, and accurate.
By: (INSERT YOUR NAME)
Signed________________________
Date____/____/____
Title____________________________
Passport Number ________________

6. COMPANY CERTIFICATE OF INCORPORATION

Not Required if you enter the Program in Your Personal Name

Insert Company Incorporation Certificate Here

Must be Good Clear Photo and NOT Sanitized with Information Obstructed or Hidden

I, (INSERT YOUR NAME), hereby declare with full personal and corporate responsibility under penalty of perjury that the company certificate of incorporation above is mine and is true and correct, genuine, and accurate.
By: (INSERT YOUR NAME)
Signed________________________
Date____/____/____
Title____________________________
Passport Number ________________

7. PROOF OF FUNDS

Provide 1 of the following Acceptable Proof of Funds Formats:

a. Bank Statement stamped and signed by a Bank Officer
b. Certified copy of Bank Statement Notarized by a Lawyer or Notary Public
c. Bank Letter signed and stamped on Bank letterhead which includes Bank Name and address, Client Name and address, Account Number or IBAN and SWIFT Code

Insert Full Color Photo of your Proof of Funds Here

I, (INSERT YOUR NAME), hereby declare with full personal and corporate responsibility under penalty of perjury that the Proof of Funds above is true and correct, genuine and accurate as of the date I have signed this declaration and that the funds above are under my direct control, earned freely and legally, are not from any criminal activity or origin and are unencumbered and available to complete any transaction the corporate resolution in this application requires.

By: (INSERT YOUR NAME)

Signed______________________

Date____/____/____

Title________________________

Passport Number _______________

8. BANKER EMAIL

Provide a copy of an email from your Bank not more than 7 days old that confirms the current balance in your account.

Insert Banker Email Here

I, (INSERT YOUR NAME), hereby declare with full personal and corporate responsibility under penalty of perjury that the Banker Email above is true and correct, genuine and accurate as of the date I have signed this declaration and that the funds above are under my direct control, earned freely and legally, are not from any criminal activity or origin and are unencumbered and available to complete any transaction the corporate resolution in this application requires.

By: (INSERT YOUR NAME)

Signed____________________

Date____/____/____

Title______________________

Passport Number _____________

9. BANKER BUSINESS CARD

Provide a Color Photo of your Bankers Business Card

Insert Full Color Photo of Bankers Business Card Here

I, (INSERT YOUR NAME), hereby declare with full personal and corporate responsibility under penalty of perjury that the Banker Business Card above is true and correct, genuine and accurate as of the date I have signed this declaration and that the funds above are under my direct control, earned freely and legally, are not from any criminal activity or origin and are unencumbered and available to complete any transaction the corporate resolution in this application requires.

By: (INSERT YOUR NAME)

Signed____________________

Date____/____/____

Title______________________

Passport Number ____________

10. NON-SOLICITATION, NON-CIRCUMVENTION, NON-DISCLOSURE, NON-DISPARAGEMENT AGREEMENT

PARTIES AND PURPOSE

The undersigned are potentially and mutually desirous of doing business with respect to the arranging a financial transaction in cooperation with one another and with potential third parties for the mutual benefit of all. It is their intention that the information exchanged among the signatories in the course of doing business, as well as the documents which will be generated subsequent to the execution of this Agreement, including but not limited to Buyers, Financers and Sellers identity, their websites or any electronic information and data, letters of intent, full corporate offers, bank comfort letters, contract terms and conditions, project plans and details, business and finance plans, financial and banking details or pre-advised payment instruments, and/or any information contained in such documents, will not be passed, under any circumstance, to another intermediary or broker or trader of any other company or private person who is not an end buyer or end supplier, without prior specific written consent of the party or parties generating or without proprietary rights to such information and/or documentation.

This Agreement shall obligate the undersigned parties and their partners, associates, employers, employees, affiliates, subsidiaries, parent companies, nominees, representatives, successors, clients, and assigns (hereinafter collectively referred to as 'The Parties') jointly, severally, mutually and reciprocally for the term of and to the performance of the terms and conditions expressly stated and agreed to below. Furthermore, whenever this Agreement shall be referenced in any subsequent document(s) or written agreements, the terms and conditions of the Agreement shall apply as noted and shall further extend to any exchange of information, written, oral or in any other form, involving financial data, personal or corporate names, contracts initiated by or involving the parties and any addition, renewal, extension, rollover amendment, renegotiations or new agreement that are in any way a component of what shall hereinafter be referred to as 'The Project' or 'The Transaction'.

NOW, THEREFORE, IT IS MUTUALLY AGREED AS AN AGREEMENT NOT TO DEAL WITHOUT CONSENT.

The Parties hereby legally, wholly and irrevocably bind themselves and guarantee to one another that they shall not directly or indirectly interfere with, circumvent or attempt to circumvent, avoid, by-pass or obviate each other's' interest, or the interest or relationship between The Parties, by means of any procedures, sellers, buyers, consultants, dealers, distributors, refiners, shippers, financial instructions, technology owners or manufacturers, for the purpose of changing, increasing or avoiding, directly or indirectly, payments of established or to be established fees, commissions, or the continuance of pre-established relationships, or to intervene in un-contracted relationships with manufacturers or technology owners, intermediaries, entrepreneurs, legal counsel, or to initiate and buy/sell or any transactional relationship that by-passes one of The Parties in favor of any other individual or entity, in connection with the subject Transaction or Project or any related future Transaction or Project.

RELATIONSHIPS AND PREVIOUS RELATIONSHIPS

If either Party has already established a previous relationship with the parties to a transaction or the contract introduced in the specific transaction, the Party with the previous relationship or transaction will immediately notify the other Parties by email or fax outlining the prior relationship and in that specific case, the Party with the previous relationship or transaction will be exempt from the non-circumvention clause of this Agreement. The other Party reserves it abilities and right to dispute the existence of prior relationship. Furthermore, The Parties agree that this Agreement shall not be construed to impede the development of normal day to day business relationships regardless of the existence of a pre-existing relationship on the part of either Party, such as, other direct seller's portfolios and including but not limited to lenders and other mortgage brokers.

AGREEMENT NOT TO DISCLOSE

The Parties irrevocably agree that they shall not disclose or otherwise reveal directly or indirectly to any unauthorized individual or entity any confidential information provided by one party to another, including but not limited to contract terms, product information or manufacturing processes, prices, fees, financial agreements, schedules and information concerning the identity of sellers, producers, buyers, lenders, borrowers, consultants distributors, refiners, manufacturers, technology owners, or the representatives of any of the above, as well as names, addresses, principals or telex/fax/telephone numbers, references to product or technology information and/or any other information deemed confidential or privileged within the broadest possible scope of The Project or The Transaction without prior specific written consent of the party or parties generating or with proprietary rights to such information.

AGREEMENT TO HONOR COMMISSIONS

The Commissions will be paid between the Parties to this agreement as agreed to for each separate and individual transaction which will be detailed in a separate written Agreement. Commissions shall be paid through the designated paymaster, at the close of the transaction. All Parties herein unconditionally agree and guarantee to honor and respect all such irrevocable fee agreements.

AGREEMENT TO INFORM

In the specific situation where a Party acting as an agent of the parties to this agreement or a buyer's representative and any associated parties to this the seller to deal directly with one another, said Party 2 in this agreement shall be informed of the subsequent development of all transactions between the buyer or the buyer's representative, and shall be provided timely copies of all pertinent developmental and/or transactional correspondence and documentation relative thereto by the buyer or the buyer's representative and/or the seller.

NON-DISPARAGEMENT

Party 1 agrees to act with Privacy and Confidentiality by protecting the personal and professional reputation of Party 2 by agreeing that, neither it nor any of its Affiliates, employees, investors, family, friends or Associates will directly, indirectly or anonymously, in any capacity or manner, make, express, transmit speak, write, verbalize or otherwise communicate in any way (or cause, further, assist, solicit, encourage, support or participate in any of the foregoing) including web sites, media, or social media, any remark, comment, message, information, declaration, communication or other statement of any kind, whether verbal, in writing, electronically transferred or otherwise, that might reasonably be construed to be derogatory, disparaging, critical of, or negative toward Party 2 or any of its directors, officers, affiliates, subsidiaries, employees, agents or representatives or any party associated with any transaction being facilitated by Party 2. In the event Party 1 breaches this Non-Disparagement Clause, Party 2 is immediately and automatically to be awarded liquidated damages of $1,000,000 (One Million) USD for each proven public disparaging statement and $500,000 (Five Hundred Thousand Dollars) USD for each proven private disparaging statement and Party 2 will have the full legal right to pursue any and all legal remedies against Party 1 including court action to enforce this clause and collect any liquidated damages amounts owed by Party 1. Nothing in this clause shall prevent any person from testifying when subpoenaed or required by law by a Government Agency.

TERM

This Agreement shall be for ten years commencing from the date of this Agreement. This Agreement may be renewed for an additional ten years, subject to and upon the terms and conditions mutually agreed between and among the signatories. The Parties agree not to make contact with, solicit, deal with, or otherwise to be involved in any transaction(s) with regard to source, contact, trust, strategic partner and/or any other entity that the other Party introduces to or discusses with the other Party for a period of 18 months after termination of this Agreement. The term may be extended automatically if the project is not closed during that time. This Agreement shall apply to: All transactions originated during the term of this Agreement;

and all subsequent transactions that are follow up, repeat, or extended transactions or renegotiation(s) of transactions originated during the terms of this Agreement. Each Transaction shall be registered by the parties or their representatives and a record maintained of Date, Party, project, and results and sent to all parties as it changes. This agreement supersedes any prior agreement.

INJUNCTIVE RELIEF AND PENALTIES

The Parties agree that in the event there is a violation of this Agreement, the Non-Violating Party is entitled to immediate injunctive relief as awarded or instructed by an Arbitrator under the terms of the Arbitration clause in this agreement. Furthermore, any violation of this Agreement is enforceable by a penalty of actual damages, per incident and such penalty shall apply to any and all subsequent transactions with that source, contact, trust, client, strategic partner and/or other entity. This penalty shall survive the term of this Agreement and all extensions and rollovers.

AGREEMENT NOT TO CIRCUMVENT

The Parties agree not to circumvent or attempt to circumvent this agreement in an effort to gain fees, commissions, remunerations or considerations to the benefit of the one or more of The Parties with the full knowledge and acquiescence of all necessary Parties, whether or not such fees, commissions remunerations or considerations gained through circumvention would otherwise be deemed the rightful property of any one or several of The Parties.

ARBITRATION

All disputes arising out of or in connection with this Agreement with the exception of the Non-Disparagement Clause shall be fully and finally resolved by arbitration in accordance with the appointment of one professional Arbitrator in the country of Nevis as decided by Party 2. All such arbitration awards shall be binding on all Parties and enforceable by law. Party A in this agreement consents willingly to waive all rights to engage in any legal action in any court in any jurisdiction and agrees that any and all disputes between the parties with the exception of the Non-Disparagement Clause will be resolved solely by way of Arbitration.

The Parties further agree to carry out the terms of any arbitration award without delay and shall be deemed to have waived their right to any form of alternative recourse in court by or through any other means, in so far as such waiver can validly be made.

Each of Parties named in an Arbitration proceeding and/or required to appear under such a proceeding, unless otherwise agreed, shall be responsible for its own legal expenses. The prior sentence notwithstanding, any Party adjudged by the Arbitrator to be in material breach of this Agreement shall compensate in full the aggrieved party, it's heirs assignees and/or assigns, for the total remuneration received as a result of business conducted with the Parties covered by this Agreement, plus, subject to the determination of the Arbitrator reasonable arbitration costs, legal expenses, and other charges and damages incurred relative to its dealings with banks, lending institutions, corporations, organizations, individuals, lenders, or borrowers, buyers or sellers that were introduced by the aggrieved party, notwithstanding any other provisions of the awarded.

FORCE MAJEURE

Each of the Parties shall not be considered or adjudged to be in violation of this Agreement when the violation is due to circumstances beyond its reasonable control, including but not limited to Acts of God, natural disasters, civil disturbances, war, fire, pandemics, floods, strikes and failure of third parties to perform their obligations to either Party. As a condition to the claim of no-liability the party experiencing the difficulty shall give the other prompt written notice, with full details following the occurrence of the cause.

AGREED AND ATTESTED

Each representative signs below guarantees that he/she is duly empowered by his/her respectively named company to enter into and be bound by the commitments and obligations contained herein either as an individual, corporate body or on behalf of a corporate body.

NOTE: Initial, Date and Sign all pages in sequence including all parties representing the Party 1 and Party 2.

Party 1:

Company Name: ______________________________

Address:

____

____

Phone: ___________________________________

Email: ___________________________________

Signature___________________________

Signature Date____/___/___

Print Name & Company Position

____

CHAPTER 8

WHAT IS A PRIVATE PLACEMENT MEMORANDUM?

A private placement memorandum, also known as an offering document and offering memorandum, is a financial legal documents that companies use to attract prospective investors. It offers information about the company selling securities and related terms and conditions according to the Securities Act of 1993. This information helps investors perform their due diligence towards their stakeholders.

The Private Placement Memorandum (PPM) is the document that discloses everything the investor needs to know to make an informed investment decision prior to investing in a Regulation D Offering. Unlike a Business Plan the PPM details the investment opportunity, disclaims legal liabilities and explains the risk of losses.

The PPM is important because it provides the investor with all of the prescribed data they will need to make an investment decision and includes the actual documentation to effect the investment transaction. PPMs are designed as a stand-alone document - meaning that there need not be other information presented to the investor for them to make an accurate investment decision.

Private Placements or Private Stock Offerings are "private" equity/debt transactions and are considerably less expensive to complete than an initial public offering such as an IPO (for the purpose of raising capital).

Benefits of private placement memorandums include:

- Issuer is not subject to the US Securities and Exchange Commission (SEC) regulations
- Ability to raise capital quickly
- Lower costs versus preparing a prospectus
- Permissible to maintain confidentiality
- Can raise smaller amounts from a large pool of investors
- Private placement markets are considered more stable versus common stock
- Personalized options and flexibility

There are several key advantages associated with private placement memoranda. They can help your organization or startup raise capital. However, there are disadvantages to using PPMs as well, so way your options carefully.

Here is an article about the Securities Act of 1993.

Purpose of a Private Placement Memorandum

The purpose of a private placement memorandum is to help investors understand the investment security or instrument. Smaller and emerging markets, typically involving startups, utilize a PPM when raising capital from a specific group of people. These individuals tend to be high net worth institutional investors.

Examples of when to use private placement memoranda include:

Example 1. Raising business capital for a startup

Example 2. Taking advantage of fraud protection statutes

Example 3. Offerings above $5 million with unaccredited investors

Example 4. Soliciting angel investors with a formal approach

Example 5. Negotiating with a large group of investors over fixed terms

Example 6. Investing with a lead investor or smaller markets

As you can see, a PPM is not right for every situation. However, they are helpful when raising capital. You should seek immediate, in-state legal advice if you are still trying to decide if this approach is right for you.

Types of Private Placement Memoranda

While private placement memoranda are used to raise capital, they also come in many forms. Several company types can sell unregistered securities versus going through an initial public offering (IPO). For the best result, use the PPM type that is right for your situation.

Types of private placement memoranda include:

- Corporation common stock sales
- Count financing authority bond sales
- Mutual fund shares held in trust
- Limited liability company (LLC) promissory notes
- Mortgage broker business notes

If you are thinking about using private placements to raise money, you must draft a PPM that complies with current regulations. You have the right to use private placements, but only if you meet specific conditions. Otherwise, you could be on the hook for SEC violations.

Key Parts of a Private Placement Memorandum

Private placement memoranda are formal documents. They are not a business plan since they do not address the business entirely. The most critical point to drive home if you draft a PPM is to ensure that it complies with SEC requirements and that you follow them carefully.

Key parts of a private placement memorandum include:

Part 1. Investors' notice

The investors noticed should outline important disclosures that prospective investors anticipate seeing. Some common investors' notices include high-degree of risk, securities transfer restrictions, and company rights. These notices are generally offered following the rules and regulations of the SEC.

Part 2. Executive summary

An executive summary is a letter to the investors that summarizes the PPM and points out other critical details. The executive summary should be crafted to entice investors. You should share the top three most important information facts you want to share so that they can refer to them later quickly.

Part 3. Overview and purpose

The overview and purpose section allows you to introduce your organization and describe what you are using the proceeds for. You can also share your market knowledge, planned operations, and SWOT analysis results. This part will give investors an understanding of who you are, your company's greater purpose, and how you plan to move ahead.

Part 4. Terms and conditions

The terms and conditions of your PPM are critical to learning about how the deal is structured, including your dilution and dividend policy. Other elements to address include voting rights, liquidation rights, and information rights. If you hire an attorney, they will provide you with a checklist of considerations regarding this section of your private placement memorandum.

Part 5. Risk factors

Risk factors are the most component of your PPM. Potential investors may skip to the section immediately to learn about your company's risk factors. Statements related to risk should be short, simple, and in bold typeface.

Part 6. Financial Statements

Your financial statements and a summary therein share with investors how your company has performed in the past. This section can signal to investors that you can turn a vision into a reality, which is an attractive attribute. Your accountant can provide you with the necessary financial statements that you will need.

Part 7. Use of Proceeds

The second most important section is how you plan to use the capital raised. Break your anticipated expenses down into several categories. These categories should match the ones contained within your pro forma documents.

Also, it is worth sharing that the Securities and Exchange Commission routinely warns investors about the warning signs of a potentially fraudulent investment scam or scheme. If your PPM is poorly written, formatted, or generally sloppy, you could turn prospective investors away. Inattention to detail is a significant red flag to an investor.

Private Placement Memorandum vs. Prospectus

The difference between a private placement memorandum vs. prospectus is that a private placement memorandum explains the terms and conditions of a private placement. A prospectus is an offering document that performs the same function but for publicly traded issues, such as companies selling common stock or introducing an IPO. Given you can buy the share in the public markets, there is no need for details about the terms and conditions.

Get Help with Private Placement Memoranda

For the best result, draft a PPM with business lawyers. They will help you avoid legal mistakes while maximizing your opportunities. Errors can result in expensive consequences and fines in the future, which means you should seek legal advice before utilizing a PPM, prospectus, or other offering documents.

Knowledge and Skills

Business attorneys are well-suited to guide you through the process. They have the knowledge, training, and skills that you want when approaching investors. Solo practitioners and small firms in your state can offer personalized attention, competitive rates, and institutional knowledge.

Personalized Attention

Another benefit of business attorneys is that they offer full-service, personalized attention. They can field calls, write letters, discuss your objectives, and answer questions on-demand. Solo practitioners generally can customize their offerings quickly versus large law firms.

What Should be Included in a Private Placement Memorandum?

A PPM provides the offering structure, the share structure of the company, SEC disclosures about the shares being purchased, company information, information on company operations, risks involved with the investment, management information, use of proceeds, information on certain transactions that could affect the investor, and investor suitability data. A typical PPM will include the following sections:

- Important Notices
- Disclaimers
- Jurisdictional (Nasaa) Legends
- Summary of The Offering
- The Company
- Management
- Terms of The Offering
- Plan of Distribution
- Description of Securities

- Use of Proceeds
- Capitalization Statement
- Management's Discussion and Analysis of Financial Condition And Results Of Operations
- Fiduciary Responsibilities of The Directors and Officers of The Company
- Risk Factors
- Principal Shareholders
- How to Invest
- Investor Suitability Requirements
- Litigation
- Forecasts of Future Operating Results

PRIVATE PLACEMENTS: SCAM OR REAL?

They are REAL but like everything else you must do your research to make sure you are not getting yourself into a bad situation. Whether you feel the agent or principle disclosed everything about the company or investment strategy, do your own research in addition to the prospectus that is provided. Doubt everything until it is confirmed! I suggest that you deal with only reputable agents (now that's an oxymoron) or at least companies and syndicates that are visible and very assessable. That's important if you need to go "postal".

I personally only deal with organizations where I get to know the principles. In the mid-90s, I participated in a several private equities offering with USA Technologies (OTC: USAA). Over the years since that period, management would invite me to participate, usually packaging up a treasure trove of warrants and other hard to turn away from goodies. Regulon Global, a pharma focused on really innovative cancer drugs headquartered in Greece is a great opportunity for the long-term hold investors.

I did a private placement investment to fuel their European clinical trials when they first developed their premier drug. I later tried brokering an acquisition deal with Wyeth Ayerst and GlaxoSmithKline but the Regulon CEO at the time got cold feet. It's hard to get some eggheads to see the bigger and more profitable picture at times.

When I was a venture capitalist, I learned that some people really just don't care about money. I personally don't trust anyone who doesn't care about money. I'm not saying I'd respect you more if you were some greedy little weasel but one shouldn't lose perspective of the benefits that money offers. If their actions and thoughts aren't contingent on making a dollar and they are motivated by something that is senseless or something you really can't identify, then who knows what they will do next.

Trading Platforms: SCAM or REAL?

REAL but watch out because there is an overwhelming number of scammers out there praying on anyone with a little green looking to double their savings and or retirement. The legitimate and performing trade platforms are very difficult to find out about. Noticed I said LEGITIMATE and PERFORMING. The real deals are closely guarded secrets and participation is usually by invitation or association with the right uber rich financier. Those programs that you may have heard about from a guy who heard something from another guy or an obscure LinkedIn posting most likely ARE SCAMS.

At a minimum, it takes a $100 million to enter into a LEGITIMATE trade program. Any amount being marketed that is less than that is hopefully pooled by the platform's program manager until $100 million is reached. Why such a large amount in order to enter the trade? The tremendous profit spread could never be achieved without such sums being invested SUCCESSFULLY. This is why these "small cap" programs (anything under $150 million) market such generous profits to investors.

Very few programs exist that allow participation below $10 million. I have found a few platforms that do offer programs with a minimum investment of $50K to $2 million. The problem with the small cap programs is that they seldom last more than a few months before significantly raising the minimum investment or disappearing altogether.

If you are fortunate enough to possess the funds to invest in a trading platform, you must do your homework! Just because the broker or marketing materials mention that big name banks are involved someway in the deal means absolutely nothing. So what if the transactions are executed from the Bank of America Trading Desk. Knowing that doesn't make me feel any better about the risk. No matter how many controls may be in place to hedge risk, there is ALWAYS a chance that something may go wrong. There are strategies that you can do to reduce risk but make no mistake that small fraction of a half percent is still an element of risk.

Try to mitigate the risk of your investment vaporizing before your very eyes by first doing your research and getting verification that the people or organization you may do business with are who they say they are and that they possess all the necessary governing legal documents, regulatory filings and licenses to do what it is that they claim they do. All of these trading platforms operate and or are transacted off-shore due to strict US regulations. Just because the deal is off-shore doesn't mean that there aren't regulatory conditions and or mandatory filings in order to transact that type of business or service. If the platform is in China, verify that everything and that all the "i"s are dotted and the "t"s are crossed per that Country's jurisdiction. If there are multiple jurisdictions involved within multiple countries VERIFY that everything is of public record; trade licensing, corporate filings, assets under management, offers, etc.

While you are doing your homework, ask the agent or principle to provide proof that the program is performing. Copy of a SWIFTs is not proof of anything. Trading desk receipts are proof, paymaster escrow accounts verified are proof, etc. If the program doesn't offer it ask for non-depletion accounts that only YOU control and verify it with documentation. Also, ask for an insurance wrap on the funds. The wrap should also cover third-party allocations of funds. If they don't offer the insurance get a policy yourself. I can't stress it enough, verify EVERYTHING, especially what they claim and what is written in their contract. Make sure the contract addresses every possible situation including what happens if the program fails to perform. If so, aside from them hopefully and voluntarily returning your principal, try to negotiate some concessions for lost opportunities, interest, penalties, etc.

I know I most likely have precluded you from investing in a trading platform, but at least you know the intense steps you must take to secure your money in the hands of potential criminals. Obviously, I have been around and have had both good and negative experiences with the program managers, agents, brokers, paymasters, etc. You have to stay on these S.O.B.s.

There are all types of trading platform structures; leveraged instruments, bank guarantees (BGs), escrow funding, leveraged loan financing, bullets, buy/sell, etc. Unless you can afford to potentially lose millions, I strongly suggest you invest in a "Buy/Sell" program for two reasons:

The risks are virtually non-existent if mitigated by some of the earlier suggestions; and they tend to be small cap programs requiring less capital to participate. The downside is that they typically don't pay the kinds of ridiculous returns as the others. Most small caps I have encountered pay a return between 8% to 10% monthly. Yes, monthly. Not bad if you are able to find a consistent performer. Generally, trading platform contracts are for one-year and do not auto-renew.

My first trading platform investment was a small cap gold buy/sell program where my funds were placed in a non-depletion escrow account and used as a proof of funds for buyers who wanted raw bullion directly from the mine. The agent representing the buyer would use the proof of funds to verify that the buyer is real and possesses the necessary cash deposit in order for the order to be filled. Once the order is filled, the bullion is delivered to the buyer COD. I received 10% monthly from that platform. After receiving returns like that for just providing the front money, I was hooked. I took my profits and jumped into a more sophisticated small cap program that paid out a 1000% in six months.

Unfortunately, not all the programs I invested in were as straight forward or successful. The good news is I actually made a nice return and to date have never lost my principal. The bad news is that two of the programs did not perform as marketed. The bottom-line is you must do your research and ask all the questions you can think of, even the dumb ones.

SCAMS

From time to time you may hear about scams (or potential scams) in the High Yield Investment Programs arena. One of the conditions that facilitate scams in this business is due mainly to the non-solicitation environment and the private approach required that forces information to remain as pure whispered gossip ready to be expressed aloud at any time. That fact facilitates a diffuse level of ignorance in this matter where scammers are in their element.

Possible scams include:

- The intermediary asks for up-front fees (in a real situation no one will ask for up-front fees to the client).

- You are asked to transfer the money into an escrow account not in full control of the client.
- You are asked to buy a bank instrument against the funds to start the program (that later will be discovered to be of no value).
- You are asked to pool the funds together with other little clients.

The internet is now full of different money-making opportunities that promise to return a high yield on the small client's money. In most cases such programs are Ponzi schemes (pyramid schemes). And even if a few might be managed by honest people who are trying to aggregate enough funds in order to enter this kind of trading, they are doomed to fail. First there is the problem with pooling a €100M minimum. In many countries, it is illegal to pool money with promises of a high return. Factor in the problems with high numbers of participants being managed, the trust factor, and clearance issues, trading may never begin...

However, the main scams are usually made or attempted with small clients that never will qualify as PPOP clients. Usually, it is very rare that an honest client with €100M can fall into this kind of trap. Larger clients are investment savvy and can utilize the knowledge of other financial experts to drive the deal on a "safety road".

USE OF LAWYERS FOR ADVICE AND GUIDANCE

It is the writer's opinion that lawyers and accountants are engaged to serve as people who execute agreements or financial reports between the principals in support of the client's business decision made between two parties. In most general cases, their advice is solicited, however, it is rare to find an attorney who is intimately familiar with PPOP's. As a result, almost always, the client is poorly advised by practicing attorneys who are not sufficiently educated in this arena. Would you go to a podiatrist to get advice on having brain surgery?

Too often, because of their well-deserved achievements to become a legal or accounting professional, they are additionally asked to guide and direct the client's decisions. Whilst they are trained professionals in their respective fields, they are not the ones who should be in charge of or direct the client's ultimate business decision. As a result, typically ill-advised input comes from a lack of understanding in this arena, and many clients who otherwise would have benefited well are told to stay away by their 'advisors'. Even though they will believe or state they are 'protecting the client', the lost opportunity because of that advice is extraordinarily costly. Both have their place, but should not be guiding a decision in this world if they are not experts. The final decision rests with the client.

WARNING ON SCAMS

It is very common to find so-called "Official Reports" warning the public that this business does not exist and any of these offers are scams.

The reports in question could have been written by the SEC, FBI, ICC, or any other regulatory authority. You should be aware that official documents like the "Commercial Crime Services' Special Report on Prime Bank Instruments Frauds" by the ICC Commercial Crime Bureau are widely spread and used as a reference by banks, accountant firms, lawyers, SEC, FBI, and other authorities around the world. So, if the ICC says that this is a scam, and your accountant says that this is a scam, and your banker says that this is a scam, is it a scam?

Understand, most people working at banks, securities houses, and accountant firms have no insight into this kind of trading. So, if the SEC, FBI, and others say that this is a scam, then they believe it to be so.

PRIVATE PLACEMENT PROGRAM TERMS

As an experienced team of economists, lawyers and bankers specialized in the financial sector, De Micco & Friends is one of a small number of law firms which provide qualified assistance and consulting in Private Placement Programs (PPP). More than twenty years of experience in private and public financial transactions makes the group a good partner for investors, institutions, and banks.

Administrative Hold: A term usually used by brokers. It refers to the investor's bank reserving funds in favor of another individual, without actually encumbering or moving the assets.

Asset Backed: A note or bank instrument which is collateralized by hard assets, not liquid assets such as gold, art,, diamonds, or other rare valuables.

Assignment: Transferring ownership, or rights to use the collateral, to another individual for a specific period of time.

Bank Instrument: A debt instrument issued by banks to access immediate liquidity, providing an annual interest and face value for the purchaser such as BGs and MTNs.

Beneficiary: The individual listed as the owner of a debt instrument, such as a medium-term note (MTNs) or bank guarantees (BGs).

Best Efforts: This term (contract with trader) states that the trader, or investment manager, will use their best efforts to achieve high profits. For example, a contract may say "profits will be achieved on a best-efforts basis".

Blocked Funds: A phrase which refers to blocking liquid assets in favor of another person. This is most commonly achieved via a Swift MT-760.

Broker Chain: Also known as a "daisy chain", this frequently-used term describes the "layers" of brokers that one must go through before one reaches a trader.

Bullet Program: Phrase used by brokers that describes "short-term" private placement programs, promising high returns in less than 30 days.

Cash Backed: Assets which are backed by cash, the most common type of backing.

Collateral: An asset guaranteeing the line of credit the bank gives, which can be seized upon default from the loan terms. Bank instruments, such as cash and MT-760s.

Commitment Holder: An individual/institution who is contractually obligated to purchase a bank instrument at an agreed upon value.

Compliance: The process of completing due diligence on a new investor. At this time, the investor must complete the required documentation, usually referred to as the "compliance package".

Corporate Resolution: A compliance document which asks the client to formally state their relationship to the business entity they represent.

Cutting House: Term referring to a bank which creates, issues, and backs discounted bank instruments. The instruments are "cut", and sold to traders at discounts, who then sell them at a higher price to "exit buyers".

Discount: The concept that bank instruments can be purchased at a discount from face value, leaving the opportunity to profit from resale or the difference from the face value.

Due Diligence: Phrase referring to the process of qualifying people or companies, verifying and investigating their financial and legal background.

Escrow: An escrow service is a licensed and regulated company that collects, holds, and sends money, according to conditions specified by both the investor and service provider.

Euroclear: The world's largest settlement system for securities transactions, covering bonds and equities, as well as bank instruments. This system allows transactions to be completed directly and remotely, while ensuring safety for both the buyer and seller of the asset.

Exit Buyer: The "buyer in place" purchasing the bank instrument at a higher value from the current owner.

Fishing: When a "prospect" contacts a broker or advisor with little to no intent to move forward, but plenty of detailed questions in an effort to investigate (fish) for information.

Free and Clear: Also known as "unencumbered", there are no liens or debt obligations associated with an asset.

Fresh Cut: Phrase referring to a recently issued bank instrument that has had only one owner over the course of its existence. They are accessed at a steep discount from the face value.

Gate-Keeper: An individual who claims to be in direct contact to a trader with a private placement program.

Hypothecate: The process of assigning a monetary value to an illiquid asset, and then extracting liquidity in the form of a loan, using the illiquid asset as collateral.

In-Ground Assets: Land areas which have been appraised based upon geological assessments of the assets which lie beneath.

Intermediary: Anyone involved in a private placement transaction, either through introduction or compensation, who is not the trader, program manager or investor.

Junk Bond: A bond issued by a company or institution which has poor financial integrity, making the bond effectively worthless.

Ledger to Ledger: A transfer between two accounts held by the same bank.

Letter of Authorization: A compliance document required for all private placement investors, allowing the trade group to verify the investor's assets from bank to bank

Line of Credit: Volume of a Bank loan.

Managed Buy/Sell: Managed buying and selling of bank instruments by a private placement trader.

MT-103: This is an improved version of the original Swift MT-100, which is similar to a wire transfer.

MT-760: Swift message used to block funds in favor of someone other than the investor, collateralizing the asset while enabling loans against it.

MT-799: Swift message used between banks to communicate in written form and is usually referred to as "pre-advice". Usually, the MT-799 will be used before the MT-760.

MTN: Medium Term Note, a tradable and discountable debt instrument issued by banks to collect annual interest before expiring upon maturity with a specified face value.

Non-Depletion Account: Article, used in private placement contracts which guarantees that the funds of the client will never be depleted by the trader.

Paper: A synonym used by private placement brokers referring to several bank instruments such as bank guarantees or medium term notes.

Paymaster: A lawyer/attorney or notary elected by intermediaries who will receive the commission payments on a financial transaction and distribute them in accordance to the agreement between the parties.

Piggyback Program: Pooling of investors to meet the minimum capital requirements of a private placement program.

Ping: Leaving funds in an account while the trading bank verifies the full balance is still present on a daily or weekly basis. A ping verification system is NOT a guarantee to obtain a loan from a third bank without the Swift MT-760!

Power of Attorney: A document signed by an individual or a company which gives authority for someone to act on their behalf, as specified in the agreement.

Program Manager: An individual who is directly connected to a trader or a trader group with a private placement program, accepting all applications and questions from investors.

Promissory Note: A LOU (letter of understanding) given from one party to another, stating debt repayment obligations and terms.

Seasoned: Bank instruments, such as medium-term notes (MTNs) and bank guarantees (BGs), which have been previously owned by several different beneficiaries.

Shopping: When a representative/broker sends out an investor's compliance package to several "program managers" at the same time. This is not recommended!

Signatory: An individual or company who legally represents the assets/services of another person, entity or themselves.

Slightly Seasoned: A bank instrument which has been traded, having more than one owner over its lifespan before maturity. This is a bank instrument which is discounted and sold at a value of 65-80% of its face value.

Swift: A system of communication between banks. (MT-100, MT-103, MT-760, MT-799.)

Tabletop: Face to face meeting between a buyer/investor and a seller/trader.

Trade Program: Synonym of "private placement program", this is used by brokers and program managers.

Trader: A person with a direct contact to banks which are issuing discounted bank instruments that will later be sold to a pre-defined "exit buyer" for a higher value.

Trading Bank: Bank where the trader receives the collateral or assignment from an investor. This bank also provides the loan to the trader.

Unencumbered assets: These assets have no liens or debt obligations to third parties.

CONCLUSION

Private placement trading programs are the opposite of public investments. Unlike public investing opportunities, only a small number of qualified people will be invited to invest privately in a company's business interests. From there, investing in private placement trading programs results in a profit for investors. The private transaction typically takes place between two parties and a middle facilitator. When it comes to all the investment opportunities that exist, this is truly one of the most lucrative options available to you. This kind of trading is based on the fractional reserve banking system, which is not a difficult concept to understand once you learn how it is tied to this kind of investing.

Once you have a clear understanding of what investing in this kind of programs involves and how fractional reserve banking comes into play, you must discover a way to get into a trading platform. This step near the beginning of the process can be the most difficult of all. This is because private placement trading is exactly that-private and secret. If you want to get involved with these programs or other alternative investment opportunities, you need to get in touch with an investing and trading company.

Getting started in investing in trading programs can yield huge returns. Placements typically start at more than $1 million and there is no cap as to how much you can invest. With this amount of money, you may be given estimates from brokers of unbelievable possibilities in return amounts. It may sound too good to be true, and it probably is. To keep yourself from becoming greedy, you need to keep a realistic view on your investment and potential returns. Some opportunities may indeed yield incredible returns because this is a lucrative investment opportunity, but others many not meet up to your expectations. This is simply the nature of investing in private placement trading programs.

The best way to make money with trading programs is to find a genuine opportunity. The last thing you want, after all, is to be strung into a deal that ends up being illegal or illegitimate in some way. To spot an opportunity that you want to avoid, see if national brokerage firms refuse to become involved in the private placement program. When this happens, it may be the case that the brokerage firm has been bitten when investing in private placement trading programs before and they want to avoid a repeat occurrence.

www.ingramcontent.com/pod-product-compliance
Lightning Source LLC
LaVergne TN
LVHW010320220926
848484LV00004BB/817
* 9 7 8 1 9 1 6 8 9 6 5 4 3 *